Council for eco-philosophy

Nature & Culture
A Change
empowered by Joy!

||| Clink Street

Date of publication

Place of publication or printing

Published by Clink Street Publishing 2022

© *Authors and illustrators*

First edition.

ISBN :
978-1-915229-41-0 - paperback
978-1-915229-42-7 - ebook

Editing and graphic design: Torbjørn Ydegaard, Nils Faarlund and Aage Jensen

Illustrations: Book cover: Erik Skabo, Page 24: Asgeir Kvalvik. Page 27: Jon Bruskeland, Page 38: Tindegruppa. Page 167: Sigrid Buene. Pages 58, 79, 134, 174 and 223: Sigmund Kvaløy Setreng. Page 83: Peter Wessel Zapffe. Page 118: Marius Kramer. Page 219: Karl Erik Harr Page 114: Peder Balke

The book is an abridged version of Council for eco-philosophy (eds.): Arven og gleden, Tapir Akademisk Forlag, Trondheim 2010.

Grants from the Norwegian FRITT ORD Foundation and Norges Høgfjellsskole and donations from Houdini Sportswear AB, Sweden, and Aclima AS, Wool Specialist, Norway finally made this book possible.

FOREWORD

The Mountains Are Calling

DAVID ROTHENBERG

Norway is a paradoxical and beautiful country. Famed for its natural beauty and a culture built strongly on this closeness to the Earth, it has become one of the world's wealthiest nations on a foundation of petroleum extraction, the single worst industry for the future of our planet. Norway has made so much money from offshore oil that it can guarantee prosperity for all of its citizens for at least a hundred years after the whole industry collapses.

The world's moneymen quake in their alligator boots when they hear that this country plans to divest its giant national fund from all fossil fuel companies. But wait… didn't Norway make all of its money from fossil fuels?

Like I said, it is a paradoxical place. But a nation that can and should show the way forward beyond our climate crisis, so that there just might be a way for humanity to survive the turbulent century we've got ahead of us.

Now it wasn't always like this in Norway. I first arrived there in the 1980s, where businessmen and everyone else wore black and brown leather backpacks on Karl Johansgate, and the city was glum and gray, even inside restaurants and cafés. All that oil had yet to be found, all those tunnels through the mountains had yet to be dug.

I came to this beautiful place for its mountains, its music, and above all its special people, already then committed to celebrating a loving, joyful connection to the fjords and viddas, to the waterfalls and the wind. I am so glad I got to meet and climb mountains with such unique ecological visionaries as Arne Naess, Sigmund Kvaløy, Nils Faarlund, Finn Alnæs, Erik Dammann, Johan Galtung and Øystein Dahle. It is wonderful that so many of these great thinkers and outdoorspeople are still going strong in their eighties and nineties. *Friluftsliv* is good for you!

The mountains still call to us, and there we must go. And if we cannot go, let the mountains come to us. Poet David Ignatow wrote years ago that "I wish I could look at a mountain for what it is and not a comment on my life." Our lives are actually comments on the lives of mountains. If we honor them, we gain the right to keep living and sustaining on this planet. As all statistics point closer and closer to a disaster signaling the end of the human project on this planet. Warming, schwarming, the planet will do fine without us, rest assured about that, the ultimate human tragedy as Peter Wessel Zapffe knew so many years ago.

There should be no separation between the goals of humanity and the future of the Earth. We have been wrong about this split for so long… The value of nature is the value of people, those that honor and enjoy and dance and smile in the wake of it. Don't mean a thing without that swing, said the great jazz fans Faarlund and Kvaløy in Trondheim so many years ago. We need to learn and feel enough to improvise our way through all the crazy challenges we shall face in the decades to come.

"I am optimistic," grinned the white-haired bouldering sage Arne Naess in one of his later essays, "for the twenty-second century, not the twenty-first." The world looks good if we can imagine a world still here one hundred years from now. Think deeply we must.

To that strange peak with its stark flat top, if you can't climb up there than simply imagine it, and slowly read the Stetind Declaration and see if you too can sign on to it. We sure do possess a great capacity to create and to destroy. Watch out for that – use all your abilities to promote life as we chart a way forward beyond all the bad news, back into the mountains, into greener cities, into better and new forms of energy creation and energy saving.

I salute all the unique and colorful voices in the book before you. These are not your usual environmentalists bogged down in bad news and sinking statistics. There is an optimism here that we all would do well to learn from and to share. If the whole human project has truly begun to falter, as Bill McKibben recently writes, the only way to pull out of this precariousness, is with a rigorous plan based firmly on joy and beauty found with the Earth, a path the inspiring texts in front of you are ready to guide you on.

Dare to have fun tackling the most serious problems our species have ever had to face.

Always the Mountains, David Rothenberg

ACKNOWLEDGEMENTS

In 2010 the Council for Eco-philosophy published the book *Arven og Gleden* (The implied meaning is *The Nature Heritage and a Change Empowered by Joy*). In all these years after the release, it has been constantly talked about publishing an English version of the same book. With an unwavering stubbornness and persistence, Nils Faarlund has constantly kept the dream of an English edition alive. In the early years as a loose talk, but gradually more and more specifically through the establishment of contact with Authoright and Gareth Howard who patiently responded to all questions about acid-free and recycled paper and non-toxic glue. The book had not been realized without Nils' glow and enthusiasm and Gareth's helpfulness.

But it is a financial boost to publish such a book. At first, everyone thought that in the "oil-rich" country of Norway, the money for such a project would be loose, but we were wrong! Old supporters were no longer in position or the money-wells had dried up. Eventually we received support from the Fritt Ord Foundation. Although we were hoping for more, of course, we are very grateful for the support we received. Moreover, we are once again grateful to the Norwegian School of Mountaineering, which has contributed with a preliminary support. A crown-roll among dedicated readers gave us some more money. All of you who have contributed small or large amounts must also be thanked for giving a financial contribution and seeing the importance and value of an international publication of a book with this theme. The world is probably facing problems of such a kind we have never experienced before.

A strong and warm "Thank you" goes to the Swedish Houdini Sportswear and the Norwegian Aclima Company. They are both known for producing nature-friendly outdoor clothing. Without their economic support it would have been very difficult to realize this project.

We found that it would not be a good book by translating directly *Arven og Gleden*. The texts in this book are written for a Norwegian audience and are therefore characterized by being local, but also partly characterized by being typical of the time. We wanted now a book that should be broader and appeal to other readers. The book should however not lose sight of the special and peculiarity of using the joy and nature-friendliness as the dominant changing force. After a long and tedious process, we came to the conclusion that the best solution had to be to contact most authors from *Arven og Gleden* with the offer to write an English version of their original text, but processed and adapted so that it suited better for an international audience. We want here and now to say thank you to all of you who have written new texts!

But some writers found it difficult to write in English, which meant that some of the texts had to be translated into acceptable English. Some of the old texts from *Arven og Gleden* were also translated directly. In this work we have received very good help from Ivan Georg Chetwynd, Harald Lorentzen and Gro Mari Liland. We are very grateful for the help you have given us.

In the entire process leading up to a final manuscript, Leiv Sandven must also be mentioned. He has always been an invaluable supporter and opponent with clear opinions about the content and edit of the book. We thank you for the glow and interest in this work.

Editing *Arven og Gleden* we had the privilege to work with a university publishing house. As this was beyond reach for our English version of the book, we had no alternative but to turn to BoD publishing. We were offered favorable support for the presentation of our book internationally but met with unexpected difficulties with the special editing procedures of this trade. After struggling for months and months, Torbjørn Ydegaard, a former student of Norwegian *friluftsliv* and eco-philosophy and since years an accomplished author and publisher by BoD, stepped in and made wonders for the editing process. Thank you so much, Torbjørn!

Last but not least the Council of Eco-philosophy sincerely thanks Aage Jensen for his tenacious work as a coordinating editor alongside with Nils Faarlund. With inventiveness and diplomacy Aage has contributed essentially to make real a condensed edition of our 2010 anthology about the Norwegian eco-philosophy tradition and a cultural change empowered by joy.

CONTENTS

INTRODUCTION

The Council for Eco-philosophy was founded in 2008 and one of the first initiatives of the Council was to work out the Stetind Declaration. The mountain Stetind became very early a symbol for the eco-philosophy movement in Norway. You can read more about this in the article written by Nils Faarlund. The Declaration was originally written in Norwegian but became very soon translated into English, French, German, Japanese and Northern Sami. A website was established, and it became possible to sign the Declaration. All over the world thousands of people signed it. The Stetind Declaration ends up with the manifest by rewriting Gandhi:

> *There is no path to harmony with nature.*
> *Harmony with nature is the path.*

The Council for Eco-philosophy decided to publish a book in Norwegian called *Arven og Gleden* (The implied meaning is *The Nature Heritage and a Change Empowered by Joy*). The content of the book was inspired by the Norwegian outdoor tradition called *friluftsliv* that literally translated means "free-air-life" and is characterized as a life – simple in means, rich in ends. The basic idea was to focus on the joy of being in nature. The idea is very simple: To change our way of living, we should pay attention to the importance of joy. Living in a nature-friendly way is a source of joy. Different people from all over Norway were invited to write about how they have experienced the joy in their nature relationship and write about how they mean joy can be a changing agent. Those who were asked were very enthusiastic to contribute to the book. The second part of the book contains stories written by different persons selected because of their commitment and role in the Norwegian society and how they have experienced and look upon joy in their relationship to nature.

Since then, it has been a strong desire to make an English edition of the Norwegian book. Now the book is here and was given the title: *Nature and Culture – A Change Empowered by Joy*. Our hope is that the focus on joy and a change with joy towards a nature-friendly life can be an important contribution to cope with the crises our planet is facing. In the first part of the book we are presenting the roots of the Norwegian tradition of eco-philosophy, its characteristics and how and why this happened in Norway. The second part of the English book has the same content as the Norwegian book – different persons engaged in nature protection, are writing about their experiences and looking upon joy in their relationship to nature.

THE NORWEGIAN ECO-PHILOSOPHY TRADITION – A RETROSPECT

The Norwegian eco-philosophy tradition – a retrospect

NILS FAARLUND

Beyond doubt – the worldview of Modernity brought us affluence but caused a planetary crisis. In 2019 this is well documented in authoritative reports by IPCC and IBPES: A Special Report on Global Warming of 1.5 °C (SR15) by the Intergovernmental Panel on Climate Change (IPCC) was presented in October 2018. A 1.5 °C target is possible but would require "deep emissions reductions" and "rapid, far-reaching and unprecedented changes in all aspects of society".

The key findings of the IPBES Global Assessment – the definitive global synthesis of the state of biodiversity, ecosystems and nature's contributions to people – was launched in May 2019, concluding: "Following the adoption of this historic report (…) We can no longer continue to destroy the diversity of life. This is our responsibility towards future generations."

The natural sciences, the rigorous, modern way of thinking, which was developed by René Descartes (1596–1652) and colleagues, paved the way for the industrial revolution in Europe in the nineteenth century. In one way a smashing, economic success, but at the cost of free nature, being degraded to a *resource*, which means serving as "raw material" and "recipient" of pollution. The east ends of stylish European cities were changed into the most miserable slum quarters for the workforce, whereas the surroundings of the towns were more or less left as battlefields.

A protest movement came into being. The initiative did not come from people in power in politics or clergy, not from the business world, not from the consumers and also not from a striking workforce. It came from master painters like C. D. Friedrich and I. C. Dahl and master poets and thinkers like J. W. Goethe and F. W. Schelling. But the fortress of "primary qualities" (cf. John Locke) – i.e. number, extension, motion of the natural sciences – could not be overcome by means of "secondary qualities" – i.e. color, sound. The disastrous weapons of Modernity, serving two world wars, survived as the preferred frame of mind – even for the liberal democracies. Efforts made by organizations for nature prevention in the spirit of the Romantic movement have most often been brusquely rejected.

The naturalist John Muir (1838–1914) achieved a Pyrrhic victory, when he with diplomacy established the institution of national parks. Yellowstone in the US was the first "wilderness" to be protected by law in 1872. Since then, most nations on the Planet have copied the American system. The national parks represent a Pyrrhic victory because the paradigm of Modernity still has an unlimited control of the lion's share of the landscape in the country, which is not protected.

The American forester Aldo Leopold (1887–1948) is said to be a pioneer in taking advantage of the evidence-based science ecology in the defense of free nature. His book *A Sand County Almanac* (1948) allowed for an introduction of "primary quality" arguments among conservationists. But it was not before the biologist Rachel Carson (1907–1964) published her sensational book *Silent Spring* (1962) about the dramatic effects of chemicals intended to kill undesirable insects and plants, also called weed, that an "environmental" movement started to grow in the US. On April 22, 1970, Earth Day I, 20 million Americans took to the streets, parks, and auditoriums to demonstrate for a healthy environment in massive coast-to-coast rallies. The 68-er generation included the threat of a senseless misuse of the weapons of Modernity in their protest movement, eventually achieving effect in US legislation.

The Norwegian philosopher Arne Naess (1912–2009), University of Oslo, made a presentation in Bucharest at the Third World Future Research Conference 1972, where he discussed the longer-range background of the new environmental movement and its concern with an ethic respecting nature and the inherent worth of other beings. This is acknowledged as the birth of "Deep Ecology", becoming a new trend in American philosophy in the 1970s and 80s as well as a backing of the vivid US environmental movement. At home, Professor Naess, also an accomplished mountaineer, had already six years earlier been a founding father of the Norwegian tradition of eco-philosophy.

At the Arctic wonderland of rock, Stetind (1392 m), during a fortnight of Big-Wall climbing initiated by Nils Faarlund, a graduate from 'The Norwegian Institute of Technology' (NTH, now NTNU), they came up with a new formula for defending beloved mountain landscapes against damming: The natural science ecology to counter hard core economic growth politics, governed by a Spinoza-inspired inherent values philosophy. The merging of "hard" science ecology, which Nils had hit upon 1959 at a technical university in Germany and Arne's normative premises for interventions in free nature also safeguarded against the misuse of ecology-based arguments for nature-damaging practices – since 1969 named eco-philosophy.

This is what in retrospect is called the Stetind perspective. Having watched the Norwegian mountains being brutally transformed into an *Apparatenlandschaft*, viz. the mountaineer and philosopher Peter Wessel Zapffe (1899–1990), Nils Faarlund dropped his biochemist career and established Norges Høgfjellsskole/The Norwegian School of Mountaineering in 1967. Already convinced that mountaineering "by fair means" was the most captivating way of making friends with free nature, a combination with eco-philosophy as a frame of mind appeared to him as an Aristotelian "Give me a place to stand, and I will move the world."

The concept worked and soon was expanded to an all-embracing learning and leadership training in free nature at sea level, in the woods and up to the snow and ice of the high mountains – eventually at all levels of learning in accord with the Norwegian tradition of *friluftsliv*. This beloved and nonpareil cultural trait has its roots in the Romantic movement paradigm of the eighteenth century. It turned out that the Spinozaian values orientation of the sixteenth century also were the core values of this protest movement against the industrial revolution. Thus, the Stetind perspective could be brought a jour in a time of globalization in supporting eco-philosophy by the ethos of the world's first efforts for nature prevention – cf. the essays : "The Place of Joy in a World of Fact" (p. 35) and *"Friluftsliv* A Way Home" (p. 48)

Sigmund Kvaløy, a PhD student at Arne's Institute for philosophy and a member of the Stetind group, initiated the first University seminar on eco-philosophy "Man and Nature" 1969. A hard core of mountaineers was joined by young academics and students in philosophy, sociology, biology, technology and architecture. Beforehand he established the "Cooperation Groups for Nature and Environmental Protection" which in Norwegian was abbreviated to (snm). His haste was due to new, threatening hydroelectric power work projects in our beloved mountains. In the following year (snm) prepared a Gandhian nonviolent action to defend the watercourse of Mardøla with the spectacular Mardalsfossen – among the highest waterfalls in Europe. Unfortunately, the strong media impact and spontaneous supporters visiting the high camp by the hundreds, taking part in sit down actions, did not impress the Government. They sent in the police to clear the camp. We lost the battle over freedom for nature in Eikesdalen, but we eventually won the "hearts and minds" of our countrymen.

Spurred by a maturing eco-philosophy a "greening of Norway" happened in the 1970s.

Our new grassroots movement rejected Norway's membership in the European Economic Community (EEC) in the 1972 referendum on membership, against the interests of fully-fledged, economic growth machinery. At the parliamentary elections of 1973, three political parties, which had gone through a change of paradigm and turned green, got 20% of the votes.

The most prominent example of a "Green Shift" in Norway in the 1970s was the end of the hydroelectric power work era after the Alta nonviolent action 1979–1981. In (almost) every other country in the world this seems counterproductive for a nature-friendly future, but in "the-other-place" – Norway – we have since many years had an overproduction of renewable energy (!). Only by running an immense energy-intensive industry and recently by exporting electricity, has it been possible to keep the kWh-price at a profitable level. To better understand the "Green Shift" in Norway, read the essays "Gaia versus Servoglobe", "The Ash-lad" and "My Pal Sigmund".

Since the 1990s the impact of eco-philosophy has faded due to an invasive oil fever.

Our green counterculture lost momentum because of the consequences of the oil extraction in the North Sea. The increase of the CO_2-concentration in the atmosphere did not infer in a personally impressive way like damage done to a beloved landscape. The organizations for the prevention of nature responded by turning to sensational media stunts to evoke attention, leaving out the philosophical message, which of course had no spearheading effect in the boulevard press. As there were nobody with the necessary standing and political appeal to follow up the leadership of Arne and Sigmund in their spheres, only the in the meantime institutionalized work with "conwaying" values orientated learning and leadership in the Norwegian tradition of *friluftsliv* went on.

Børge Dahle, associate professor emeritus of *friluftsliv* at the Norwegian School of Sport Sciences (NIH) was among the professionals and volunteers, who refused to give in. As a student of sport sciences at NIH in 1968–1970, he was inspired by the novelty to academic institutions in Norway at the time – eco-philosophy – and later devoted his life to forward nature-friendly lifestyles. He has unhesitatingly come up with new initiatives to counter the consequences of the 'Industrial Growth Society' (Sigmund's 1970-term for the neoliberal economic system). In 2007 he launched a research project where one element was to retrace the development of the Norwegian tradition of eco-philosophy. The other was to edit an anthology, containing the history and selected essays on how to create a paradigm shift with joy.

The anthology *Arven og Gleden* (The implied meaning is *The Nature Heritage and a Change Empowered by Joy*) appeared on Tapir University Press, Trondheim 2010, sponsored by the Norwegian Ministry of the Environment. Børge invited three members of the 1966 Stetind group (Sigmund, Siri and Nils), bishop emeritus Finn Wagle, retired Standard oil industry director Øystein Dahle (later leader of the Norwegian Trekking Association) and colleague Aage Jensen, assistant professor at NORD University, Campus Levanger, to make up an editorial group for the anthology. The editors, named Council for Eco-philosophy, also got the assignment to elaborate an updated version of the Norwegian tradition for eco-philosophy, resulting in the Stetind Declaration.

The Council for Eco-philosophy concluded their work with a *one-page* text. The radical 2010-edition emerged from studies of utopian manifestos, i.e. Marx et al., which have ended in historical catastrophes. That is why the Stetind Declaration focuses on embodying the inherent values of free nature and of humans – cf. the UN Human Right Concept. The driving forces of our crises are known. Repeating once more is of no use. And: Is there a force stronger than the joy of finding solutions to questions without answers? What we need for a paradigm shift is motivation for personal creativity – the Ashlad's serendipity – governed by mutual *normative* premises – keel and rudder for thinking and acting. The Stetind perspective, thanks to Arne Naess, gave us the Spinozian values orientation of universal and eternal validity. After ten years of doubt and toil we at last, thanks to Aage Jensens's diplomacy and tenacious work, have managed to share our ideas and experiences in a condensed edition of the 2010 anthology *Nature as the Home of Culture and a Change empowered with Joy*.

THE STETIND PERSPECTIVE

Hard-science Ecology and Deep-joy philosophy united against mountain landscape damage
NILS FAARLUND

Yes, we love with fond devotion
This our land that looms
Rugged, storm-scared o'er the ocean,
With her thousand homes.

From *Ja, vi elsker* –
Norwegian National Anthem,
Bjørnstjerne Bjørnson, 1858/1869

Norway – where, what?

Since 1905 a kingdom on the Scandinavian Peninsula, bordering the North Sea, the North Atlantic and the Arctic Ocean. It is among the world's most northerly, and one of Europe's most mountainous countries, crowning the many scenic fjords. Norway has been internationally top ranked for Quality of Life, (The Human Development Index - a composite statistic of life expectancy, education, and income per capita indicators) and together with Switzerland in later years topping the list of per capita nominal GDP (Gross domestic product). If Planetary Pressures – adjusted, Norway falls back 15 places.

Hundred years ago, Norway was a developing country

Haraldr hárfagri (850 – 893) established Norway as a kingdom 872. From 1319 to 1537 Norway liaised with Sweden and Denmark in a variety of 'personal unions', then became a vassal state (1537 – 1660), later an autocracy (1660–1814) under Denmark. Norway at last regained its independence as a nation from a union with Sweden, lasting from 1814 till 1905.

Due to Norway's subordinate political role for almost four hundred years, the country did not take part in the European industrial revolution as the ruling neighbours found it more opportune to grab our country's natural wealth for use at home. Thus, Norway one hundred years ago belonged to the category of developing countries.

Six years after Norwegians became masters in own house Norwegian University of Science and Technology (NTH) was in operation to enable Norway to benefit from modern technology. Like other countries with an economy relying on the primary sector, it took time to catch up with the developed countries. Two World Wars, economic crises and a cumbersome paradigm shift also hampered the changeover.

The Driving Force behind the Norwegian *Wirtschaftswunder*

The transition of Norwegian culture into an efficient modernity machine, *i. e.* as demonstrated by the recent international economic top rankings, did not occur till after WW 2. Under the auspices of social democratic leadership, which had turned technocratic under the impressions of a war fought by means of the knowledge of the natural sciences, Norway produced nothing less than a *Wirtschaftswunder* (conf. post WW 2 "economic miracles" in Germany). This was not effectuated by *high tech* production, but by relying on the use of the national 'comparative advantage' of cheap electric energy for basic, electrochemical engineering, *i.e.* electrolysis of aluminium.

Motivated by the German scorched-earth policy in Arctic Norway at the end of WW 2 and the need of restoring the rest of the land after five years of occupation, the whole population took part in the spirit of the Norwegian volunteer-work tradition – *dugnad*. The key to this engineering *tour-de-force* was the construction of state-of-the art hydroelectric power works throughout our beloved mountains.

The tremendous damage done to *our land that looms/ Rugged, storm-scared o'er the ocean* (Bjørnson) was to start with tolerated as a necessary sacrifice for restoring housing and infrastructure as well as raising the affluence of the people and building a strong welfare state. In the 1950s though protests were heard from people *with fond devotion* for 'The Home of the Giants' with its grandiose waterfalls. The Norwegian Society for the Conservation of Nature, (NNV) founded in 1914, argued for prevention – but in vain. Although NNV was an established organization with respected citizen their points of view were disqualified as 'sentimental' and 'nostalgic'. When professor Rolf Nordhagen, a botanist with international reputation, opposed the damming of Aurlandsdalen by threatening that it might mean the end of wild Rhubarb in Norway, he was made a fool of. The gift of ample precipitation from the surrounding oceans of two thousand kilometres of Norwegian mountains was an outstanding slot machine, which nobody should dare to question.

Why the pledge to respect free nature in a modern, prosperous Norway

Many observers from abroad are puzzled by the fact, that Norwegian's profound way of communing with nature – friluftsliv – has survived the post WW 2 paradigm transformation, boosted by the oil fever. Recently Alice Wilkinson, reporting for The Telegraph in February 2017, notices that friluftsliv » ... is rooted in Norwegian culture and tells us that the key to (our) wellbeing lies, not just outdoors, but in a close connection to nature.» Four representative surveys since the beginning of the 1990s document the persistence of this close connection: 9 of 10 take part in friluftsliv in the Norwegian tradition. The motivation is far beyond the use of nature as a 'sparring partner': 9 of 10 state that they enjoy the silence found in the mountains, in the woods and on fjords/at sea, whereas near to 1 of 2 appreciate "the mystery of nature".

Over the years the grassroots friluftsliv culture of post WW 2-Norway has in tune with democratic practices developed strong non-profit advocacy organizations, i. a. The Norwegian Trekking Association (DNT – now more than 300.000 members) and Norsk Friluftsliv – a cooperation between 16 outdoor organizations (almost one million members or about 1/5 of the Norwegian population). Thus, the conditions for expressing the values of *friluftsliv* in the Norwegian tradition today are more favourable, than in the 1950- and 1960s. Since 1968 *friluftsliv* is also established as an *academic* field of study at all levels: BA, MA and PhD. In 2018 seven Universities and nine University Colleges were providing more than twenty different programs.

A bird's view of Stetind with the sunlit 1000 m high South face

A 'radicalization' of the *friluftsliv* culture emerges in the 1960s?

In the 1950- and 1960s the academic, economic and political power behind the hydroelectric offensive in our beloved mountains was of the kind military analysts today call 'an asymmetric conflict' – systematic, structural violence against a *grassroots friluftsliv culture powered by* passion. It was this hopeless situation, that provoked the genesis of the Norwegian tradition of eco-philosophy. So how could a 'radicalization' to enable a potent defence in the *friluftsliv* spirit come about?

Searching for the answer, we must pay attention to the great variety of *friluftsliv* in the Norwegian tradition – here stressing Norwegian – because we have the word in common with Swedes and Danes. Partly due to the mountainous nature in Norway and partly rooted in the in political history, there is a salient difference of *fond devotion* for wild mountain landscapes in the Scandinavian countries. Mountains may be harsh neighbours and they are for sure strict mentors, but they also *cultivate strong passions. If you follow the call of the mountains* with an alpine character, it means all or nothing. The deadly danger is obvious; thus, you are forced to relate in an all-embracing

24

way to reality – to nature – *free* nature with no restricted enforcement against seasonal, diurnal or growth rhythms is since 1977 our preferred term.

Scholars studying our forefathers' ways of life tell us, that the evolution of our ability and motivation for learning has a history of more than 11 million years. Situated learning in face of lethal danger has been a lasting necessity through the ages. Thus, we have inherited the talents for mastership in this art. According to the recent insights given by studies of such processes, the driving forces of learning are very powerful drugs, i. a. dopamine – known to cause addiction.

Origin of a Norwegian uprising against *Apparatenlandschaften*

This explains why mountaineering may 'radicalize' people, who without compromising, commit themselves to the intimacy with free nature, which since some generations has been cultivated as an absorbing branch of *friluftsliv*. When you are at 'the sharp end' of the rope, engaging 'by fair means' (no technical aids) in an instant rapport with rock, snow and ice, a strong friendship is created and confirmed. Dedicating yourself over years to this 'steep-land-art' (an art where nature plays a key role) causes addiction – passion for nature in possession of its multitude of undisturbed patterns in the rock, the snow, the ice, the weather – and the manifold of life encountered in a steep world.

It was not by chance that the Artic granite wonder Stetind (1392 m) became the birthplace of the Norwegian tradition of eco-philosophy (notice that the tree line this far North is at 500 m). The South Face has the dimensions of El Capitan (2307 m) in Yosemite, California, the almost one thousand meter high 'studio' for advanced mountaineering on rock since the 1950s. Stetind was also the place where the Nestor of Norwegian philosophy, Arne Naess, practiced the new 'hardware' belaying methods enabling hard climbs on blank rock, that he had learned in the Austrian and Italian Alps during his years as a doctoral student in Vienna in the 1930s.

Thirty years later, tirelessly studying the abundance of philosophic literature available around the world, the professor was a still-going-strong mountaineer. Having met Arne for the first time in the *Klettergarten* of our young mountaineering club – "Tindegruppa" – at Norwegian University of Science and Technology for the first time in 1960, I kept in touch to take advantage of his universe of knowledge as well as his experiences from mountains worldwide. Sometimes we met in the mountains, sometimes at The University of Oslo.

During one of my visits at his Institute of Philosophy in the winter of 1966 I emptied a bag full of precious pieces of blacksmith art on his desk. It was a collection of ingeniously made pitons (belaying equipment to be hammered into cracks in the rock) from the masters on rock in Yosemite. I had a dream: To convince Arne to join a small group of keen members of our mountaineering club at the University in Trondheim for two summer weeks of 'steep-land-art' at Stetind in the summer to come. Obvious to mountaineers I wanted Arne to share secrets about great lines up the Giants awe-inspiring face. But most of all I wanted an ideal opportunity to ponder over how to counter the prevailing politics of turning our beloved mountains into *Apparatenlandschaften* (an expression coined by Peter Wessel Zapffe, Arne's friend, philosopher and mountaineer, who was an early defender of free nature – often by means of refined irony).

Reputed philosopher and mountaineer Arne Naess joined in

Today I cannot remember exactly if Arne took time or not to make up his mind. Knowing his enthusiasm for the use of pitons and his appreciation for the music they made, when he hammered them home, I had no doubt. The marvellous ironwork of the Californian hippie blacksmiths would overwhelm him. They instantly promised a new era in belaying – and the pitons could be used over and over again. Arne's response was YES! He came with his wife Siri and daughter Lotte (8 years). And loads of books – because a professional philosopher, according to Arne's strict work regime, had to practice at least every other day to be fit for the demanding work of thinking.

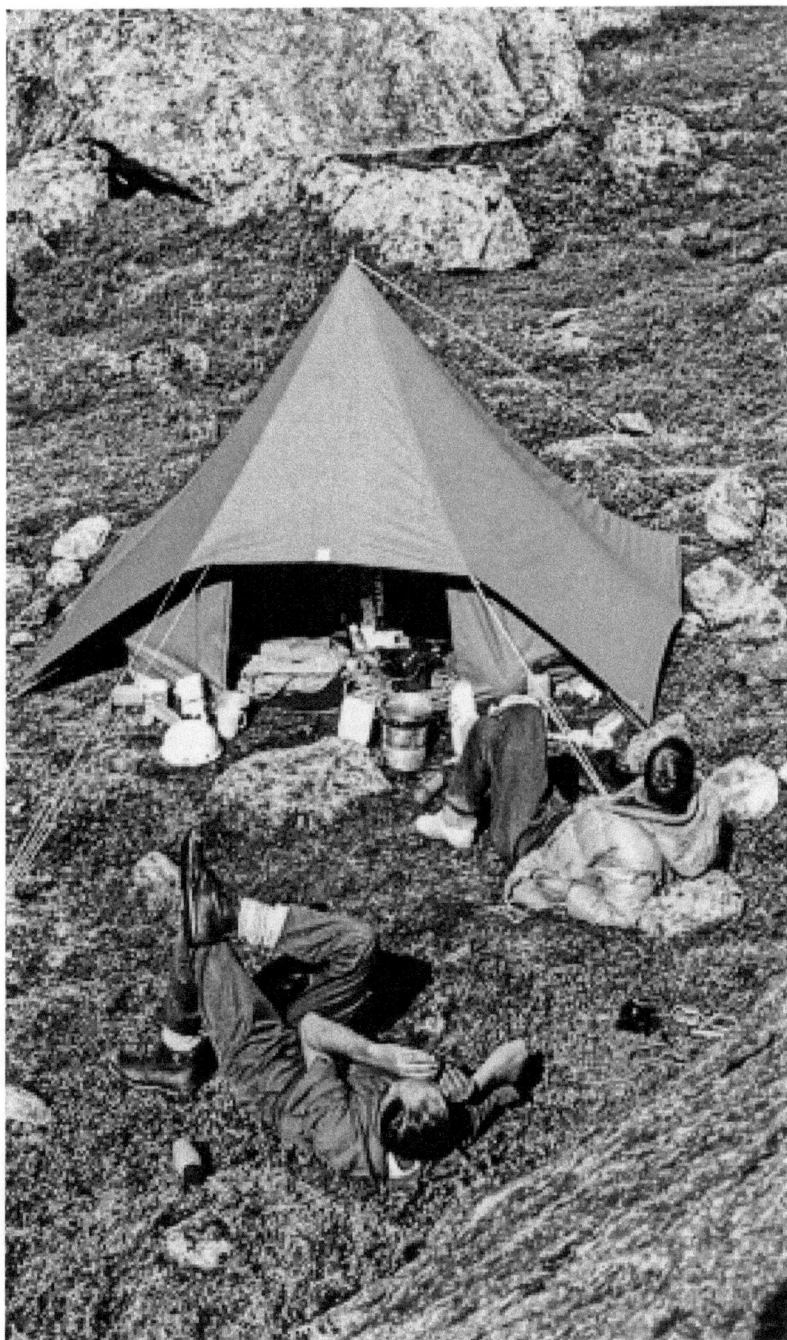

Arne Naess (1912 – 2009) looking for promising rock formations in the 1000-meter high South wall of Stetind (1392 m).

Although the grandeur of Stetind and the quality of the rock equals El Capitan and its neighbours, the climate in Arctic Norway adds limitations to when and how long you can enjoy the freedom of movement on dry and sunny rock. We were lucky to find 'weather windows' to dance our way up new lines on the superb rock in state-of-the-art big wall style. When we pitched our tents at the foot of the towering South Wall, we read with excitement the ornaments made through the ages by ice forcing cracks in the solid granite – like reading a map. Leaving two weeks later after intimate contact with the mountain 'at the sharp end' of the rope, we all felt a hearty familiarity with The Giant. Bjørnson, a colleague of Ibsen by the way, expressed our feelings with his introduction to our national hymn:

Yes, we love with fond devotion…

I came to Stetind with devotion for the free nature of alpine landscapes. My enthusiasm for mountaineering had downed upon me after a summer of guiding on a glacier in the centre of Jotunheimen when I was halfway through my MA-studies in biochemical engineering in Trondheim. By good luck I was the following year, 1958, awarded a one-year scholarship at Leibniz University Hannover, Germany, enabling me to do an apprenticeship with accomplished mountaineers in the *Alpenverein* of the region. During our ventures on The great Wall in the vicinity of Narvik it occurred to me that my 'destiny' now was to become a professional mountaineer to enthuse my fellow countrymen for the secrets of this at that time in Norway less known branch of *friluftsliv*.

The Stetind perspective: Defending free nature with ecology, governed by philosophy

This said, there is obviously more to tell about our visit to Stetind. I had the intention to use the rainy days, which were not suited for refined mountaineering workmanship, to ponder over how to counter the prevailing politics of turning our beloved mountains into *Apparatenlandschaften*. Being aware of Arne's dislike of small talk – he set the standard for preciseness for generations of Norwegian students – I chose to consult him on two for me at the time most essential questions (in the professor's special 'sociolect' also named 'seminar'):

(1)   Mountaineering – WHY?

and

(2) HOW to stop the damming
     of the Norwegian mountain world?

Today in the age of the *selfie* culture and climbing as indoor fitness activities, competitive sports, package tours to the highest mountains and 'high sensation seeking', my question number one is out-dated. Lacking a hundred years old tradition of a pass-time where 'conquers of the useless' (Lionel Terray, legendary, French mountain guide) put their life at stake, this was a recurring question for people with 'steep interest' in Norway some fifty years ago. As a family father and the person responsible for establishing "Tindegruppa" at NTH, the first open mountaineering club in Norway, I felt the need for support from a professional. Arne had the best of qualifications as a credible reference, being an accomplished mountaineer and a reputed philosopher.

Arne answered my first question head-on by an introduction to the philosophy of Baruch Spinoza of The good Life, which to him was a pursuit of *hilaritas* or Deep joy. Spinoza (1632 – 1677) advices us as individual, *small selves* to engage in all-embracing, creative ways of life towards an identification with *The great Self.* The great Self was for Spinoza synonymous with free nature, creation. His God was wholly 'immanent', in some sense synonymous with free nature. Mountaineering in the tradition of the Norwegian *friluftsliv* is thus in accord with Spinoza's advice of pursuing Deep joy in an all-embracing, creative steep-land-art way.

Admittedly a reference to a philosopher of the 16th century some tree hundred years later seems out-dated. On the contrary – a qualified, contemporary critic of the philosophy of the enlightenment with its *cogito ergo sum* dichotomy (Descartes) was Arne's judicious choice for answering the question of The good Life in the Age of Modernity. Spinoza had studied Aristotle, Plato and his contemporary, Descartes. He was an inspiration for Goethe and his followers in the Romantic movement, *i.e.* Rousseau, Schelling – and Haeckel (originator of the natural science ecology 1866). Today we know that he also had followers like the *primus inter pares* physicist Einstein and recently even the up to date leading neuroscientist Antonio Damasio.

Damming – an obstruction to all-embracing, creative steep-land art

We have already noticed that a mountaineer is "forced to relate in an all-embracing way to reality – to nature". Remembering that 'forced' in this context means an individually chosen exposure to the forces in alpine mountain terrain, mountaineering in the *friluftsliv* tradition fits nicely into Spinoza's patterns of thoughts about Deep joy and relating to The great Self. The damming of the mountain landscape does not, which prompted my second question for Arne about HOW to stop this brutal damage.

After WW 2 Arne as a philosopher turned away from his Vienna Circle inspired, positivistic perspective towards pluralism. In these early cold war days one of his primary projects was to work out a systematic ethics for peace on the basis of Mahatma Gandhi's life and practice. To further democratic practice and peace he also contributed to interpretation and preciseness. Generations of students in Norway have been influenced by this work. Thus, Arne's response to my second, far-reaching question were comments on how to achieve an efficient dialog in the spirit of Gandhi, conducted with preciseness and respect for facts.

So far so good, but as long as we were not able to come up with 'hard' science in defence of our beloved mountains, to match the economic and engineering expertise, demonstrating good manners was not of much use. Professor Rolf Nordhagen introduced his 'soft' natural science of botany to back the threatened wild Rhubarb in Aurlandsdalen and flopped. Thanks to the scholarship I got from Leibniz University in 1958 I stumbled over a natural science discipline called ecology. I was curious about this 'hard' science, which describes the relationship between the organic and the physical world. It was unknown to me these days – not so strange, because the landscape architects at the technical university of Hannover pioneered this field of study in Europe as a guide to the consequences of landscape interventions.

The revelations I got from the study of ecology fitted well into my apprenticeship as a mountaineer but remained dormant the following years of my busy professional and family life – topped by any free time spent in the mountains. But my criss-crossing of the alpine mountain world to make new acquaintances at home and in the Alps eventually became a wake-up call for using the perspective of ecology to oversee the extent of damage done by damming. Thus, I was aroused to contribute to the new deal needed in Norwegian nature prevention under the eagle-like shape of the Stetind South Face.

Eureka: Hard-science Ecology and Deep-joy philosophy united

With his thorough understanding of the philosophy of science, Arne immediately saw the potential of introducing ecology in an uprising against the idea of *Apparatenlandschaften.* Both of us having a professional background for the comprehension of the possible misuse of the power of sciences based on the principle of objectivity, *i. e.* Einstein's $E = m \cdot c^2$ and the construction of the atomic bomb, we right away went on to ponder how to handle this dilemma. In his profound work concerning the ethics of Spinoza and Gandhi, Arne's solution was to add *normative* premises to the descriptive.

Having clarified the perfect fitting between mountaineering in the Norwegian tradition and Spinoza's philosophy, there was an obvious solution to our recognized dilemma:

> *Make sure that objective, ecological knowledge is always practiced in keeping with subjective* fond devotion *for our dear mountains i. e. the inherent value of humans and of free nature.*

With these founding ideas of a strategy against further advancement of dam(m)age in/to the Norwegian mountain landscape, I left Stetind with the firm conviction, that the 'seminars' with Arne had brought forth nothing less than a discovery of an 'Archimedes lever' for calling off the hydroelectric offensive in our beloved mountain world – Archimedes: "Give me a place to stand and I will move the world". Admittedly my rope mates did not quite share my optimism. The reason why this did not cool down my enthusiasm was simply; I think in retrospect, that the potential of ecology was difficult to grasp at short notice as long as this science was still unknown in Norway in 1966.

After travelling for two days and one night homewards by bus and train back to the University College near Oslo, where I was studying microorganisms in forest soils, I unveiled for my wife, Helga, what for me had come out of the Stetind weeks. To my immense relief she agreed to leave a life in an academic culture bubble in an urban setting and settle in a small community in a landscape suitable for establishing a mountaineering school. In support of my idea of arranging courses in mountaineering in summer and winter to foster nature-friendship I reminded of the experience after hundred years of mountaineering of the power of the all-embracing steep-land-art 'to win the hearts and minds'.

Thus, I resigned from my research position in the autumn and welcomed the first participants in our mountaineering courses on rock and ice/glaciers – later known as Norges Høgfjellskole – in Hemsedal in July 1967. The enthusiasm created hands-on in the mountains opened for the reception of ecological knowledge and Spinoza's philosophy of intrinsic value of free nature. The concept worked!

Skier tragedy made way for eco-philosophy to nature protection

As fate would have, 16 skiers were killed in the mountains during their Easter holidays 1967 triggered the understanding that Norwegians not anymore were born mountaineers. This tragedy suddenly opened up for a full winter program of accident prevention at our brand-new school for teachers, leaders of trekking organizations, scouts, mountain rescue volunteers, army officers, students at University colleges and more. No participant left without an introduction to eco-philosophy: The hard-science ecology and deep-joy philosophy according to Spinoza united against landscape damage (our Council for Eco-philosophy added the hyphen in 2010 to make clear that the values philosophy is guiding the use of objective knowledge).

Aroused by the national tragedy of 16 people killed when skiing during their Easter holidays and the sensation of a Norwegian school of mountaineering headed by a white collar *drop out*, the media also spread the message of the eco-philosophical approach to the protection of free nature, accompanying a campaign for safety in the mountains. When a close friend from ski jumping in our domestic hills with whom I later shared college years, Sigmund Kvaløy (later Setreng), 1969 initiated the first University seminar on eco-philosophy "Man and Nature". The student uprising in 1968 had created a 'carrier wave' of critical thinking.

Sigmund Kvaløy opened for Eco-philosophy at University level

Sigmund, a mag. art./PhD student of Arne's, was also a member of the Stetind group. Due to his overshadowing interest for the philosophy of jazz at the time (the subject of his degree), his burning engagement for eco-philosophy took a year or two to develop. Arne supported Sigmund's "Man and Nature" seminar idea and we got started in the autumn semester of 1969 with a University level seminar. A hard core of mountaineers was joined by young academics and students in philosophy, sociology, biology, technology, and architecture. Sigmund did not have the patience to wait till the opening of the autumn semester, thus in spring he took the initiative to establish (snm), the acronym for "Cooperation Groups for Nature and Environmental Protection". His haste was due to new, threatening hydroelectric power work projects in the mountains. Top priority was given to Aurlandsdalen.

The cryptic acronym (snm) symbolizes our collective work style in tune with the 68ers' movement. Whereas the student uprising followed Marx, Lenin and Mao, our lead philosophers were Spinoza, Bergson, and Gandhi. The use of lover-case letters and parenthesis for the logo symbolizes the priority of the creative process over enforcing structures of the organization of the work, which soon gave the 'cooperating groups' a strong momentum. The "Man and Nature" seminar followed up the experiences made by (snm), working out a WHAT-WHY-HOW pattern for a Gandhian non-violent action for defending watercourses against rigorous damming projects.

Journalists reported eco-philosophy word by word from Mardøla

Our first target was the mentioned Aurlandsdalen, a valley subsidiary to the longest fjord in Norway of World Heritage quality, Sognefjorden. Realizing that we were too late to prevent the damming by practicing Gandhian non-violent methods in this stunning valley, we turned to the watercourse of Mardøla near Romsdalen with the magnificent Trolltindene – Aiguilles of the Trolls. The Mardøla waterfall was among the ten highest waterfalls in Europe with a spectacular upper drop of 358 meters.

Because the Mardøla non-violent action was well timed to 'the slow news season' for the media, the (snm) tent camp above the tree line near the crest of the waterfall was crowded with journalists for two weeks. As tabloid journalism was not yet invented in Norway fifty years ago, the campers with Sigmund as the mentor of philosophy enjoyed the privilege of speaking to journalists, who reported the eco-philosophic message word by word. It certainly added to the great public interest for the Mardøla struggle, that it was an action of civil disobedience – once introduced by Henry David Thoreau.

Unfortunately, the media impact and spontaneous supporters visiting the high camp by the hundreds, taking part in sit down actions, did not impress the Government. They sent in the police to clear the camp. The battle over freedom for nature in Eikesdalen and the neighbouring *land that looms Rugged, storm-scared o'er the ocean* was lost, but we during the 1970ies won 'the hearts and minds' of our countrymen.

Two years after the Mardøla-action the first Norwegian referendum on membership in the European Economic Community (EEC) was staged. On the last evening before the election the final battle was fought in the studio of our sole TV station. 'Everybody' watched. The secretary of state for the environment, representing the social democratic party, defended the YES-point of view. The spokesperson for the NO-movement was a reader (of professor competence) of history of ideas in Arne's institute, who based his arguments on an at that time well elaborated eco-philosophy. Our grass roots movement won by a (very) small margin. It is not obvious that our values-based use of ecology, which now had nurtured a vigorous protest movement against a fully-fledged, Norwegian economic growth machinery, alone was the 'Archimedes lever'.

The 'greening of Norway' in the 1970s spurred by eco-philosophy

But eco-philosophy transformed into 'ecopolitics' with Sigmund as a figurehead.

And the fact is, that we at this time already had three political parties, which had turned 'green'. At the Parliament elections of 1973 they were supported by 20% of the voters. During the following years every political party in our country went through a 'greening' process. The adoption of ecopolitics was of course also stimulated by The European Conservation Year 1970 and The *United Nations* Conference on The Human *Environment* 1972.

The most prominent example of a 'Green Shift' in Norway in the 1970ies was the end of the hydroelectric power work era after the Alta non-violent action 1979 – 1981. In (almost) every other country in the world this seems counterproductive for a nature-friendly future, but in '*the-other-place*'-Norway we have since many years had an overproduction of renewable energy. Only by running an immense energy-intensive industry and recently by exporting electricity it has been possible to keep the kWh-price at a profitable level.

Other examples of the 'greening of Norway' in the 1970s is the shift from an enforced evacuation of scattered rural settlements, as practiced in Sweden, to supporting agriculture and other productive undertakings in the periphery. Collective transport and a turn towards nature-friendly production were other corrections of the post WW 2 techno-optimistic culture. Fighting pollution was also given priority, *i. e.* acid rain/sulphur dioxide, perfluorocarbons, and sodium fluoride from the aluminium production. But then the oil age took off in the 1980s and an eco-philosophic world view was blurred by a buoyant and dazzling affluence.

The impact of eco-philosophy faded due to an invasive oil fever

For people busy embodying the Spinozian philosophy of the inherent values of free nature as well as of humans it took some time to recognize that our parliamentarians again were consequently adjusting to the economic growth ideology – in line with the trend of globalization. Our green counter-culture lost momentum because of the consequences of the oil extraction in the North Sea and the increase of the CO_2-consentration in the atmosphere did not infer in a personally, impressive way like damage done to a beloved landscape. The organizations for the prevention of nature responded by turning to sensational media stunts to evoke attention, leaving out the philosophical message, which of course had no spearheading effect in the boulevard press. As there were nobody with the necessary standing and political appeal to follow up the leadership of Arne and Sigmund in their spheres, only the to some extent institutionalized work with 'conwaying'[1] values orientated learning and leadership in the Norwegian tradition of *friluftsliv* went on.

Børge Dahle, associate professor emeritus of *friluftsliv* at The Norwegian School of Sport Sciences (NIH) was among the professionals and volunteers, who refused to give in. As a student of sport sciences at NIH in 1968 – 1970, he was inspired by the novelty to academic institutions in Norway at the time – eco-philosophy – and later devoted his life to forward nature-friendly lifestyles. He has unhesitatingly come up with new initiatives to counter the consequences of the 'Industrial Growth Society' (Sigmund's 1970-term for the neo-liberal economic system). In 2007 he launched a research project where one element was to retrace the development of the Norwegian tradition of eco-philosophy. The other was to edit an anthology, containing the history and selected essays on how to create a paradigm shift with joy.

'Industrial Growth Society' challenged with the *Arven og Gleden*

The anthology *Arven og Gleden* (The implied meaning is *The Nature Heritage and a Change Empowered by Joy*) appeared on Tapir University Press, Trondheim 2010, sponsored by the Norwegian Ministry of the Environment. Børge invited three members of the 1966 Stetind group (Sigmund, Siri and Nils), bishop emeritus Finn Wagle, retired oil industry director Øystein Dahle/later leader of The Norwegian Trekking Association and Aage Jensen, assistant professor at NORD University, Campus Levanger, to make up an editorial group for the anthology. The editors, named Council for Eco-philosophy, also got the assignment to elaborate an up to date version of the Norwegian tradition of eco-philosophy, resulting in the Stetind Declaration.

---

1   *Con-way-ing*: *Con* is latin for (together) with, thus *conwaying* means situated learning in smaler groups, being accompanied by a mentor (*viz.* Greek tradition).

The Council concluded their work with a *one*-page text. The radical 2010-edition emerged from studies of utopian manifestos *i. e.* Marx *et al.*, which have ended in historical catastrophes. That is why the Stetind Declaration focuses on embodying the inherent values of free nature and of humans – *cf.* The UN Human Right Concept. The driving forces of our crises are known. Repeating once more is of no use. And: Is there a force stronger than the joy of finding solutions to questions without answers? What we need for a paradigm shift is motivation for personal creativity – the Ashlad's serendipity – governed by mutual *normative* premises. The Stetind perspective, thanks to Arne Naess, gave us the Spinozian values orientation of universal and eternal validity. After ten years of doubt and toil we at last, thanks to Aage's diplomatic and tenacious work, have managed to share our ideas and experiences in a condensed edition of the 2010 anthology of Nature as the Home of Culture and a Change empowered by Joy.

The place of joy in a world of fact[2]

ARNE NAESS

The solution of environmental problems is presupposed in all utopias. For example, every family is to enjoy free nature under Marxian communism. "In communist society," Marx says in a famous passage in *The German Ideology*:

> Nobody has one exclusive sphere of an activity, but each can be accomplished in any branch he wishes. Society regulates the general production and thus makes it possible for me to do one thing today and another tomorrow: to hunt in the morning, fish in the afternoon, tend cattle in the evening, engage in literary criticism after dinner, just as I have in mind, without ever becoming a hunter, fisherman, shepherd, or critic.

The complete individual is not a specialist; he or she is a generalist and an amateur. This does not mean that the person has no special interests, never works hard, or does not partake in the life of the community. The complete individual does so, however, from personal inclination, with joy, and within the framework of his or her value priorities.

In the future society, whether outlines by Marx or by more bourgeois prophets, there will be people who might use most of their energy doing highly specialized, difficult things, but as amateurs – that is, from inclination and from mature philosophy of life. There will be no fragmentary men and women, and certainly no fragmentary ecologists.

We all, I suppose, admire the pioneers who, through endless meetings held in contaminated city air, have succeeded in establishing wilderness areas in the United States. Unfortunately, their constant work in offices and corridors has largely ruined their capacity to show, *in action*, what they care for; otherwise, they would spend much more time (and even live) in the wilderness. Many people verbally admire wilderness areas, but have not stepped down from their exalted positions, as chairs of this or that, to enjoy these areas at least part of the year.

---

2   This essay was written in 1982 and revised in 1991. It was originally published in The Deep Ecology of Wisdom (Dordrecht: Springer, 2005) (SWAN, vol.10), 395-419.

Arne Naess (1912 – 2009) studying the philosophy of Baruch Spinoza in a high camp during the first ascent of Tirich Mir East (7692 m).

What I say here about advocates of wilderness seems, unhappily, to be valid for advocates of a better environment in general. Ordinary people show a good deal of skepticism toward verbally declared values that are not expressed in the lifestyle of the propagandist. Environmentalists sometimes succumb to a joyless life that belies their concern for a better environment. This cult of dissatisfaction is apt to add to already fairly advanced joylessness we find among socially responsible, successful people and to undermine one of the chief presuppositions of the ecological movement: that joy is related to the environment and to nature.

In short, the best way to promote a good cause is to provide a good example. One ought not to be afraid that the example will go unnoticed. For example, Albert Schweitzer hid himself in Africa, but his public relations prospered and so did the sale of his books.

So much for utopias. My next concern is with how to get nearer to our utopias. I shall take up only one aspect: the relation between personal lifestyle and teaching.

The Lifestyle of Environmentalists

Joy is contagious. If we only talk about the joys of a good environment, though, it is of little avail.

I know that many *have* turned their backs on more lucrative careers and life of security, cultivating well-established sciences. This is not enough, however. Life should manifest the peaks of our value priorities. Working for a better environment is, after all, only of instrumental value. We remain on the level of techniques. What criterion shall we use to follow the lead of our personal priorities? We do have one that is underrated among conscientious, responsible people: joy.

Joy according to "pessimistic" philosophers

Suppose someone adhered to the doctrine that there cannot be too much cheerfulness under any circumstances – even at a funeral. The sad truth is, I think, that he or she would be classified as shallow, cynical, disrespectful, irreligious, or mocking.

Søren Kierkegaard is an important figure here. He *seems* to take anguish, desperation, a sense of guilt, and suffering as necessary, and sometimes even sufficient, condition of authentic living, but he also insists upon continuous joy as a condition of living. Whatever is done without joy is of no avail. "At seven thousand fathoms' depth," you should be glad. At seven thousand fathoms, one should retain "a joyful mind." He sometimes calls himself Hilaritus, the one permeated with *hilaritas* (Latin for "cheerfulness").

Dread is the technical existentialist word for the kind of anxiety that opens the way to a deeper understanding of life. According to Heidegger (another hero of modern pessimism), dread is not an isolated, negative sensation. The mind is in a complex state in which dread cannot exist without joy; that is, one who thinks he or she has the dread experience but lacks joy suffers from an illusion. Dread has an internal relation to joy.

Our problem is not that we lack high levels of integration (that is, that we are immature and therefore joyless), but rather that we glorify immaturity. Do the most influential philosophers of our time and culture represent high degrees of maturity and integration? I have in mind not only Heidegger, Sartre, Kierkegaard, and Wittgenstein, but also Marx and Nietzsche. Tentatively, I must answer no. There are lesser-known but perhaps more mature philosophers, like Jaspers and Whitehead.

Should the world's misery and the approaching ecocatastrophe make one sad? My point is that there is no good reason to feel sad about this. According to the philosophies I am defending, such regret is a sign of immaturity, the immaturity of unconquered passiveness and lack of integration.

The remedy (or psychotherapy) against sadness caused by the world's misery is to do something about it. I shall refrain from mentioning Florence Nightingale but let me note that Gandhi loved to care for, wash, and massage lepers; he simply enjoyed it. It is very common to find those who constantly deal with extreme misery to be more than usually cheerful. According to Spinoza, the power of an individual is infinitely small compared with that of the entire universe, so we must not expect to save the whole world. The main point – which is built into the basic conceptual framework of Spinoza's philosophy – is that of activeness. By interacting with extreme misery, one gains cheerfulness. This interaction need not be direct. Most of us can do more in indirect ways by using privileged positions in rich societies.

There are clear reasons for us not to concentrate all our efforts directly on extreme miseries, but rather to attack the causes, conditions, and other factors indirectly contributing to this misery. And, just as important, we need to encourage the factors that directly cause or facilitate the emergence of active (and therefore cheerful) work to alleviate misery.

Behind the prevailing widespread passivity found throughout the world is a lot of despair and pessimism concerning our capacity to have a good time. We tend to enjoy ourselves (except during vacations) in a private world of thoughtlessness, well insulated from the great issues of the day.

One of the strangest and next-to-paradoxical theses of Spinoza (and Thomas Aquinas and others) is that knowledge of evil, or of misery, is inadequate knowledge. In short, there is no such object, whereas there is something good to know. Evil is always an absence of something, a lack of something positive. Their theory of knowledge holds that objects of knowledge are always something. When you say that you see that the glass is transparent, what you see, for example, is a red nose behind the glass. You do not see the transparency, which is not an object of perception.

In any event, while I do not think that the positive nonexistence of evil things can be shown without a great redefinition of words, I nevertheless do not consider this view totally ridiculous. Like so many other strange points of view in major philosophies, it has an appeal and points in the right direction without perhaps stating anything clearly in the "scientific" sense.

Spinoza on joy

Spinoza operates with three main concepts of joy and three of sorrow. *Laetitia, hilaritas* and *titillatio* are the three Latin terms for the positive emotions of joy. Translation of these terms are, to a surprising degree, arbitrary, because their function in Spinoza's system can be discovered only by studying the complex total structure of his system. Isolating one concept from the others is not possible. Moreover, the system is more than the sum of its parts. From a strict, professional point of view, you must take it or leave it as a whole.

I translate *laetitia* as "joy" – a generic term comprising several important sub-kinds of joy. The main classification of joy is *hilaritas* (cheerfulness) and *titilatio* (pleasurable excitement). *Hilaritas* is the serene thing, coloring the whole personality, or better, the whole world.

Spinoza defines *hilaritas* as a joy to which every part of the body contributes. It does not affect just a subgroup of functions of the organism, but every one, and therefore the totality of the organism. Spinoza contends that there cannot be too much *hilaritas*.

The other main kind of joy, *titilatio*, affects a subgroup of the parts of the body. If very narrowly based and strong, it dominates and thereby inhibits the other kinds of joy. Accordingly, there can be too much of it. Here Spinoza mentions love of money, sexual infatuation, and ambition. He also mentions other sources of joy that are all good in modern degrees if they do not hamper and inhibit one another.

A second classification of joy is that derived from the contemplation of our own achievement, creativity, or – more broadly – activeness, and the joy

41

derived from the contemplation of the causes of joy outside us. The first he calls satisfaction, or response in ourselves (*aquiescentia in se ipso*); the other he calls *amor*. There can be too much of them, however, because they sometimes refer to parts, not to the whole.

According to Spinoza, what refers to the whole of the body also refers to the whole of the conscious mind and to the whole of the universe or, more generally, to the whole of Nature, insofar as we know it. This is understandable from Spinoza's so-called philosophy of identity, which proclaims the ultimate identity of thought and matter, and from his theory of knowledge, which relates all our knowledge of the world to interaction with the body – just as biologists tend to do today.

Lack of self-acceptance (*aquiescentia in se ipso*) accounts for much of the passivity displayed by an important sector of the public in environmental conflicts. Many people are on the right side, but few stand up in public meetings and declare how they, as private citizens, feel about the pollution in their neighborhoods. They do not have sufficient self-respect, respect for their own feelings, or faith in their own importance. But they themselves do not have to fight for the changes; it is only necessary that they state their feelings and positions in public. A small minority will then fight with joy – supported by that considerable sector of people.

The distinction between pervasive joy (covering all) and partial joy need not to be considered an absolute dichotomy but rather one that exists in degrees. Joy may be more or less pervasive. Clearly, higher degrees of joy require high degrees of integration of the personality, and high degrees of such integration require intense cultivation of the personal aspect of interaction with the environment. It requires a firm grasp of what we call value priorities – which Spinoza would call reality priorities, because of his resolute location of value among "objective" realities. Spinoza distinguishes degrees of realness and perfection. That which is perfect is complete. Integration of personality presupposes that we never act as mere functionaries or specialists but always as whole personalities conscious of our value priorities, and of the need to manifest those priorities in social direct action.

The specific thing to be learned from Spinoza and certain modern psychologists is, however, to integrate the value priorities themselves in the world. We tend to say "the world of facts", but the separation of value from facts is, itself, mainly due to an overestimation of certain scientific traditions stemming from Galileo. These traditions confuse the *instrumental* excellence of the mechanistic worldview with its properties as a whole philosophy. Spinoza was heavily influenced by mechanical models of matter, but he did not extend them to cover "reality". His reality was neither mechanical, value-neutral, nor value-empty.

This cleavage into two worlds – the world of facts and the world of values – can theoretically be overcome by placing, as Spinoza does, joys and other so-called subjective phenomena into a unified total field of realities. This, however, is too much to go into here. I am more concerned with the place of joy among our total experiences. The objectivist conception of value is important, though, in any discussion in which technocrats tend to dismiss cheerfulness in the environment as something "merely subjective".

Spinoza makes use of the following short, crisp, and paradoxical definition of joy (*laetitia*): "Joy is man's transition from lesser to greater perfection." Somewhat less categorically, he sometimes says that joy is the affect by which, or through which, we make the transition to greater perfection. Instead of "perfection", we may say "integrity" or "wholeness".

Of central importance, in my view, is the difference between these formulations and subjectivist ones proclaiming that joy only *follows* or *accompanies* these transitions to greater perfection. For Spinoza, the relation between joy and increase in perfection is an *intrinsic* one. That is, the two can be separated only conceptually, not in practice. Such a realistic view of joy suggests that joyfulness, like color, attaches to and forms part of objects, but, of course, changes with the medium and must be defined in terms of interaction with organisms. Joy is linked intrinsically to an increase in many things: perfection, power and virtue, freedom and rationality, activeness, the degree to which we are the cause of our actions, and the degree to which our actions are understandable by reference to ourselves. Joy is thus a basic part of the conceptual structure of Spinoza's system.

An increase in power is an increase in the ability to carry out what we sincerely strive to do. Power does not presuppose that we coerce other people; a tyrant may be less powerful than some poor soul sitting in prison. This concept of power has a long tradition and should not be forgotten. What we strive to do is defined in relation to what actually happens; thus "to save the world from pollution" is not something anyone strives to do, but rather a kind of limited effort to save the things around us.

Cheerfulness (*hilaritas*) requires action of the whole integrated personality and is linked to a great increase in power. In the absence of joy, there is no increase of power, freedom, or self-determination. Thus, lack of joy should be taken seriously, especially among so-called responsible people furthering a good cause. The joy of work, like any other partial joy, can dominate and subdue other sources of joy to such an extent that the overall result is stagnation or even decrease in power. In Spinoza's terminology, this means a loss of perfection or integration and increased difficulty in reaching a state of cheerfulness.

"To be happy" is often equated with enjoying oneself, laughing, or relaxing in the sense of being passive. Enjoying oneself by becoming intoxicated, which decreases the higher integrations of the nervous system, results in resignation. It means giving up the possibility of joyfulness of the whole person. Cheerfulness, in the Spinozistic sense, may not always be expressed in laughter or smiling, but in concentration, presentness, activeness.

The example of Buddha may illustrate my point. Buddha was an active person, but had great repose in himself (*acquiescentia in se ipso*). Long before he died, he said to have reached Nirvana, which, properly interpreted within Mahayana Buddhism, involves supreme integration and liberation of the personality, implying bliss or (in the terminology of Spinoza) *hilaritas*. Research by F. Th. Stcherbatsky (1974) and others concerning the term *dukkha* (conventionally translated as "pain") shows that so-called pessimistic Buddhism also has a doctrine of joy as a central aspect of reaching freedom in Nirvana.

One may say, somewhat loosely, that what we now lack in our technological age is response on oneself. The conditions of modern life prevent the full development of the self-respect and self-esteem that are required to reach a stable high degree of acquiescentia *in se ipso* (the term *alienation*, incidentally, is related to the opposite of *in se*, namely, *in alio*, wherein we repose in something else, something outside ourselves, such as achievement in the eyes of other – we are "other directed.")

Humility, as defined by Spinoza, is sorrow resulting from the contemplation of one's own impotency, weakness, and helplessness. A feeling of sorrow always involves a decrease of perfection, virtue, or freedom. We can come to know adequately more potent things than ourselves. This gives us such a joy because of our activeness in the very process of knowing them. The realization of our own potency, and our active relation to the more potent, result in joy:

- first, the joy resulting from the contemplation of our own power, however small, which gives us *acquiescentia in se ipso,* self-respect and contentedness
- second, the joy resulting from increased personal, active knowledge of things greater than we are
- third, the joy resulting from active interaction, which, strictly speaking, defines us (as well as objects or fragments) in the total field of reality (or in Nature, in Spinoza's terminology)

44

Adequate knowledge always has a joyful personal aspect because it reveals a power (never a weakness) in our personality. In Spinoza's words:

> *Therefore, if man, when he contemplates himself, perceives some kind of impotency in himself, it does not come from understanding himself, but from his power of action being reduced ... To the extent that man knows himself with true rationality, to that extent it is assumed that he understands his essence, that is, his power.*

We say with some haughtiness that Spinoza belongs to the age of rationalism, to the pre-Freudian, pre-Hitler era. Nevertheless, Spinoza in many ways anticipated Freud, and his term *ratio* must not be translated into our term *rational* or *rationality* unless we immediately add that his *ratio* was more flexible and internally related to emotion. Rational action for him is action involving absolutely maximal perspective – that is, where things are seen as fragments of total Nature – which is, of course, not what we tend to call rational today. Spinoza was not an intellectual in the sense of modern Anglo-American social science.

Pity and commiseration (*misericordia* and *commiseration*) are not virtues for Spinoza, and even less so for Gandhi, although they may have some positive instrumental value. Spinoza says that:

> *Commiseration, like shame, although it is not a virtue, is nevertheless good in so far as it shows that a desire for living honestly is present in the man who is possessed with shame, just as pain is called good in so far as it shows that the injured part has not yet putrefied.*

A modest function, but nevertheless of instrumental value! Tersely, Spinoza adds that "a man who lives according to the dictates of reason strives as much as possible to prevent himself from being touched by commiseration." People who are crippled are among those who practically unanimously agree.

Commiseration is sorrow and therefore is, in itself, an evil. According to certain conventional morality, a duty should be carried out even if there is no joy. This suggests that we had better disregard our duties if we are not permeated with joy. I find this interpretation rather fanatical, however, except when one adds a kind of norm concerning the high priority of developing the *capacity* for joy. "Alas! I cannot do my duty today because it does not fill me with joy. Better to escalate my efforts to experience joy!" Spinoza does not stress the remedy to the above situation – greater integration – but he presupposes it. The case of humility shows how *ratio* changes sorrows to joys: Spinozistic psychoanalysis tries to loosen up the mental cramps that cause unnecessary pain.

Freud worked with the tripartition of id, ego, and superego. The superego, through its main application in explaining neuroses, has a rather ugly reputation: It coerces the poor individual to try the Impossible and then lets the person experience shame and humility when there is no success. In Spinoza's analysis, the *ratio* also functions as a kind of overseer, but its main function is rather one of consolation. It directs our attention to what we can do rather than to what we cannot, and eliminates feelings of necessary separation from others; it stresses the harmony of rational wills and of well-understood self-interests.

A major virtue of a system like Spinoza's is the extreme consistency and tenacity with which consequences, even the most paradoxical, are drawn from intuitively reasonable principles. It meets requirements of clarity and logic of modern natural science. The system says to us: "You do not like consequence number 101? But you admit it follows from a premise you had admitted. Then give up the premise. You do not want to give up the premise? Then you must give up the logic, the rules of inference you used to derive the consequence. You cannot give them up? But then you have to accept the consequence, the conclusion. You don't want to? Well, I suppose you don't want clarity and integration of your views and your personality."

The rationality of a total view like Spinoza's is perhaps the only form of rationality capable of breaking down the pseudo-rational thinking of the conservative technocracy that currently obstructs efforts to think in terms of the total biosphere and its continued blossoming in the near and distant future.

The philosophical premises of environmentalism

Personally, I favor the kind of powerful premises represented in Chines, Indian, Islamic and Hebrew philosophy, as well as Western philosophy – namely, those having as a slogan the so-called ultimate unity of all life. They do not hide the fact that big fish eat small ones, but stress the profound interdependence, the functional unity, of such a biospheric magnitude that non-violence, mutual respect, and feelings of identification are always potentially there, even between the predator and its so-called victim. In many cultures, identification is not limited merely to other living things but also to the mineral world, which helps us conceive of ourselves as genuine surface fragments of our planet, fragments capable of somehow experiencing the existence of all other fragments: a microcosm of the macrocosm.

Another idea, right at the basis of a system from which environmental norms are derivable, is that of self-realization. The mature human individual, with a broadened self, acknowledges a right to self-realization that is universal. Consequently, he or she seeks a social order, or rather a biospheric order, that maximizes the potential for self-realization of all kinds of beings.

Level-headed, tough-minded environmentalists sometimes stress that it is sheer hypocrisy to pretend that we try to protect nature for its own sake. In reality, they say, we always have needs of human beings in view. This is false, I think. Thousands of supporters of unpolluted so-called wastelands in northern Labrador wish simply that those lands should continue to exist as they are, for their own sake. The wastelands are of intrinsic, and not only instrumental, value. To invoke *specifically* human needs to describe this situation is misleading, just as it is misleading to say that it is egotistical to share one's birthday cake with others because one *likes* to share with others.

Self-realization is not a maximal realization of the coercive powers of the ego. The *self* in the kinds of philosophy I am alluding to is something expansive, and the environmental crisis may turn out to be of immense value for further expansion of human consciousness.

In modern education, the difference between a world picture – or better, a world model – and a straightforward description of the world is glossed over. Atoms, particles, and wave functions are presented as parts or fragments of nature or are even presented as *the* real, objective nature, as contrasted with human projections into nature – the "colorful" but subjective nature.

So-called physical reality, in term of modern science, is perhaps only a piece of abstract mathematical reality – a reality we emphatically do not live in. Our living environment is made up of all the colorful, odor-filled, ugly, or beautiful details, and it is sheer folly to look for an existing thing without color, odor, or some other homely quality. The significance of this subject is a broad cultural one: the rehabilitation of the status of the immediately experienced world, the colorful and joyful world. *Where* is joy in the world of fact? Right at the center!

Literature:

- Karl Marx and Friedrich Engels, *The German Ideology* (London: Lawrence and Wishart, 1970)

- F. Th. Stcherbatsky, *The Central Conception of Buddhism* (Delhi: Motical Banarsidas, 1974)
- Benedict (Baruch) de Spinoza, *The Ethics* (New York: Hafner, 1955), 226-227. The passage was translated from Latin by Naess. All passages in this essay are from The Ethics and were translated by Arne Naess.

Friluftsliv – a way home

NILS FAARLUND

Contemporary Norwegian culture – European culture, Western culture – has become estranged from the *home* of mankind. We belong to cultures that have failed to *recreate* a sense of *free* nature as our true home – archetypical nature, recognized by its rhythms and tides. Because our cultures have failed to pass on this precious understanding, free nature has lost *standing*.

Where humans are left without a home, made fugitive in the world, we feel lost, alone. Modern culture, instead of reintroducing us to nature, encourages our solitude by insisting that it is a *virtue* to be *outstanding*, a "separate individual", a true, objective *observer*. Alone, we are prey to anxiety, we *are afraid*. Afraid, some turn *aggressive* towards the foreign – other humans, or nature. Some reject a confrontation, becoming *followers*. Either they follow the aggressive, or feeling hopeless and powerless, they turn cynical, or even mad.

In cultures where free nature has lost standing, people release aggression through their work, but also through their leisure, especially in outdoor recreation. Where nature has lost standing, it usually becomes the victim of aggression – humans think of themselves as Descartes' *maître et possesseur de la nature*. Coupled with the technological prowess made possible by the Newtonian natural science, it is no surprise that the world today is in the throes of an ecological crisis.

If you are one of those who feel at home in free nature, there is no need to persuade you of the consequences of this crisis; you have probably been feeling them for some time.

If you are an objective but attentive "observer" of nature, you might be persuaded of the gravity of the situation by "crisis literature" such as *Mankind at the Turning Point* (Mesarovic and Pestel, 1974).

If you see nature as a resource, nothing less than a crisis, which breaks into your daily life – massive fish kills, a dying forest – will suffice to wake you up.

But the future is not uniformly black. There are still ways out of the crisis, ways opened by a sense of joy with nature. In Norway the tradition of *friluftsliv* is a way of recreating understanding for nature, of rediscovering the true home of mankind. *Friluftsliv* (pronounced "free-loofts-leave", and meaning literally:

"open-air life") is similar to, but not exhausted by the English term "outdoor recreation": it has resonances in the French *la vie en plain air*, in the English "nature-life" or in the archaic English term "nature-*faerd*."

Whichever way it is translated, *friluftsliv* draws on traditional crafts, tools, and lore from a Norwegian culture, which was still consonant with the rhythms of free nature. Its roots and values are in harmony with the *poesophy* (poetry/philosophy) in the European Deep Romantic Movement of the last century.

Fridtjof Nansen (1861–1930), polar explorer and humanitarian, was an especially strong inspiration towards *friluftsliv*. In 1888 this national hero had skied across Greenland, and in 1895 he set out in an (unsuccessful) attempt to reach the North Pole on skis. As Norway's ambassador to the League of Nations, he worked tirelessly to bring peace to a war-torn continent – and in the meantime inspired many Europeans to take up skiing!

Nansen urged that an alternative rising of youth should avoid the tendency towards "tourism" – superficial acquaintance – in all aspects of life. In addition, he contended that the use of technology in outdoor life had to be "appropriate", and that only an ample opportunity for life in free nature would foster responsible and mature people. Nansen's writing revealed a sense of cooperation with nature's awesome power, and equally important, a sense of joy in being in nature. And his belief that free nature was our true home was explicit:

> *That which could revive us and lead us back to a more human*
> *existence is to take up a simple life in nature; in the forest, plains*
> *or mountains, on the high plateaus, in the great, lonely emptiness,*
> *where new and greater thoughts stream into us and leave a mark*
> *that cannot be easily erased… one feels something basic, something*
> *that feels like one's real self, and one comes back with a fresher and*
> *healthier view of life than we have in the city.*

Mountaineer-poet Carl Wilhelm Rubenson (1885–1960) was also a source of *friluftsliv* philosophy. "There is much in a person," he wrote after returning from a long pilgrimage through the Himalayas,

> *that present-day life, especially in the cities, does not call use; half-*
> *forgotten abilities and instincts from a time when man lived together*
> *with nature, and had to struggle with nature's power to maintain his*
> *existence – we don't have to do that today. But there is still something*
> *left in us from those times, in every healthy human being there is*

*a deep need to feel at home in nature, to show himself that his mind
has roots, roots which have not yet lost their grip in the earth. It is
that need which drives us city-folk out to the sea, into the forest, and
up onto the mountains.*

A sense for the Norwegian mountains "soaring out of the sea" is expressed in our national anthem written by Bjørnstjerne Bjørnson. Henrik Ibsen's poem "Paa Vidderne" introduced the word *friluftsliv* in 1869 to Norwegian literature in a paean to the rough purities of "nature-life".

Besides words, other media have also been used to convey a feeling of the intrinsic values of free nature. The music of Kjerulf, Nordraak and Grieg gave diversity and fullness to the expressions of a folk tradition with roots firmly in the land. Finally, artists like I. C. Dahl and H. Gude tried to portray nature's magnificence on canvas.

Something these artists, composers and writers have in common is that they all were part of the Deep Romantic tradition of the nineteenth century. At a time when the industrial revolution was threatening to do its utmost to tear man *away* from his natural surroundings, the Romantic Movement celebrated the possibility of man's *identity* with nature. It hearkened to the joys found in unadorned nature, and claimed that man could find fulfillment of his deepest urges *immediately*.

The message of Nansen, Rubenson, and the Deep Romantic Movement was not to be mistaken: they were pointing to a *re*discovery of free nature. The Romantic Movement struck a deep chord in the soul of Norwegians, and lead to a revival of national identity – *this* is Norway, this free nature, and we are unique as Norwegians to have it. The German philosopher Schelling's "Nature is visible Spirit, Spirit is invisible Nature", epitomized this reawakened sensitivity to land. The implication, of course, was that contemporary Norwegians in cities – and Europeans in general – had *already* lost that identity with nature. And this irony is reflected out by the beginnings of *friluftsliv* as a social phenomenon. Like the Romantic artists who travelled around Norway in search of subjects to paint, those who streamed out of the city in their wake were *urbanized* men and women. The natives of the countryside had, in a sense, never left the land, and thus felt no need to be reunited with it. Instead, rural people played "interpreter"; accompanying city-folk around so that the latter could "find their roots".

This sometimes presented an amusing spectacle, but the sincerity of these city dwellers should not be doubted. Even in those early days, the "civilized" inhabitants of Norway were realizing the heavy toll of being excluded from "real" Norway – the country that was sung by the poets on the continent and of their own land.

This urge to regain citizenship in the "real" Norway still touches Norwegians deeply. Swedes and Danes use the term *friluftsliv* too – but apply it also to races on groomed tracks, painstakingly marked trails through rural farmland, or cabin cruising through crowded archipelagos. On the other hand, most Norwegian outdoorspeople react quite strongly if told they are *not* engaged in "genuine" *friluftsliv*. In Norway the word has a more limited usage, applying to the experience of *free* nature.

Above all, *friluftsliv* is an expression of Romanticism. Rather than laying down fixed rules for what it includes, we can say that we show respect for natural processes and for the realization of all life. It takes place in (relatively) free nature, without the use of technical means of transport (e.g. motor vehicles). *Friluftsliv* presents a diverse range of challenges to the total person, and is an opportunity for emotional, physical, and intellectual engagement. The extent and quality of the *friluftsliv* experience is a free choice of the participant, according to his or her own abilities.

Carl Gustav Jung argues throughout his work in psychology that fundamental to all humans is a recollection of archetypes. Having lived for a hundred-thousand generations in an environment where the non-human, rather than the human, was dominant, it should be hardly surprising that many of our archetypes involved free nature. To understand ourselves, then to realize our potential for being a human being, we must communicate intimately with that which is – in some sense – the most inhuman: wild, undeveloped nature. *Friluftsliv*, in challenging us to respond in body, mind, and spirit with the rhythms of the natural environment, is our best opportunity for that development.

Friluftsliv is a paradigm shift: away from a dominant "objective" view of nature and towards an emotive identity with its characteristic of Romanticism. By using the Romantic tradition as an example, I do not mean that we should become "romantic about the past". Rather, I mean that the search for a more multisided relationship with nature *need not* be exclusively in Eastern traditions or in the "new physics". We have the roots for such a relationship in our traditional cultures – and they are not completely lost.

We might get a feel for what *friluftsliv* is by naming a few things it is not. It is not *sport*, in the sense of physical activity in a selfish, competitive way; staying fit to compensate for an otherwise unnatural and unhealthy lifestyle. It does not take place in carefully prepared arenas designed to smooth out the "vagaries" of nature and ensure "fair competition" and exciting action.

Nor do I mean that *friluftsliv* is *tourism*, in the sense of the business and practice of rapid transit through different places. Such trips are inspired by and produce a sense of alienation from our "environment" and the people around us.

Friluftsliv isn't a *scientific excursion* teaching about the "scientific" processes in nature, collecting specimens of objective interest. This approach to nature eliminates an emotive sense for nature, a poesophic appreciation that friluftsliv encourages.

Neither is *friluftsliv* a "trade show" style of grand Himalayan mountaineering expedition, display windows for sponsors, equipment, wealth, tourism, competitive adventure, using nature as a "sparring partner" and the like.

Finally, *friluftsliv* should not be modelled as *outdoor activity*, in the sense of a safety valve for a fundamentally anti-natural lifestyle or aggression. It is not meant to shore up our modern way of life, but to help us – as individuals and as a society – *out* of it.

Friluftsliv evokes such strong responses in Norwegian society because it evokes a *national* identity, a sense of really "belonging" to their land, a sense that predominated in Norway as recently as the Second World War. In the nineteenth century, it was also a kind of statement of fashion consciousness – little Norway, on the outskirts of Europe, was finally in tune with the Romantic fervor sweeping the rest of the Continent. *Friluftsliv* conveys *social* identity in a similar two-edged way, but as a "real" Norwegian and as a member of the upper class who must go *back* to nature. Finally, it conveys an *individual* identity in the same way that Nansen described, by paring a persona built in the city down to some sort of "essential self".

In the Norwegian context, *friluftsliv* is a living tradition for re-creating nature-consonant lifestyles. It implies making friends with nature, and passionately recreating free nature's standing in our culture. It is an unselfish "I-Thou" relationship that tries to come away from anthropocentrism of a nature-dissonant society.

More than just an individual pastime, *friluftsliv* is a Norwegian tradition inspiring an active response to an ecological crisis. It points towards a new way of living with other people and with our planet – consonant with the Norwegian tradition of eco-philosophy.

It is a poor "media event" in the eyes of the networks. In its proper perspective, though, *friluftsliv* is more significant than an event at the Olympics – it is as much *social* movement as physical activity. It is a step towards a lifestyle in which there is no *need* to seek our home through *friluftsliv*. In this sense, the goal of *friluftsliv* is to make itself obsolete.

"There is no way leading to peace," wrote Gandhi, "peace is the way." *Friluftsliv* is not an armed battle, not a sports event, not an academic discipline, but a move towards lasting cultural change. It is a *process* – a process of joy. There is no force stronger than joy. *Friluftsliv* as a way Home is a way of joy. Go for it!

Gaia versus Servoglobe[3]

SIGMUND KVALØY SETRENG[4]

Introduction

The core content of this article was originally given as a talk at an international conference on the "Gaia theory", arranged by ECOROPA in Cornwall, England in 1987[5]. My interest in globalized microprocessor control goes back, however, to the early fifties, initially embracing the concept with science fictioninspired enthusiasm. Over the years that attitude changed radically, and it finally came to a head during my stay at Columbia University, New York, in 1967. I was there to study and produce something on "The aesthetic and communicational problems of electronic and computer-generated music". New York is also the Mecca of jazz music, and I was deeply struck by the contrast between the two forms: constructivism versus improvisation; they appeared finally as two different worlds, and that became the starting point for the development of the concepts 'complication' and 'complexity' (defined below)[6].

I left New York and the Ecophilosophical Group was formed at the University of Oslo in 1969: We watched the expansion of the European Economic

---

3   This is from a special edition from" Filosofisk institutt publikasjonsserie 43. NTNU." I et filosofisk terreng – festskrift til Sverre Sløgedal".

4   He was born and named Sigmund Kvaløy, but after he had settled on his mother's farm, he added to his family name, the name of the farm. From then on, he called himself: Sigmund Kvaløy Setreng. This happened around 1990.

5   The" Gaia theory" was an invention of the British specialist on atmospherically chemistry, James Lovelock, in 1969. It proposes to view the earth's biosphere as one organism and an entity that actively changes itself to survive under shifting circumstances. Since then, a growing interdisciplinary team of scientists has been active in elaborating the theory.
ECOROPA – The Campaign for an Ecological Europe – was started in 1977 (This writer was one of the founding members).

6   The ground for this line of thinking had been laid, however, during the years 1955 – 58, when I worked as an aircraft technician in the Norwegian Air Force. In the middle of that period, we had to be re-schooled to the American" Technical Order System"., under which everything we did had to fit into a pre-arranged, hierarchical order scheme. It gave us an explanation why Vietnamese improvisers won out against the world's mightiest industrial power – at the war's last stage putting its faith in computers. That made things worse, and the jungle guerrillas just kept on eating up the pyramid.

Community (EEC) inspiring the concept 'Industrial Growth Society' (later designated ACID; see below), and in 1972, seven of us produced the book *Økopolitikk eller EEC?* (Ecopolitics or the EEC?), which sold 10 000 copies to our surprise, since it was somewhat on the philosophical side. One of the books the group had discussed was Christopher Hodder-Williams' *A Fistful of Digits* (see bibliography), giving us the idea of "Servoglobe"; he uses the designation "Servex" which we also used in the beginning, until we were threatened to be sued in court by the washing machine company SERVEX.

That made us invents the word Servoglobus (Servoglobe), which, anyway, turned out to cover the intended meaning better than the earlier term. Other analyses that helped form our own were those made by Jacques Ellul (*The Technological Society*), Lewis Mumford (*The Myth of the Machine*), Peter Wessel Zapffe (*"The Norwegian apparatus landscape"*), Norway's earliest ecophilosopher, philosopher and sociologist Dag Østerberg (*Forståelsesformer* "Forms of Understanding"), as well as the more ecophilosophical parts of the British monthly *New Scientist*. (Additional sources see the bibliography).

Inspired by these, and my collaborators in the ecophilosophical group (Arne Vinje, Paul Hofseth, Ivar Mysterud, Per Gaarder, Nils Faarlund, Erling Amble, Jon Godal, Karl Georg Høyer and Arne Naess and Dag Østerberg as important satellites to the group), still being politically naive but thinking we had a message of overwhelmingly serious significance, I approached members of the Parliament around the mid-seventies as batches of new communication and surveillance systems were put into space (notably satellites etc. of the National Security Agency (NSA) arguably the world's most secret global espionage organization). I was met with friendly nods but it quickly became clear that I would need a week or two of talking space to establish communication on the issue, and of course the Parliamentarians' space available for me was ten minutes at the most.

Anyway, our book on Ecopolitics and the EEC has turned out to have a great predictive value, e.g. that the socioeconomic process let loose by the EEC's founders was a self-strengthening spiral (a positive feedback affair) towards a union (the leading opinion makers scoffed at this possibility in 1972, and, strangely, still do it today (1999), when the Union is more or less a fact).

Gaia:
complex

SERVOGLOBE:
COMPLICATED

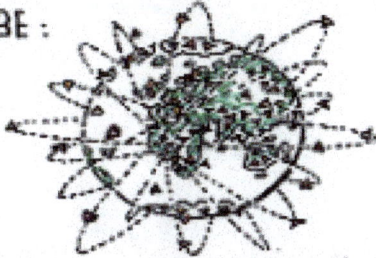

Disney-world:
Pseudo-complex

In later years I have had the opportunity to meet and discuss the main ideas of this paper with some of the authors who helped inspire it in the first place, like Hubert Dreyfus, and Theodore Roszak in California (see bibliography), the Dalai Lama as well as Buddhist philosophers of Bhutan, and most prominently, Helena Norberg Hodge, founder and director of the *International Society for Ecology and Culture*, as well as Edward Goldsmith, editor of *The Ecologist* a leading ecophilosophical journal.

Of course, I am mentioning the interaction with these people to try to convince the reader that the Servoglobe prediction is not just the product of a mind gone astray in the face of the contemporary turmoil. Anyway, Norway appears to me to be the country where society's computerization has been accepted with the greatest naïveté. Now and then up through the passing years, returning again and again with inspiration from abroad, I have attempted to start a debate in my own country, using available opportunities in the various media; it always came to nothing. Our academic environment is small and we largely lack politically engaged generalists to face the specialists.

Lately, however, the law professors Thomas Mathiesen and Ståle Eskeland have tried to raise awareness of and an opinion against the Big Brother scheme of the European Union (Schengen, Europol, etc.). No political reaction seems to be forthcoming. Georg Apenes, the Director of Datatilsynet ("Data Watch") a state institution that watches and can stop computer violation of privacy is almost the only one in Norwegian society who manages to stir up a little debate now and then. None of these, however, appear to have gone into the psychosocial and ecopolitical impact of the computerization process in its global reach.

The present attempts at interdisciplinary team research at all four of the Norwegian universities are, if anything, positive towards computerization, revealing how this new trend lacks in depth. To argue that failure of insight is the substance of this paper.

Summary of Main Points

1. "Servoglobe" is a name given to a supra-nationally run "global supercomputer" an "artificial intelligence" system coupled to a global network of information gathering and electronic data-processing systems, surveillance satellites, regional expert terminals, etc., semiautomatic in operation created partly by economic globalization forces, and partly to serve mankind's survival in the face of a destructively simplified natural biosphere (Gaia) and the threat of political and social chaos.

2. There are strong scientific, technological, economic, administrative, and political forces at work on all sides of the various global conflict fronts to reach efficiency in repairing and managing the increasingly unmanageable mess created by Western Industrial Society or rather: the Advanced Competitive Industrial Dominion ACID (to be defined). There have been various research projects in operation for more than thirty years to coordinate this effort through micro-processing networks of increasing sophistication. Various feedback loops are involved in this process, gradually producing a selfpropelling impetus of such a force that it is hard to see what would stop it, even if there were any

public awareness of what is happening. There is not. Projecting this development into the future, the end point is Servoglobe.

3. Part of the strength of this selfpropelling process has its root in the impossibility of managing a natural dynamic "system" as if it was a system of static machinery (the 'complex' as if it was 'complicated', see below), but *these are the only means that science and technology have given us.* The result is a build-up of chaos-potential, and at an accelerating rate larger quantities and more refined versions of the mechanistic "medicine" are applied. Instead of changing the medicine, which is beyond the horizon of ACID, a steadily greater effort is put into widening its application: The thinking is that "there are loopholes in the systems" which must be closed to achieve a completely rational functioning of it. Among other things, human political activity is treated as "sand in the machinery" that must be removed to obtain a smooth running. So are old borders between nations. Servoglobe is the "Endlösung" (Final solution) to these problems.

4. Finally, nature the biosphere, Gaia must also be conceived by this thinking as too messy for rational management. After all, she is seen primarily as a collection of resources for human material needs. So, the impetus is strong toward a replacement of Gaia i.e. the biosphere's natural self-regulation by an artificial system of global compass.

5. Servoglobe, however, is an impossible goal, a breakdown of the mechanistic control network will happen before that endpoint is reached. The reason for this is the later mentioned lack of "interface" between *'the complicated'* and *'the complex'*. These concepts are defined (this is the central part of the presentation, which everything else hangs on): Gaia is complex; ACID tends inherently towards perfected complication.

6. ACID may go far in this grandiose attempt and the further it gets; the more devastating will be the resulting chaos (Prigogine is counter argued). To create awareness of this development is therefore an extremely vital project.

Central Concepts

Computers large and small abound and proliferate exponentially. Even my own country, Norway, reputed as housing an exceptionally down-to-earth nation, has been hit by an almost frantic propaganda for their use in all possible corners of society, the schools being the prime target. We must bring our people quickly into the computer age, otherwise we'll lose out in the international competition. Not only economically, but culturally too.

A decade ago, we saw one TV program after another telling us that we should watch the children "*they* are not afraid!" "Just try for a while, and you'll be convinced!" and we were promised new jobs, as well as a new creativity and even liberation from *angst*, from chaos, from war. By now, we are convinced; very little of the old fear remains. The media hardly ever publish any critical comment. Directly, and indirectly, in many ways, we are led to believe that computers and human brains belong to the same class of phenomena, reducing the "interface" problems to something almost negligible, around the next corner the computer will exist as a natural extension of the human mind. Both to blue/red industrialists and green "New Age" followers, interconnected computers will solve our problems on a global scale.

For those of us who think that we are here in for the most consequential and unfathomable upheaval of society that human history ever witnessed, among other things, due to the speed and universality with which the computers take over vital functions, it's high time we sit down and try to grasp as well as we can the depth of what is happening. Time is, in my opinion, far overdue for green associations, like the intra-European ECOROPA, and The International Forum on Globalization, to do this, since what we see here is, in effect, an attempt to replace the naturally flowing ecosocial system with an artificially controlled, mechanistic scheme.

I will mention three concepts that to me have been useful on distinguishing various elements that the pro-computer advocates mix up to everybody's confusion. I label these concepts *complexity, complication and pseudocomplexity*; in the latter case I also, depending on the context, use the expressions "Amusement diversity" and "Disneyland Effect". This handful of concepts have been helpful to me in clarifying, among other matters, how computers and living entities differ to the extent that they belong to different worlds. As will be seen, the concepts contain hypotheses about nature, society and machines.

By "complexity" (CX) I mean the dynamic, irreversible, non-centrally self-steered, goal-directed, conflictfertilized manifoldness of nature and as a particularly refined and intricate version of that the human mind/body entity.

By "complication" (CC) I mean the static, reversible, externally and unicentrally steered, standardized structure-intricacy of the machine. The computer is a particularly refined and intricate version of that.

"Pseudocomplexity" (PCX) is, like CC, a human design-product, but unlike CC it mimics CX in order to set up various arrangements and activities to keep people occupied in a diverse manner, through mass media, hobbies, tourism, schools, etc. so that it replaces complex challenges; it occupies people on the shallow level that is exemplified by the amusement park, i.e. without offering training or development that equips them better for creative interaction with nature and society. Environmental PCX often functions as a "safety valve" outlet for the inner urge towards complex integration with the larger world that every human being is born with; it offers, however, only the sort of interaction that leaves the personality without further development or maturation after the event.

CX can be described only by reference to qualities (where, however, quantitative perception and assessment is included as one segment of the spectrum of qualitative mediations between the individual and her/his environment) kinds and sorts of differentiations and border-crossings, shades and hues without fixed boundaries, dialectical buildups and breakthroughs, etc.

CC can, in any situation, be completely described by reference to the five mechanical parameters: height, breadth, depth, mass, and locomotion modeled through spatial diagrams, mathematics and formal logic, and quantified according to fixed numerical scales.

CX is thought of as something existing, as being real as concrete, imperfect, practice related goings on in the human body-mind and its world, and as something already given and presented when "consciousness wakes up" and starts to formulate concepts. It's in large measure pre-intellectual.

CC is a product of the human intellect and manifests itself as abstract model collections, describing ideal, theoretical, perfect machinelike structures. Since Pythagoras and Plato, and modernized by Descartes, CC has largely been taken to express the real world[7], and that is still dominating Western thought, making it easy to accept the computer as an extension of the living.

Time

To understand CX and CC and their difference, it is useful to apply two different time concepts, "organic time" as a part-characteristic of CX and "mechanical time" (or "clock time") as the "time" of CC. Organic time is the group of modes of change related to the various subjects and actors and groups of such in nature, it expresses itself through rhythm, expands and contracts, is created as part of natural processes, does not extend into the

---

7   A. N. Whitehead's "Fallacy of Misplaced Concreteness" is related to this.

future, nothing moves through it; it is movement itself. Organic time is concrete; it has no existence separate from material-spiritual events ("being-processes" is one tentative word that might be useful to get away from the Cartesian split between matter and spirit). It cannot be "objectively" measured, because any kind of measuring rod would change with it, but among humans it can be illustrated and talked about concretely, clearly, and with abundant communicability. Available to us for such communication are innumerable human sensual, emotional, aesthetic, and ethic experiences ("I arrived earlier than my uncle, who was actually walking very fast red-faced and puffing, but strong despite his heart condition", etc.!).

Mechanical time is a human intellectual invention. It was historically prepared through the observation of the rhythmical pulses of day and night and the seasons, but came into consequential being as something different from organic time only with the invention of a reliable mechanical "timekeeper" (a device that conserves time) the clock. It is used to quantify natural time or, rather, to substitute mechanical coordination for rhythmical living in approximation with the sun's rising and setting tides in the sea, and various rhythmical body functions. Mechanical time is regarded as being the same for all natural processes; it's "objective" not "subjective", we speak as if we are "moving through it", it is supposed to stretch out into the future (it is actually constituting the concept 'future' in Western civilization a sheet of paper, a map, now a screen, on which the *planners* trace their lines), as if what has not yet happened is already "there" "some place" (it's embryonically also the basis for the belief in precognition and time travel strengthened today through science fiction where H. G. Wells' *The Time Machine* is the classic). It keeps us in captivity since it's a fenced-in path for our steps, but it is abstract not dependent upon concrete events, and so lacks qualitative aspects. It is the basis for the notion of reversibility of processes, and it is the only time concept relevant to the construction of the physical computer and the programming of it as well.

Human culture as we know it, can hardly function without the coordination of mechanical time. The trouble is, however, that it has a tendency to hide natural time, and as *the dominant* time concept of industrialism it has made Western man almost lose awareness of natural time a fact of deep consequence, including the notion that the human brain/mind relationship is a kind of computer/computer program ("software") system. Logically, mechanical time is a *spatial* parameter it is the measuring rod for locomotion shift of location in geometrical coordinate systems. As said, it psychologically tends to eliminate (natural, real) time. Only space is left. In accordance with this perspective, the

Advanced Competitive-Industrial Digit-Society (ACID), the social system that like acid simplifies complex entities, is an extreme experiment in testing how far it is possible to go in spatializing the human universe, an attempt that started in classical Greece (Pythagoras, Parmenides, Plato, Xenon, etc.).

Two Cultures two-time concepts

As an illustration of this historical development, the modern Western house, an engineering perfection of the Greek temple has a smooth, geometrically perfect appearance, seemingly timedefiant. If a crack appears in its shining surface an attack of organic time it looks terrible because decay is supposed to be irrelevant to its conception. It is an expression of a "stoptime aesthetic". In contrast, if we take a look at say a Sherpa house in Nepalese Himalaya, it always appears "unfinished", a creation that never reached "its destined geometrical perfection ". This, however, is the modern Western perception of it that of the visiting tourist or development aid expert. We stop at the entrance of the village and say: "The poor ignorant Sherpas, they can't do a better job."

But, from the traditional Sherpa point of view, the beauty and, intimately connected with that, the utility of his house may only be discovered if you settle down for a couple of generations, build such a house yourself, take responsibility for its daily care, live with the house instead of being its architect, repair it when (that frequent) need arises, add to it or subtract from it as the requirements of your family and your animals may be, etc. The modern Western building is given an adequate expression through a snapshot photo, while there's another modern Western devise that might help you to an initial appreciation of the quality of a "Sherpa type house", the cinematic film camera. You mount it on a tripod in front of the house and let it expose one frame every day for, say, a hundred years. Finally, you develop the film and let it run at normal cinematic speed. What will be revealed to you, is not a house in the western sense, but an organic structure, its wall stones and roof material will be moving about and changing, likewise the shape and the size of the structure; the vegetation clinging to it, the animal and human life around it will expand and contract, speed up and slow down, shift in kind and variety all in subtle coordination with changes appearing in the house itself. You are viewing a total, complex process, where all elements in the environment and economic/social conditions prevailing in the locality, quickly and flexibly are mirrored in the house.

This is a house that is decaying every day, a fact that is *accepted* by the people that are part of this "house-hold" a material, pliable dough, responding to both the immediate and the long-term challenges of local life. The people of the house let it decays, always, to some extent, so that it can bud and sprout every next spring, but at any *moment* moving to be something new. This house behaving like a living organism is the expression of a culture that also accepts illness, age, and death that even finds security in accepting that nature is an insecure place, a process. Strengthening that, the Sherpas have a religion Buddhism founded on the premise that nothing is permanent. The result is that quality of self-reliance, resourcefulness, ability to improvise, and flexible cooperation which makes the Sherpa's help so attractive to Western mountaineers engaged in the world's most demanding ventures in wild nature, summit climbing in the Himalayas.[8]

Why wouldn't the computer be of any help here, but rather a hindrance? Because we are faced with a particularly clear case of Gaia's demands on natural, complex man. The challenges facing the Himalayan mountaineer are hardly ever complicated. But in principle, these demands are no different from, say, those facing someone bringing up a child anywhere, even in the West (which tends, however, to "complicate" that issue too). In both cases, complex growth is the challenge. Correspondingly, the computer may be useful in constructing and running a modern Western office building, while it is a total miss in a Sherpa village life process. And the office building, in order to stay smooth, as a daily sign of corporate reliability, continuously demands resources far beyond what the neighborhood can give. The same goes for the Western urban system as a totality and any attempt at keeping a complicated structure smooth!

Meaningful, complex work versus complicated employment in the Gaian perspective

There is, from what I have said, justification in using the expression "real time" for natural time, since it is irreducibly concrete - movement itself as experienced by each individual, while mechanical time is an abstraction - a reducing of time to geometrical space. Under the heading "a complicated system (like the

---

8   The ability to improvise, individually and collectively, is now (1999, 2000) being studied at the University of Trondheim, Norway, through the project "Improvisation in interdisciplinary light". Various cultures are here being compared. Metaphors, enlightening to the problematique, are the jazz band and the European symphony orchestra, contrasted.

computer) is incapable of handling real time", there is one aspect where "natural man's" incompatibility with the computer is particularly consequential. To my thinking, the concept of *meaningful work* is central to understanding of the unfoldment of human personality, and I am here talking about something specifically human. It is the aspect of "human-ness" that- before anything - is the product of man as an inventive socioecological creature. "Meaningful work" - as I will define it - is "human work", in contradistinction to "mechanical work" or "complicated employment". Again: The complex versus the complicated.

I define *meaningful* - or *humanly appropriate work* (mfW - where "mf" also stands for manifold-ness, i.e., complexity) as follows:

1. It is an activity *necessary* for the human being's material survival (through this, it possesses a direct, clear seriousness not shared by any other activity except defense against disruptive social conflict).
2. Its *fruit* of products (goods, services…) are such that do not damage but rather strengthens life (human society and nature) with no envisaged time limit - which means that Gaia is always - more or less consciously - on the horizon.
3. It poses such challenges that bring the potential *complexity* of capabilities - including the ability to improvise, i.e. alertness to organic time - in the human individual and her group to bloom.
4. It demands of its partakers the building of *solidarity and loyalty* and practical, flexible techniques for cooperation; and
5. In general it engages *children* (as the most important group - but any other, like old people, as well).

Years of active life filled with mfW establish constant awareness of organic time, including personal, dialectical shifts, -i.e. conflict-fertilized maturation.

Work roughly corresponding to this concept has as a matter of fact been the normal basis of society - its economy, education, artistic and political ability world-wide and as far back as we are able to trace human history. *The first society to completely lack this basis* is ACID, and the computer perfects this state of affairs: it employs people, i.e. segments of them, to some extent, but robs them of work. A complex society, with complex process- attachments to Gaia entails complex persons! Sums of specialists or segment-persons won't do. To state very briefly one of the many lines of argument involved in the matter: A society built on the basis of mfW is a society that in principle thrives on meager resources in energy and materials while energy/materials abundance blocks its realization.

Contrary to ACIDic thinking (also in greener branches, New Age, "Over-centralized Regionalism!" etc.), microelectronics presupposes an energy-intensive, international heavy industry economy, factually accelerating the depletion of the world's resources: The word "postindustrial" stands in my analysis for idealistic wishful thinking!

The main point here is that mankind's greater teacher is Gaia in her manifoldness, always up to something new; but she will fulfill that function only if her complex challenges are not replaced by complicated problem tasks, posing as the easy way out usually through the ready availability of specialists. (Wo)man is by birth preeminently gifted towards being a continuously creative Gaia-being in body-spirit, but that creativity is a complex affair, which as a general, social characteristic is brought to flower only in cultures that have their basic flow-structure determinate through meaningful work, posed as a challenge necessary for survival. This line of reasoning owes nothing to the "Christian/ Protestant work ethos" a generation or two back, but is founded on empirical observation, comparing how societies live and develop within various cultures. The point is that a human animal is free, even in the sense that it may "choose" the easy way out, if its environment offers that, like ACID. Then it may expand in a pseudo-complex manner, or just "go to pot", ashes-like.

I am here largely in keeping with E. F. Schumacher in the chapter "Buddhist Economics" from the book *Small is Beautiful*, where he stresses the point that to my mind has paramount importance, viz. that "man needs work *as much as* he needs food", and that "man without work is in a desperate situation" where the concept 'work' is closely related to mine (except for point 5 the requirement of children's participation, which of course is indispensable if we want to restore to work the role as society's foundation).[9] Taking this point seriously constitutes an elementary step towards the much-sought-for Green Paradigm. In spite of its extremely well-twined historical roots, it is a truly radical, concrete and forceful departure from ACID - one that we cannot possibly avoid if our course is to de-serve the label "social" or Gaiadirected.

In contradistinction to this, the computerized society model furthers isolated individualism as it is spelled out, e.g. in Zbigniev Brzezinski's grand vision of a "Technetronic Society"[10], a "society" that in my analysis would be economically dependent on mechanistic schemes replacing organic processes producing an alienation to nature that also means human self-alienation. It offers an abstract

---

9   Schumacher explains that he got this set of ideas from a study of Burmese Buddhist culture.

10   Zbigniev Brzezinski: *Between Two Ages: America's Role in the Technetronic Era*, Penguin 1977, Green wood 1987. Brzezinski was a special adviser to President Jimmy Carter.

world in replacement of a concrete, a complicated for a complex, machine-directed employment instead of work. It represents the last stage of a western civilization that for centuries increasingly regarded work purely as a means toward an end - survival, and, if possible, affluence: Work acquired meaning *only* from the end it was to serve, - from itself only as a chance byproduct. The socialist workers' revolution happened within this historical context, and for that reason, partly, meaningful work - work in itself possessing the promise of human bodily/intellectual and emotional expansion - never became an important fighting issue to the socialist movement. If it had been the case, computerized employment would have had a much harder time in gaining labor's acceptance than we see today. Let's call this "Karl Marx's blind spot". Due to historical urgencies in his time, we can't blame him. His day required the red so much that it had to blot out the green. In my opinion - after thirty years of discussing work and social change on three continents (admittedly a short time - clockwise), Green's central key is meaningful work, as defined.

MfW requires (wo)man to accept insecurity as a normal state of affairs, and it trains the individual or the group to be broadly prepared for new challenges, to improvise - to be creatively one with organic time. That is why mfW shares a common departure with Buddhism, which in some of its historical branches represents the world's most radical eco process philosophy. (This is *not* the case with the *Avatamsaka Sutra* story of *Indra's Net*, often quoted by New Age people. Instead, we have here to do with a sort of Far Eastern "Spinozistisk" eternalism, where everything reflects everything else in a perfect manner. The crystalline world net mentioned in the story is rather some sort of "supercomplication", inspired in its way by meditation, which at its deep level is quality-free[11]...) In those branches of Buddhism where its originality is kept fresh *nothing* is permanent, everything is change and movement; - the idea that anything is enduring, like even the most highly cherished objects, the human soul and God - is an illusion.

In keeping with this, but transposing Buddhism to our time and place, I define the human personality through *activity*, more or less creative, and the individual's activity as it ties in with another individuals' activity. The individual is here thought of as a process - it's being is its activity, slow-moving and gradual or creative by leaps, only hazily distinguishable from other individuals' activity-processes (unlike Indra's Net, nothing is ever a copy, the world is full of mutually over-lapping, reciprocally inspired individualities,

---

11   The difference between the Chinese and the Indian branches of Buddhism, where the latter was dynamically oriented, was reflected already at the famous Council of Lhasa a thousand years ago, where the Chinese were thrown out on the ground of their static interpretation!

new ones and new constellations forever emerging - human, animal and plant. This kind of reality explains why the scientific method, as we know it, can never grasp more than distorted fragments of the world). The "other individuals" may here be either animal or vegetable, or even non-animate - like a mountain, a desert, or a river. Everything concretely nature-given is movement, perceivable through characteristic rhythms and modes of rhythm shifts, while the world of mechanistic science is static, mathematical and abstract (I do *not* say that mathematics is non-creative or useless!).

Even though new approaches may be appearing in modern microphysics, the way science is taught and practiced is still mechanistic, which it must be anyway as long as it serves ACID. The computer is part of the latter, regardless of its vastness in electronic miniaturization. Either digital or analogue, it's still qualityless - complicated not complex: The computer functions on the basis of sharply defined boundaries, the individual it represents is either an abstract-binarily catalogued "cat" *or* a "dog", never the doglike cat that crossed my way as I left the farm to start on the complicated and complex journey to an ECOROPA meeting. A robot can never be any sort of open-ended, inventive activity-presence, at every stage redefining its character, as any member-being of concrete Gaia. Computer-locomotion is reversible - as long as it fulfills its expectations, Gaia's and man's activity is not.[12]

Ecology was at one time defined by the American ecophilosopher Paul Shephard as "the subversive science". Today students, by the hundred thousand, learn about "nature " in front of a computer, displaying various "simulations". They learn about something complicated instead of something complex, and are hardly ever led on to the idea that there might be a difference. It's now an overdue and extremely important task for the ecopolitical movement and for ecophilosophical pedagogics to stir up a debate within the field of education in general about the practice of representing complexity as complication. A critical attitude to the computer would - as things have developed - has to be the central part of such a project. The computer draws the whole ACIDic development together - makes it finally crystal clear where it's all been leading us, what kind of a hole machine thinking has dug out for us.

Treating nature and human society as problems of complication plus Disneyland means giving the wrong answers at every stage, step by step

---

12   In 1985 I visited the Artificial Intelligence laboratory at the University of Texas, Austin, and interviewed its director. Philosophically still in the 17th century, he was convinced that at the next step computers would feel and value, the interface with living entities being near to perfection. It was just a matter of miniaturization and parallel processing. My quoting Hegel where he says that he who lacks a knowledge of the history of philosophy is doomed to repeat it, just produced a blank stare; any discussion of basic presuppositions did not have a chance.

aggravating the situation. What we see is a self-propelling spiral towards disaster. One expression for this - perhaps unnecessarily mechanistic - is "positive feedback". Systems governed by positive feedback tend positively in the direction of a basic change of systems, which in human social affairs might mean disintegration. And the last spiral in ACID's historical development had to be the computer - its most refined attempt at machine control: It is so refined that ACID's propaganda manages to convince us that we are dealing with an extension of human thinking, and sensitivity and feeling as well. Even though it's intricacy boils down to a simple bipolar scheme (1 or 0, the switch on or off, the house at right angles or not), treating everything as amenable to analysis (the parts tell the whole story - the whole treated as another part), ACID's educators and politicians manage to present it as complex.

A spaceship designed to replace Gaia

ACID's way to deal with the mounting crisis that necessarily results from treating the complex as if it is complicated, is a globalization of the treatment, the thought being that we are faced with a lack of co-ordination: there are still uncontrolled zones that interfere with and disrupt the data processing network. And what can co-ordinate billions of details if not the one and only computer? The perfectly logical far end of this line of reasoning is the global computer, or a globe-spanning network of interlinked computers and "data-banks", where every computer at any time "knows" what all the others in the network "know". And what they "know", is the total collection of details about the state of the "world", mechanistically interpreted into huge crystalline patterns. I call this logical end of the road SERVO-GLOBE, from "serve"/"service" and "servo" in the sense of "automatically self-adjusting", and "global". Servo-globe is, then, the historically ultimate stage of the accelerated alienation and one-dimensionality of industrio-competitive society, a stage that means the final abdication of human control and the elimination of (wo)man's creative, meaningful activity as a contributor to Gaia's life. A global, electronic service lady replaces Gaia[13]. One of the impulses to reflect along these lines came in the early seventies, in Oslo, when I became acquainted with a man who was employed by one of the leading transnational electronic corporations[14]. This

---

13   Since I wrote the first version of this, a British computer expert, Geoff Simons, has come out with a book, *Eco Computer*, describing in detail how the global computer (ServoGlobe) is becoming a reality (Wiley, N. Y. 1987, ISBN 0 471 91340).

14   Xerox International

was before the collapse of the Iron Curtain. We seemed to have thoughts and worries in common and one evening after a few beers, he confided in me that the most interesting but also the most worrying part of his work was research on what he called "the global computer". The program is led from an American university, he said, and is supported by several electronics and communications corporations: We have affiliated a large number of researchers, engineers, sociologists, psychologists, and language experts, localized in all the major industrial and administrative centers around the world.

The idea is to use satellites for observation and communication, sensor-equipped stations on land and in the oceans as well as local human observers to collect data on the state of the world's various regions. Much research goes into solving the problems of constructing sensible formulations to express the data including social conditions and political developments - so that the computer can handle them. The world is in deep trouble, he said, and this is the only way to go to overcome those troubles; some are optimists - a few, like myself are worried. Can we do it? And that's only the first part of my worry... But what about the Eastern bloc, I queried. They are surely not part of this effort, so how can you globalize without them? They are, by steps, drifting into the same thing, he said. Besides the parties stealing each other's technological secrets, there's a lot more research cooperation than most people can imagine, and because of the sorry state of the world and resources that steadily grows harder to get at, since the ecosphere doesn't respect political territorialities, the scanning and planning systems of the East and West get more and more entwined with each other. And when things break, they break across the boundaries. So, in both camps, the global computer slowly appears as the only way to go. The top politicians are hardly aware of what is happening, and among the researchers, the cross-national inter-linkage of systems are so far mainly toyed with as interesting science projects. But the development already has so much momentum that it would be very hard to reverse the process. At this stage, when serious ruptures appear, wherever else can they turn, both, the East, the West, and the South?[15] Microelectronics is, after all, the only way they know when complication overwhelms the human mind. But do you know what, he continued, there is one very hopeful aspect to this trend: the cold war blocks might one day soon wake up and find themselves so involved with each other through this global network that they'll be forced to overcome all their serious differences; they might find their life-or-death prospects is at stake if

---

15   India has by now, 1999, one of the world's largest communities of IT developers, probably third after the US and Japan. But they are pushing in the same direction; no Indian philosophy (Hindu or Buddhist) is involved. Take note, though, so far, only 1 percent of mankind has internet access!

anything disturbs the completion of this global computer system. That will be a more powerful deterrent than the threat of nuclear war, because it might mean sudden chaos - the loss of the basis for any kind of planning and political maneuvering, even the use of nuclear deterrent as a workable political tool.

I remember the day well. We were sitting with a good view of the Oslo harbor, where a beautiful square-rigger had just sailed in - its soft, rhythmical lines reminding me of days when qualitative complexity had not yet been replaced by quantitative complication, a time when the human *cybernetics* was at least in principle - still at the helm; - the millennia before Norbert Wiener gave 'the Greek word another meaning. *Cybernetics* suddenly flashed through my mind as being the great cold turkey knife across human history, replacing Einstein's $E = mc^2$ as the signpost of Western civilization's leap into the abyss. The atom bomb is very visible - the microprocessor creeps upon us, like electrified plastic grass everywhere replacing the real thing. Before it's really noticed there's just the green plastic.

I was not, however, disturbed by the second part of his worry; answering my prodding on that, he said: -If the frightful level of complication can be overcome, the computer might take over - we'd have nothing to say anymore! That, to me, was soap opera science fiction, and it still is, because you can't ever succeed in "interfacing" the complex and the complicated. *If you have absorbed that deep distinction*, nothing stops that conclusion either.

About this dependency that you are speaking about, I asked, - a forced reconciliation of East and West certainly looks like something to be jubilant about; - but a second thought comes up: - this thing about nothing being permitted to disturb the "global computer project". The world being what it is, happily but disturbingly uncoordinated, a lot of wills moving at variance with each other, won't there always be a multitude of threats to that computer-based, globally centralized steering perfection?

Yes, of course - he replied - soft - and hardware going into the network will have to be guarded against any conceivable kind of onslaught. After all, the fate of humankind would be at stake. More would be involved than - say - with radioactive materials deposition. A well-drilled, electronically equipped surveillance police force trained in sociology and psychology - resilient but firm, would have to be constantly on the alert to keep prospective, intentional or non-intentional saboteurs at bay. But in view of the strides that are being taken towards artificial intelligence - what with the competition between Japan and US etc. - we can manage that.

This is how he thought, and I've met several computer specialists later looking this way at the world. – So, we'll end up by having a global police state? - Is that really something we should hope for as the alternative to the various global and local conflicts? I went on to ask. Well, at least we would have peace, was his reply, and again, he voiced his own worry, that we'd end up as parts of a global machine, and redundant parts at that. Finally, there would be just that machine. The perspective was amazing, coming from a serious worker within the field, and not out of a science fiction book. I guess I was gaping at him, and it took me a couple of days before I started thinking that ecophilosophy was immediately relevant to the question, and particularly the concepts 'complication' and 'complexity': "Life is complex - the machine complicated", and "the more complicated the machine, the subtler and more difficult to grasp and handle the interface problems - and the greater the consequences of not seeing and handling them properly." And "the computer is nothing but a machine, albeit an extremely complicated one". But "with a machine like that, you can repair yourself out of trouble for a long while, so that when finally, nothing can hold back the system' s ruptures, the disintegration accelerates into a chaotic state."

If this were to happen to the global system the total dependency built up in the meantime would produce worldwide shock and panic. I am not speaking of any normal kind of dependency cut-off, something within the range where history can give us a lesson. What I am talking about is a global socio-ecological crumbling produced by a systematic replacing of complexity with complication on all levels - something unprecedented in mankind' s history. That could be the outcome of ACID's last survival convulsions.

Yet we are systematically educated to accept an endless increase in computerization of our world - and our children much more so. There's hardly ever any discussion going on except in a few publicly remote academic books. The task I am proposing is one that should override most others, viz. to expose this subtle but gigantic push towards SERVOGLOBE, and its consequences.

Literature

Literature that has inspired my writing (partly referred to above), and that I would like to recommend as elaboration and substantiation of what I have said:

- Whitehead, A.N.: *Science and the Modern World* (Lowell Lectures 1925), New York: 1949.
- Ellul, Jaques: *The Technological Society*, New York: 1965 (Original edition: La Technique, 1954).
- Hodder-Williams, Christopher: *A Fistful of Digits*, London 1968.

- Mumford, Lewis: *The Myth of the Machine*, New York: vol.I 1967, vol.II 1970.
- Koestler, A. and Smythies, J.R. (editors): *Beyond Reductionism New Perspectives in the life Sciences*, London: 1969.
- Gregeseu-Roegen, Nicholas: *The Entropy Law and the Economic Process*, Cambridge, Massachusetts, 1971.
- Schumacher, E.F.: *Small is Beautiful*, London: 1974.
- Waddington, C.H.: *Tools for Thought*, St. Albans, Herts: 1977.
- Burnham, David: *The Rise of the Computer State*, London: 1983.
- Weizenbaum, Joseph: *Computer Power and Human Reason from Judgment to Calculation*, London, New York: 1984.
- Haugland, John: *Artificial Intelligence the Very Idea*, Cambridge, Massachusetts/London: 1985.
- Shallis, Michael: *The Silicon Idol the Micro Revolution and its social Implications*, Oxford/Melbourne: 1985.
- Roszak, Theodore: *The Cult of Information the Folklore of Computers and the True Art of Thinking*, New York: 1986.
- Searle, John: *Minds, Brains and Science The 1984 Reith Lectures*, London/New York: 1989.
- Dreyfus, H.L., and Dreyfus, S.E.: *Mind over Machine*, New York: 1988.
- Lovelock, J.: *Gaia a New Look at Life on Earth*, Oxford: 1987

Some of my own writings arguing or developing relevant items:
- "Kraftrom mot elvetid" (Power-Space versus River Time), in: Haagensen, K. and Midttun,A. (editors): *Kraftutbygging, konflikt og aksjoner* (Hydroelectric Development, Conflict and Actions), Oslo: 1984.
- "Mangfold og tid. Hvordan en bryter pyramidens herredømme" (Diversity and Time. How one breaks the reign of the Pyramid), in: Skönberg, S. (editor): *Grønnpepper i turbinene* (Green pepper in the Turbines), Oslo: 1985.
- "Økofilosofi versus New Age" (Ecophilosophy versus New Age), in: Gule, Laugerud (editors): *Vitenskap og verdensbilder* (Science and World Views), Bergen: 1989.
- "Servoglobus Den siste pyramiden" (Servoglobe The Last Pyramid), in: (the journal) *Kontrast*, no.122, 34, Oslo: 1990.
- "Systemkrise og krisesystem" (Systems Crisis and Crisis Systems): in: Album, Alstadheim, Andersen (editors): *Supermarked eller felles framtid? EF, økokrisen og Norges valg* (Super market or Common Future? European Union, Ecocrisis and Norway's choice), Oslo; 1991.

- "Økokrisefilosofi glimt fra det norske økofilosofiske forsøket" (Ecocrisis philosophy glimpses of the Norwegian attempt at an Ecophilosophy) in: Gjerdåker, Gule, Hagtvedt (editors): *Den uoverstigelige grense Tanke og handling i miljøkampen* (The Unsurpassable Limit, Thought and Action in the Environmental Battle), Oslo/Bergen: 1991.
- *Naturens nei* (Nature's No), Norsk Bonde og Småbrukarlag (Norway's Small Farmers Association), Oslo: 1994.
- "Inside Nature", in: Goldsmith, B. et al (editors) *The Future of Progress*, Bristol, Berkely: 1992.
- "Mother Barth 's Treasures and their Revealers An Ecophilosophical Perspective", in: Kuløy, H.K. (editor): *The Treasure Revealer of Bhutan*, BIBLIOTHECA HIMALAYICA, Series III, Volume 8, Kathmandu: 1995.

The Ash-lad
The hero of Norwegian ecophilosophy and ecopolitics
SIGMUND KVALØY SETRENG

Traditional Norwegian fairytales and legends have one dominating figure –
Askeladden – the Ash-lad. Up until recently, the Ash-lad has been regarded
somewhat as a character describing Norwegian identity. Instead of striving
and strafing in the outer world he sits by the fireplace, stirring the ashes and
watching the ever-changing flames of the fire. He is fascinated by the process,
how nothing is constant, and how he can kindle and rekindle the process but
never control it. He learns what can be useful if he is attentive and open to
everything happening around him – in nature and society.

He follows the "watchfulness of the flame" when he leaves home and
wanders off to experience the complex and creative process that is the world.
Instead of being directional and goal-seeking, he is observant and fascinated
by what presents itself along the road. To the Ash-lad the world turns out
to be a fantastic realm, full of information. All this information changes
the original goal – if it existed! This approach reminds of Gandhi's process
thinking: "The goal is the road, and the road is the goal."

The Ash-lad's older and go-for-it brothers, Per and Paul, are unsuccessful,
being fixed on a prefigured point in a future – the future as an already made
map. For the Ash-lad there is no map, but an all-changing complex reality.
He shares his meager food with old hungry people, sits down with them and
learns things that expand his grasp of the world's possibilities – everything
that Per and Paul missed.

The Ash-lad has been the hero of Norwegian youngsters for hundreds of
years. Why didn't the children of Denmark and Sweden have a leading figure
like him? My explanation has to do with historical and political circumstances:
Norway was occupied and trampled underfoot by Denmark for four hundred
years up till 1814, and thereafter forcefully brought into union with Sweden
till 1905, Throughout this time, especially under Denmark, the majority of
the Norwegians were poor, surviving only through an intimate knowledge of
nature, inventive resourcefulness and a highly developed ability to improvise.

These qualities came about as the answer to naked necessities under harsh, often unpredictable natural conditions. We see the same qualities developed among materially poor people also elsewhere in the world. Ash-lads see options where the Danish overlords (Per and Paul) marched inattentively by. An explanation for the cultural difference in Scandinavia may be explained by the fact that Norwegians were independent farmers and fishermen and not surfs under a feudal system, as were many farmers in Denmark and Sweden.

The Norwegian tradition of cherishing local and national independence and distrusting foreign regimentation has survived among the majority till this day. Illustrating this is Norway saying no to joining the European Union at the referendums in 1972 and 1994, while Denmark and Sweden said yes and are both union members – 'imprisoned' as many Norwegians see it.

The leading psychiatrist Herbert Hendin in his Scandinavian studies found that children in Denmark and Sweden were brought up under a pressure of regimentation and career pursuits, producing a number of persons unable to live up to demands, feeling themselves as failures. In contrast, Professor Hendin found that such pressures were weak in Norwegian families: children were allowed to roam around and experiment, however taking part in farming and fishing, learning by "looking and participating", not by being instructed. In a relaxed way self-reliance was built up, avoiding feelings of inadequacy and failure.

Interestingly Professor Hedin also took note of the differences in historical background of the three countries and, connected to that, differences in the kind of stories told to children. Actually, he is the one who made me notice the prevalence of Ash-lad tales in Norwegian tradition, contrasting those of Denmark and Sweden: The hero of Danish and Swedish fairytales wins out in contests through magic and miracles, while the Norwegian Ash-lad wins by his own experience-seeking and inventive action. In other words, the Ash-lad is an ideal inspiring practical and self-reliant activity and a concomitant distrust in higher spirits as helpers in difficult situations.

The Ash-lad was still the hero in Norway during the German occupation of the 1940–1945 world war. Hendin compares the different reactions to the German expansion in the three Nordic countries: The Danes gave in; the Swedes protected their neutrality while Norway's mountains sheltered guerrilla resistance. Actually, the resistance movement strengthened the Ash-lad ideology. It also inspired the rebuilding of Norway's industry, farming and fisheries in the two decades after the war. Professor Sigmund Borgan at the Norwegian University of Agriculture has shown that the surprisingly quick restoration of Norwegian industry after the war was made possible through a workforce recruited from youngsters with backgrounds in small-scale farming and fishing.

These shared the "Ash-lad approach", and in many cases solved problems through advising practical short cuts where the academically trained engineers had gotten stuck in theoretical deliberations. However, these youngsters participated in building a trap for themselves and their children: as soon as Norwegian industry reached a sophistication and size of interest to the international capitalist markets. Stressing the principle of "compete or die", Norway's economic structure changed its character. Today in the "oil age" small farms and fishing hamlets have lost their "rationality", and grand scale centralization and urbanization is happening. The mass media and the schools are preaching individualistic competition as the way to the future. Small scale farming and fishing is being replaced by a tourist economy where exotic folklore on abandoned farms is taking the place of food production, computer games instead of real games.

However, some of the Ash-lad mentality lingers: We still have a majority saying no to joining the European Union – and the present shift in the world climate might soon change all priorities, bringing the Ash-lads back.

Essay written 2007, condensed by the editors.

My pal Sigmund

DOUG TOMPKINS

I first met Sigmund Kvaløy Setreng sometime in the late 1980s when I attended some Ecoropa meetings in various places in Europe. I had already been friends with Arne Naess so I was quite prepared to listen to other Norwegian voices in the eco-philosophical circles. Immediately Sigmund and I hit it off and of course as anyone who knew Sigmund understands, he was not a difficult fellow to get to know and get to like. In the ensuing years, our paths crossed often and it could have been at his home in the Budal in middle Norway talking late into the night, climbing peaks to place plaques for Peter Wessel Zapffe, attending rallies to keep Norway out of the EU, or in London , or in the United States or he and Kirsten visiting my wife and myself at our home in Chile. Or it might have been to know Sigmund through his writings, his illustrations, his speeches and talks, or even through other colleagues who used or expanded on his ideas: As environmentalists, political activists, anti-globalists/pro-localists, mountain climbers, jazz fans and deep thinking minded types we had lots in common. It was natural that we became good friends. Above all I think we liked each other for we admired many things we found in each other. I count myself, as at least, president of Sigmund's South American Fan Club!

For many of us who have spent years as thinkers, writers, conservationists, or eco-social activists Sigmund had a profound impact. I can say for myself that he was indeed a "guru" of mine, a great teacher and if I had to get down to just a handful of great books and essays I would put in the top 4 – 5 of my extensive collection, Sigmund's essay and Schumacher lecture, "Complexity and Time: Breaking the Pyramid's Reign". This is a masterpiece and his distinction of complex and complicated are forever etched in my mind and my thinking. "Gaia Versus Servoglobe" is also one of the very best technology critiques and in the league with greats like Ellul, Mumford, Illich, Mander or Winner. Re-reading that today is to clearly understand how advanced Sigmund's thinking was. I rank him as one of the absolute greats of the last hundred years. Unfortunately, too, his ideas, his writing and thinking has not been well enough distributed outside the Norwegian/Nordic world, and hopefully this will be redressed with such publications as this.

Stetind

Like all vanguard thinkers, they are also ahead of their time and there is a "cultural lag" that takes a while for the society to come to understand the leading-edge philosophers, thinkers and writers and for events to play out in real life for their ideas to be well appreciated. What I see is that it is only a matter of time before the world will really "hear from" Sigmund Kvaløy Setreng, that this "cultural lag" is in fact catching up and catching up fast. Recently I was to give at talk in New York City and the Mega-Tech Teaching at Cooper Union and was pondering on just what to speak about. I procrastinated for months in preparing my talk and as I got more and more anxious wondering what to speak on, I re-read "Gaia Versus Servoglobe" and had a kind of reawakening to just how far out ahead of all of us Sigmund really was. I contemplated not delivering my own talk but simply address the audience with a brief introduction saying that there was not much need to labor over what would surely be a second-rate speech when I should enlighten the audience by simply reading this essay by Sigmund. After all, it was all there in that one essay what has happened within the techno-industrial culture since and Sigmund articulated it with brilliance nearly thirty years before. What use would it be to try to even improve on it now?! That essay was like good wine, it improved with age.

My recommendation for anyone interested in leading-edge thinking is to do a modicum of research and come up with all the writing and recorded speeches of Sigmund's and do the scholarship that I assure will become the basis for a rich and rewarding intellectual leap forward in one own thinking. I can guarantee it from personal experience that the time it takes to find and read Sigmund's writing will be one looks at the world. Right here in this book is a good place to start.[16]

---

16   The book he is writing about is: Henderson, B. & Jensen, Aa. (Eds) (2015). Sigmund Kvaløy Setreng Ecophilosophy Fragments: Writings – Drawings – Testimonies. Chrismar Books Publications. Uxbridge, Canada.

Reunion[17]

SCOTT RANDALL

*Modern ecophilosophy started some twenty-five years ago. For
a brief spell, some bright ideas were launched. Since then, there
has been a lot of action, but very little philosophical movement.
But we have reaped a good deal of experience through ecopolitical
activity. We need now, after all that experience, to sit down and do
ecophilosophy again, to philosophize under direct influence of the
reaped experience.*

– Sigmund Kvaløy Setreng,
1993 (Reed and Rothenberg 1993: 116)

In seminar room 90 in the HF building (where a wing of the building is
coincidentally called *Niels Treschows Hus*) at the main University of Oslo
campus at Blindern[18] there is a large round wooden table in the center of
the room, where the following are patiently seated and conversing in small
talk: Sigmund Kvaløy (Setreng), Arne Næss, Nils Faarlund, Ivar Mysterud,
Erik Dammann, Johan Galtung, Jon Wetlesen, Peter Wessel Zapffe, and
the moderator.[19] These men have been called together by the moderator in

---

17 This chapter is the same as chapter 4 in Scott Randall's master thesis "Towards a Synthesis of
Norwegian Ecophilosophy", University of Oslo, 2007. The characters in the dialog is entirely fictitious,
except where noted and referenced. There is an attempt to match each character's dialog with their actual
interests and personality in real life, but any accidental misrepresentations are done for the sole purpose of
supporting the Thesis, and encouraging the movement of discussion throughout the dialog. Quotations
will be written in italics and referenced with a footnote. Quotation marks and in-line source denotations
will not be used in order to preserve the continuity of the dialog. Text-size has been slightly diminished to
off-set the formatting style of the dialog (from font size 13pt to 12pt)
The actual meeting place of the Ecophilosophy Group. Source: (Kvaløy Setreng 1991: 102)
The moderator is left unanimous to promote the supposition that any individual could fill this role as
mediator between these wise men for the purpose of a greater eco-philosophical idea.
Literature chosen for dialogue quotations centered on the main study period for the Thesis (1968–1975),
although some quotations may be taken outside of this period to support the dialog flow, especially when
referring to the adaptations to Deep Ecology such as the 8-point platform developed in 1985. Dialog
member Peter Wessel Zapffe passed in October 1990, all other members are currently living. (2007)

18 The actual meeting place of the Ecophilosophy Group. Source: (Kvaløy Setreng 1991: 102)

19 The moderator is left unanimous to promote the supposition that any individual could fill this role
as mediator between these wise men for the purpose of a greater eco-philosophical idea.

a convincing manner that was simply explained as "critical real work that to address the persistent ecocrisis". The timeframe of the dialogue could be from 1985 all the way up to the present.[20]

Dialog Towards a Synthesized Ecophilosophy

Moderator: *God dag og velkommen!* Everyone is assembled here today to revitalize your common passionate ideas of the past that have since blown out of reach of current interest and understanding. There was a period when all seated here were locked together mentally and in spirit for the cause of greater consciousness of humans and their surroundings… it was called a crisis! The crisis of the human and natural kind has not diminished, it has only increased, and you all collectively were to bring humans closer to this understanding, but have ultimately failed. I know everyone here has not become complacent; you still share the same grandiose ideas of this "golden age", where all today continue to write and lecture about it… but you do so separately I may add. And while all have the same general focus, most have developed their own singular ideas regarding a successful eco-philosophical approach. Yes, most everyone keeps in contact here, and occasionally discusses items of interest, but when was the last time a large portion of you were gathered together for the purpose of addressing the issue everyone so adamantly wishes to have some sort of resolve? This is why we are here today – to take the collective ecophilosophy of the past, the developed singular ideas of each individual since, coupled with all of the eco-philosophical knowledge we have learned – to bring all of this together into one consistent message for the purpose of one synthesized ecophilosophy. Everyone here is getting too old to let this marvelous opportunity slip by; if we are going to do this, this is the time!

Næss: Is this congregation tantamount to Camelot and the Knights of the Round Table? Or more along the lines of The Last…

Kvaløy: Messiah?

---

20 Literature chosen for dialogue quotations centered on the main study period for the Thesis (1968–1975), although some quotations may be taken outside of this period to support the dialog flow, especially when referring to the adaptations to Deep Ecology such as the 8-point platform developed in 1985. Dialog member Peter Wessel Zapffe passed in October 1990, all other members are currently living. (2007)

Næss: ... No... Supper?... Jesus and his intellectual prophets. Speaking of Peter [Wessel Zapffe], he will be arriving shortly; I believe he is still up on Kolsås getting one last climb in.

Moderator: OK, noted. Is it possible he is stuck climbing his own "*trapp*" on the side of Kolsås? ('Zapffe's Trapp in the *Klettergarten* of Kolsås). But seriously, we all appreciate humor, but the intensity of the topic makes it a distraction.

Galtung: Humor is another source of optimism. Whereas tears, anxieties and fears may bring on apathy and despondency, smiles energize. But humor must be used with care. It is easy to neutralize issues by joking about them.[21]

Næss: Humor and play is necessary in all discussion and life!

Moderator: Well, OK, let's get started.

Galtung: A question of formality, should we invite others here to this meeting that has been doing recent work on the topic? I know a few influential thinkers that would be very interested in joining... one American in particular...

Kvaløy: It would be great if James Lovelock could join the group today, his concept of Gaia could really add value to our discussion...

Faarlund: Let's just keep this meeting limited to the original Norwegian conspirators. Only those that understand *dugnad, bunad,* and *akevitt* can truly relate to our Norwegian eco-philosophical discussion.

Moderator: Yes, I strongly agree Faarlund. The purpose of this group is to resurrect the original main participators during the emergence of organized ecophilosophy, which includes the prominent members of the Ecophilosophy Group, and of significant individuals involved in the period. But we should feel free to incorporate current ideas and trends in the greater global ecophilosophy discussion. So Kvaløy, you should bring up the principles of Gaia if you think it is relevant.

Mysterud: Quick comment... It is a little unclear to me why we have to hold this meeting under the umbrella of the Humanities Faculty, in a Humanities/Philosophy seminar room, I don't believe our group is entirely understood here, or fully appreciated by the more traditional philosophy side of the department. I propose we move to a more comfortable room at the Zoological Institute, where ecology and social issues are better appreciated.[22]

---

21   Source: (Galtung and Ikeda 1995: 21).

22   The meeting room for the original Ecophilosophy Group was moved from the Humanities Faculty to the Zoological institute for these similar reasons, showing a clear strain between the natural/social science

Moderator: OK, this seems trivial, but I am sure there is symbolic weight behind this recommendation. Let's move so everyone will be more comfortable. [*Group leaves seminar room HF 90, and regroups at a small room at the Zoological Institute, close to Ivar Mysterud's office*][23]

Kvaløy: OK, back to work here gentlemen! As a part of our purpose here today, as previously stated, there still exists an ecological crisis that originally united us in the late 1960s, and even more importantly there exists a human crisis within this. Yes, a problem with the human-nature relationship, the deeper meaning of what we 68ers[24] were initially working on… *Ecophilosophy came to life as a practical oriented philosophy – as a reaction to a global crisis that we lacked prior experience to cope with. As we defined the subject, it is crisis motivated and has its main mission to give insight, advice and training principles with the ability to begin a process moving away from the catastrophes course.*[25] We should begin at the same point where we began in 68, with a focus upon the crisis and imminent catastrophe as a motivator, and real work with how to address it.

Næss: I still believe that there exists an environmental crisis as I believed back in the early 70s when I stated that *we stand today with the possibility of a devastation of the biosphere, the living part of our planet… The word "devastation" is used as an alteration for the worse, a degradation of value.*[26]

Mysterud: As I also stated back in 71, *We are living in a world under developing and increasing pressure not only from one, but many crisis's…the threat against the 'ecological balance' is a crisis of very high intensity.*[27]

---

and philosophy of the Ecophilosophy Group. Source (Kvaløy Setreng 1991: 102).

23 Note: Kvaløy had an office at the Zoological Institute from 1976-1980, working as a researcher.

24 68ers (68-erne) is a term Kvaløy uses to describe the original founders of *(snm)* and the Ecophilosophy Group within. Reference, for example: (Kvaløy Setreng 2002: 122).

25 Source: (Kvaløy Setreng 1991: 102). Translated to English from Norwegian: "…økofilosofien kom til live som en *praktisk orientert* filosofi – som en reaksjon på en global krise som vi manglet forutgående erfaring for å hamle opp med. Slik vi definerte emnet, er det krisemotivert og har som hovedmisjon å gi innsikt, metoderåd og treningsprinsipper med evne til å starte en prosess vekk fra katastrofekursen." (Kvaløy Setreng 1991: 102).

26 Source: (Næss 1971b: 1). Translated to English from Norwegian: "Vi står idag overfor muligheten av en ødeleggelse av biosfæren, den levende del av vår planet…Ved ordet 'ødeleggelse' forstår jeg her en forandring til det verre, en verdiødeleggelse (Næss 197 1b:1)

27 Source: (Mysterud 1971: 23-24). Translated to English from Norwegian: "Vi lever i en verden under

Moderator: Yes, it is understood that all were motivated by a potential crisis, and this was not only ecological, but a crisis within ourselves as well. If Zapffe were here he could elaborate on his biosophy as it relates to a crisis of humanity....

Zapffe: Hallo! I am here; I snuck in when you all moved here from the HF building. I cannot stay long though because I am tired from climbing, my withering body is finally beginning to fail me, and my spirit is waning. But as I see it, *death always offers a way out... it can even come to seem a welcome escape from life...*[28]

Moderator: Ooops, I didn't see you there behind Næss's long philosopher's beard, that's great that you could join us, you are still with us in the living for the moment as far as I can tell, so regarding your view on the human side of the relationship...

Zapffe: Well *"cosmic panic" is basic to every human mind. The species, in this light, seems predestined to destruction, since any effort to preserve and continue life is crippled when one's undivided attention and energy is required to stave off the catastrophic pressure of one's inner being...[but] most people manage to save themselves by artificially paring down their consciousness*[29] with the four mechanisms I refer to as isolation, attachment, diversion, and sublimation. This is why I believe this dialogue is somewhat trivial, bordering on the bounds of diversion and sublimation; it's just a manifestation of our inner fears, suggesting a notion of control, which is inevitably impossible...unless we can biologically mutate again to lessen our mental capacities. So, on that note, farewell friends...

Moderator: Well, we must take Zapffe's position into consideration as we discuss further; humans have created distractions to remove themselves from nature and their raw condition, and these same distractions stand in the way of promoting ecophilosophy as well.

Kvaløy: *Peter addressed the drudgery of life with a perspective as wide as the Norwegian oceans and mountains. In everything he wrote and thought, he believed that all of us are seekers deep inside, after 'an answer to the single burning question – what does it mean to be human?*[30]

---

utvikling og økende press ikke bare fra en, men mange *kriser*... trusselen mot den 'økologiske balansen' som en estimert krise av meget høy intensitet" (Mysterud 1971: 23-24).

28   Source: (Reed and Rothenberg 1993: 48), from Zapffe's poem "The Last Messiah".

29   Source: (Reed and Rothenberg 1993: 43), from Zapffe's poem "The Last Messiah".

30   Source: (Reed and Rothenberg 1993: 40).

Moderator: Yes, and this question is relevant to our understanding of the human-nature relationship, but we cannot fully accept his approach, otherwise we must then condemn ourselves to eternal numbness, which goes against the energy which gathered us. Zapffe further elaborates the seriousness of the ecocrisis that surrounds us as a species, and which is also within us as individual humans – extending beyond just the natural ecosystem.

Kvaløy: We utilized some inspirations from Zapffe within the Ecophilosophy Group in regards to how the ecocrisis and human-nature relationship was defined, as well as using the ecocrisis as a motivator for change. *In contrast to what most people mention when talking about the ecocrisis – pollution and depletion of resources – we [Ecophilosophy Group] concluded that its most serious aspects are those belonging to the fields of human ecology…[IGS] is building up social instability at an accelerating pace…we are now anchored on a course that will entail a total qualitative change in global society, one that will be reversible only after a period of complete loss of control.*[31]

Dammann: FIOH also looks beyond the crisis simply being natural, where we believe that *we are constantly hearing that we live in a mad world…If we desire a change, we must also accept that this presupposes a change in our daily lives…[another] reason why nothing happens is that we are building upon false conceptions of reality. In order to be able to accomplish anything, we must have a true, overall picture of the situation in which we find ourselves.*[32] Finding this true picture is uncovering the "sublimation" mechanism Zapffe points to, looking deep into the human being first.

Galtung: *We must be realists in our brains while keeping the flame of idealism burning in our hearts. That is what peace research and peace-oriented action are about. Being blind to realities helps no one.*[33]

Moderator: The mention of a crisis, or social change, invokes profound reactions within individuals, and directing the aim at the individual will bring about even stronger reactions, normally of the negative – how do we resolve this dilemma?

---

31   Source: (Kvaløy 1973: 147).

32   Source: (Dammann 1979: xvii).

33   Source: (Galtung and Ikeda 1995: 18).

Dammann: We should make sure that whatever we discuss or construct in this group is in a calming format and language that the people can easily understand and relate to. We should be looking towards a philosophy for the people, not a philosophy for philosophers. *I believe that there will be more and more who feel a personal involvement in the problems of mankind, and who are increasingly concerned with finding solutions to them rather than following a given ideology. It is for these people that [Future in Our Hands] have been written.*[34] FIOH kept the message and language simple so all could understand, and this seems to have been a critical factor for general comprehension of the message, as well as for mobilizing people the best.

Moderator: I must also agree with Dammann, I feel that my unique position can keep the group in line on this issue – I see myself as a common person that is untrained in academic philosophy, just like I suppose the audience of our idea will be. We should keep the concept relatively basic for their understanding, I realize the need to indulge into philosophical argument occasionally to develop the idea, but since the academic philosophers are not our main audience, we should keep the idea itself accessible to all since everyone is our audience and our inspiration.

Galtung: I am in agreement on this point also. *Perhaps my background in life and training as a sociologist have given me a greater sensitivity to the common people than political or philosophical inclination alone could have inspired...As a result of my refusal [to military service], the Norwegian courts imprisoned me for six months. This experience brought me into contact with heroes in the struggle for day-to-day survival.*[35] I can relate to all people of all sorts, and that is who we need to address if we are interested in change, a holistic idea can only have a holistic audience, which is a part of my basis for my Development Theory which is a *holistic approach to human society, in principle, and dynamic, as the world indicates.*[36]

Kvaløy: A basic language and structure is something I believe in also, which was a main tactic of *snm* and the 68ers from the beginning; *the Ecophilosophy must not be subject-specialized and*

---

34 Source: (Dammann 1979: xviii). Note: "Future in Our Hands" replaced the original words "this book".

35 Source: (Galtung and Ikeda 1995: 6).

36 Source: (Reed and Rothenberg 1993: 196), from Galtung's essay "Development Theory: Notes on an Alternative Approach".

unilaterally abstract; one must speak the 'people's language' and be concrete through many illustrations people can relate to. Diverge from this, and the particular mission is lost. Maybe that was the cover for why the institutional philosophy found little interest in what we were doing.[37]

Næss: We should take care and learn from Gandhi and his style, *Gandhi takes care to avoid metaphors, and utters the most direct statements in the simplest of prose.*[38]

Faarlund: We seem to all be in agreement on this point gentlemen; one of the main reasons I began promoting *friluftsliv* back in the 1960s was because *it seemed clear that intricate intellectual arguments could never substitute for a firsthand experience of free nature... the most effective way to reintroduce Norwegians to the values of free nature was probably to arrange a face-to-face meeting.*[39]

Moderator: It would seem that an ecophilosophy with a language and structure understood by all people, as well as being holistic in form, would be in principle a good start to forming a peaceful and just philosophy, accepted by all that agree with its following norms, since no one is immediately discriminated.

Galtung: Sure, I believe in the *attainment of peace through peaceful means... in the nonviolent spirit of Shakyamuni Buddha and Gandhi.*[40] So if the philosophy had peaceful intentions in its all- inclusive manner, then it would have the elements of a peaceful result, this is all theoretically of course because the subject of the idea could drastically change its course.

Næss: While I have much to talk about regarding Gandhi today, I believe that we should limit ourselves here, for example, *some think that Deep Ecology should encompass questions of peace and social justice, whereas I think we should be careful to distinguish the differences between these movements, and not spread oneself too thin.*[41]

---

37   Source: (Kvaløy Setreng 1991: 102–110). Translated to English from Norwegian: "Derfor måtte ikke økofilosofien være fagspesialisert og ensidig abstrakt; den måtte tale "folkets språk" og være konkret via mange illustrasjoner folk kunne kjenne seg igjen i. Svikter den i dette, så har den mistet sin særegne misjon. Kanskje var det dette trekket som gjorde at instituttfilosofien fant det vi gjorte lite interessant" (Kvaløy Setreng 1991: 102–103).

38   Source: (Næss 1965: 101).

39   Source: (Reed and Rothenberg 1993: 160), from Faarlund's essay "A Way Home".

40   Source: (Galtung and Ikeda 1995: ix).

41   Source: (Rothenberg 1993: 148).

Moderator: Professor Næss, I think you missed the point here a little. The goal of the discussion is to take value out of everything we discuss towards one unified idea. So, by us discussing peace, or the peace movement, does not necessarily mean that it will become a main component of our synthesized idea; it is just discussed to determine if there is value for use as a small component of our created ecophilosophy.

Galtung: Regarding the inclusion of all for peace, Gandhi's *insistence on nonviolence (ahimsa), not as a mere ideal but as a practice applied to all forms of life – among animals too*[42] is a clear illustration of peace through peaceful means… applying the broad principle of nonviolence can lead to the realization of intrinsic value in all life.

Næss: Looking to Spinoza and Gandhi, *My attitude to Spinoza resembles that which I have toward Gandhi – taking account of both his writings and his life. The stories about Spinoza are just as uplifting in regard to his character as the tales of Gandhi's life. Both inspire confidence because, in part, not only did they produce words, but they acted out their philosophy of life.*[43]

Kvaløy: This is an excellent point! *If you want to contribute, "the way is the goal" – selfless, nonviolent action, found at centers of social and political conflict, and meaningful work. Those are the ways of getting started on the path to liberation.*[44] It is pivotal that we, as creators of this new eco-philosophical framework, strive our absolute hardest to live our lives in accordance to the ideals we are setting forth and agree upon. We are the creators and leaders of the idea that others must look to for inspiration and knowledge of how to possible alter their own lifestyle through action towards a healthier relationship with nature.

Faarlund: This is a principal I believe in and also practice myself, as well as teach my students… *friluftsliv*, a joyous encounter with free nature can be a turning point for both the individual and society. No force is stronger than joy.[45]

Moderator: Let's save the discussion of *friluftsliv* until the end, where it will have great significance to the finale of our discussion.

---

42 Source: (Galtung and Ikeda 1995: 64).

43 Source: (Næss and Haukeland 2002: 74).

44 Source: (Reed and Rothenberg 1993: 145), from Kvaløy's essay "Complexity and Time".

45 Source: (Reed and Rothenberg 1993: 158), from Faarlunds essay "A Way Home".

Dammann: In addition to the concept of "meaningful/real work", what we are creating must have an action component. *We shall not be launching new theories, which remain at the theoretical stage. Nor do we wish to be carried along by a wave of emotion. We hope, instead, that as many people as possible will take this seriously, and personally, and do something about it. We believe that this is the only way of bringing about the changes we want to see.*[46]

Moderator: Yes, we have established that we will maintain a balance between practicality and the deeper philosophical realm.

Dammann: FIOH *does not carry the objective of promoting a specific political ideology. It has no other objective than that of discovering a practical solution – a really feasible way out of the quagmire into which we have maneuvered ourselves... We cannot make any progress by using old concepts as the basis of comparison for new ones.*[47]

Moderator: Similar to Einstein, "We can't solve problems by using the same kind of thinking we used when we created them."

Dammann: Exactly, and regarding the FIOH, *none of the ideologies is a true objective, merely previously suggested means of achieving our actual aim...*[48]

Moderator: So far, we have all agreed on the importance of a practical philosophy, which contains basic language to target the non-philosophers; an all-encompassing idea to allow for peaceful progress, and eventual meaningful work. We have also touched on the principle that we should lead by example and strictly follow our created ecophilosophy's principles...

Næss: You forgot one important principle, which Galtung already alluded to, but I would like to stress further, nonviolent action and direct confrontation; as Gandhi emphasized *that nonviolence is a practical method, which we may, no, must, adopt immediately and without hesitation in social, political, national, and international conflicts...one should avoid violence against any living being; otherwise complete self-realization would be impossible.*[49] We will come back to self-realization soon. But

46   Source: (Dammann 1979: 170–171), from "The Future in Our Hands – Manifesto" signed by Arne Næss, Thor Heyerdahl, Georg Borgström, Helder Camara, Basil Davidson, George McRobie, Gunnar Myrdal, Dennis Meadows, and Jan Tinbergen.

47   Source: (Dammann 1979: xvii).

48   Source: (Dammann 1979: xviii).

49   Source: (Næss 1965: 8, 32).

also, one should *avoid violence, but not by avoiding the conflict… from the center of the struggle [one] tries to bring about a general reduction of violence, instead of avoiding it himself.*[50] The concepts were directly employed by *(snm)* in the 1970s.

Kvaløy: Yes, yes, they were. Also, *for us [in snm] the guiding star of Gandhi was the "norm of selfless action". Gandhi tells us that the most important source of human knowledge is not to be found at some university or meditation, but at the center of social and political conflict, the fight for Life and for Truth.*[51]

Moderator: Good points, I feel that personally I am also in the fight for Life and for Truth, and that is a substantial reason for why I thought it was so vital to bring everyone here together in this engagement, and place myself right in between. Moving on, we have stated that we should begin the evolution of the ecophilosophy with the idea that a crisis exists within the human and natural realm, as well as between the two. But where do we go from there? While we have established solid leading principles and methods, what are some additional actual components of the ecophilosophy?

Kvaløy: A principle that ecophilosophy is driven by is complexity (versus complication), which are *concepts that have been useful in our analysis of modern Western society… By 'complexity' (CX) I mean the dynamic, irreversible, self-steering, goal-directed, conflict-fertilized manifoldness of nature and – as a particularly refined and intricate version of that – the human body/mind. By 'complication' (CC) I mean the static, reversible, externally steered, standardizing structure-intricacy of the machine.*[52] – where complexity references qualities, and complexity quantities. These principles go in line with the social organization of Industrial Growth Society (IGS) versus Life Necessities Society (LNS). Where IGS *is based on steady or accelerating growth in the production of industrial articles and the use of industrial methods. [LNS] is based on producing life necessities and always tending to give priority to that.*[53]

---

50 Source: (Næss 1965: 39).

51 Source: (Reed and Rothenberg 1993: 144), from Kvaløy's essay "Complexity and Time".

52 Source: (Reed and Rothenberg 1993: 122), from Kvaløy's essay "Complexity and Time".

53 Source: (Reed and Rothenberg 1993: 121), from Kvaløy's essay "Complexity and Time".

Næss: [*shaking his head and smiling at Kvaløy*] Thank you Dr. Stockmann, be careful of your threats against society and democracy, you do not want to be labeled an "enemy of the people" [*group laughs respectfully*].

Kvaløy: Arne, you of all people know best that the foundation of this thinking is not a direct threat against society, let alone democracy per se, it is the current societal structure that is a direct threat against us! [*Kvaløy turns to Faarlund and whispers.*] The '51 UNESCO report [54], now there's a threat to democracy! [*both chuckle*].

Næss: I am again just trying to gently incorporate humor in our gathering here. I remember you all *disliked that in 1968. In the student social revolution, I was slippery in a way that I didn't seem to take it all very seriously. That was bad, of course. But I'm glad [the group] told me that. And I said 'Of course, but I'm here now to have a real talk with you, a real debate'.*[55] So here I am now, as difficult as it is, here with everyone to discuss, please be patient with me, as humor may still occasionally be a part of my presentation, but I am here in all seriousness and devotion.

Moderator: Thank you for your sincere honesty Professor Næss.

Group: [*Nods in affirmation*]

Moderator: Now back to Kvaløy's eco-philosophical components coming from his ecophilosophy, can the reliance upon these polar terms using "versus" quickly draw lines and divide people similarly as the "shallow" and "deep" terms of Deep Ecology?

Næss: Sure, *"a city" as an object does not exclude complexity, or the possibility of a lifestyle that would fit my criteria for complexity. Kvaløy has introduced complication as a negative term, complexity as a positive. For me 'complexity' is neutral if separated from symbiosis and diversity.*[56]

Kvaløy: The overlying terms are meant to be simple explanations of our goals versus mainstream reality, remember the "basic approach" we discussed before? In addition, rising from the previous two sets promoting complexity and LNS, is the division of generalists versus specialists. Specialists increase complication and only

---

54 Referencing the 1951 UNESCO report entitled Democracy in a World of Tensions, that Julian Huxley (then head of UNESCO) commissioned Arne Næss to create.

55 Source: (Rothenberg 1993: 185).

56 Source: (Reed and Rothenberg 1993: 108-109), also in (Rothenberg 1993).

promote the IGS vision, *we must seek to educate generalists – people who are rich in ego-complexity, who have some knowledge within many fields, who are trained in logical inter-disciplinary reasoning in relation to the problems of whole systems and societies, and who are able to transmit all this in a language that the non-academicians (the world's vast majority) can understand.*[57]

Moderator: I see how generalists are the ultimate holistic worker that can always envision the bigger picture, but what about the specialized field of ecology as a basis of ecophilosophy… is the entire premise of ecophilosophy not holistic then?

Mysterud: *The connection between practical fields and ecological theory is one of the most important and most challenging fields of our time. The debate at this level has shown that we need an all-encompassing analysis and explanation of ecological fundamental principles. It is also clear that to develop a "human ecology" will be impossible without bringing in value estimations.*[58] This is why I wrote an entire small book in 73 entitled *Noen Økologiske Grunnbegreper (Some Ecological Fundamental Principles),* which was also published in the *Eco-philosophical Reader* of the *Nature and Man* university seminar in the early 70s. I was laying down the ecological groundwork for the understanding of systems in order to support human ecological principles that could be used in ecophilosophy.

Moderator: I see, so you put the true "eco" in ecophilosophy.

Kvaløy: Human Ecology as I mentioned prior, and Ivar just commented on, is how I see *the study of individual human beings and of human societies as integrated parts of the greater ecosystem, a field of study in which the conceptual apparatus of ecology is adapted to the description of equilibrium relationships in human society.*[59] So this is how the field of ecology has helped to give ecophilosophy its holistic essence, I don't remember if we ever contemplated the title of "human-ecophilosophy" for our idea, that is a mouthful, but how we use ecology is in the form of human ecology anyways.

---

57   Source: (Kvaløy 1973: 153).

58   Source: (Mysterud 1975: 14). Translated to English from Norwegian: "Koblingen mellom praktiske arbeidsfelter og økologisk teori er en av tidens viktigste og mest utfordrende arbeidsfelter. Debatten på dette plan har vist at vi trenger en omfattende analyse og klargjøring av økologiske grunnbegreper. Det er også klart at å utvikle en 'humanøkologi' vil være umulig uten å bringe inn verdivurderinger"

59   Source: (Kvaløy 1973: 147).

Moderator: Understanding the role of Human Ecology will come in handy when the inevitable conversation of anthropocentrism and ecocentrism pops up, I can see Wetlesen stirring over there, waiting patiently to contribute.

Kvaløy: While we are on the subject of ecology, I must also mention Gaia, and how this concept is a perfect representation of all of ecology in a way. Gaia theory *proposes to view the earth's biosphere as one organism and an entity that actively changes itself to survive under shifting circumstances.*[60] Gaia employs the Systems Theory concept of Cybernetics, where the entire Gaia system is based on feedback loops from all material on the planet. This is the ultimate holistic view of our interconnectedness, and is an excellent tool to include in our new eco-philosophical vision.

Næss: You are right Sigmund; Gaia is an instrumental concept that can be used in our creation here. Gaia *has not only opened new areas of research, but evoked a new wave of reverence and pride. What has Mother Earth done to stay alive and keep going! She has got more friends than ever – people who gladly would pay higher taxes and whatever else is needed to support efforts to conserve what there is still of wilderness and areas in general, big and undisturbed enough to let mammalian and other evolution continue.*[61]

Moderator: Sure, but the implications of Gaia goes much deeper than mere conservation of wilderness, that is somewhat untypical dogmatic thinking you are exhibiting Professor Næss. Gaia should help us better understand our relationship with our surroundings, and the significance of a crisis therein, but any sort of policy or action efforts should come from the created ecophilosophy, not from the Gaia concept alone. Understanding Gaia should help us go in the other direction from dogmatism, questioning our actual place in the world, the true skeptical approach.

Næss: You are hitting at an internal dilemma of mine, but it is actually just a part of my personality, wandering from one pole to the other, I see too much value in all sides. But I was thinking, it would be nice if we could soon discuss the development of a solid platform. A platform such as the one used in Deep Ecology is a clear way to present the philosophies beliefs and standpoints.

---

60   Source: (Kvaløy Setreng 2001b: 1).

61   Source: (Næss and Rothenberg 1989: 138)., from Kvaløy's essay "Complexity and Time"

Galtung: No, I would urge the group against the formation of a platform. A platform of such can quickly draw lines and disturb any peace that exists. Where I think that a diagram can be a valuable starting point, or at least a good visual descriptor, a platform such as that in Deep Ecology is too dividing, exemplifying a tone of "you are either with us or without us", and "even if you are with us, and don't act as we do, then you are without us" – now this is dogmatic!

Næss: Yes, I see what you are saying, actually, this is one reason why I dislike working in groups and with other people, I have already been disregarded on some of my more prominent ideas, but if the platform does not fit the context of what we are creating, then it is not needed. Come to think about it, *I would never be good at facing people and fighting it out, so to say. I can face avalanches, but I'm not good at facing people. If they have counterarguments, I try to find reasons why these counterarguments are good. I tend to interpret them favorably...*[62]

Moderator: The purpose of our gathering is to work together collectively, in this group. Can you participate further Næss? Don't you believe in the group's common underlying value of collectivism over individualism towards one greater idea?

Næss: Yes, I believe *we need intimate interactions of a noncoercive kind. Let us use the example of Robinson Crusoe: if there are two people stranded on a desert island, it is hoped and is so much better that they find each other and work together...let us say that these philosophers, Robinson Crusoe and Friday, should at least acknowledge each other, and benefit from each other's existence.*[63] I will continue, until I feel totally coerced to stay, then I will start walking towards Tvergastein.

Moderator: OK, understood, I think we should table the idea of the potentiality of a platform until we have a better idea of where we are going [*group nods in affirmation*].

Wetlesen: Maybe this is a good time to bring up the anthropocentrism and ecocentrism argument as it relates to ecophilosophy; it will also be a good lead-in to discuss the concept of intrinsic value as well afterwards.

---

62   Source: (Rothenberg 1993: 134).

63   Source: (Reed and Rothenberg 1993: 109), also in (Rothenberg 1993).

Moderator: Sounds like a good progression… I am torn between believing if we are creating an idea that is human-centered or ecosystem-centered, it seems to me that we are constantly swaying back and forth between them, I personally feel this way in my own thinking as well. My ultimate interests lie in protecting human's home that protects us, and this of course includes protecting the ecosystem above all – this seems to be a common thread of the group as well. While this is just a technical classification, it draws great interest, and it is a subject we must address.

Wetlesen: Yes, this is necessary to discuss, and it can get real tricky, but I have done extensive research in the area, so hopefully I can shed some light upon the issue… The core of the issue comes down to the question of: *Which objects should be included in the class of moral subjects, and which should be excluded? Should we include, for instance, humans only; some or all, present or future? That would be an anthropocentric position. Or should we include nonhumans also; some or all individual living organisms (animals, plants, micro-organisms), as assumed in a biocentric position; or supra-individual wholes also (species-populations, ecosystems), as assumed in an ecocentric position? … The prevalent moral opinion in the modern world is anthropocentric.* [64]

Moderator: With that simple explanation ecophilosophy is generally ecocentric in its approach… but then again, it is ultimately anthropocentric in its inner goal.

Næss: *"Homocentrism" and "anthropocentrism" which so often have been used in a derogatory way should be qualified by an adjective, "narrow homocentrism" etc. Gradually the prospect of protecting the planet as a whole and for its own sake is seen as one of the greatest challenges ever. And it certainly is a specifically human task. A deep human need is involved…* [65]

Kvaløy: *I am more anthropocentric than Arne, and of course we have talked about it. He feels closer to animals that are far away from the human universe; it fascinates him very much, and one of my many personalities does feel the same way. But although it is important to have strong feelings about nature, we have to concentrate on the human society and the human being; otherwise everything we cherish will be destroyed.* [66]

---

64   Source: (Wetlesen 1993: 101-102).

65   Source: (Næss and Rothenberg 1989: 141).

66   Source: (Reed and Rothenberg 1993: 148), from interview with Kvaløy.

Næss: Yes Sigmund, I have believed from the start that *the equal right to live and blossom is an intuitively clear and obvious value axiom. Its restrictions to humans are an anthropocentrism with detrimental effects upon the life quality of humans themselves. This quality depends in part upon the deep pleasure and satisfaction we receive from close partnership with other forms of life. The attempt to ignore our dependence and to establish a master-slave role has contributed to the alienation of humans from themselves.*[67]

Kvaløy: Yes, well from the start we were more concerned with the greater social system and change. *Næss has put a lot of effort into proposing and discussing theories of animal rights and 'humanity as part', while the Ecophilosophy Group might be said to be more anthropocentric, spending most of their time on the organization of human societies and how human cultures develop and change.*[68]

Galtung: *Both Næss and Gandhi seem here to suffer, in my view, from the same fallacy of misplaced individualism... For Næss and Gandhi ultimate reality is somewhere in the human mind rather than in social structures.*[69]

Wetlesen: In the grand scheme, Arne and Sigmund have subtle differences, but I believe we are all in the same boat here. An appropriate explanation for our confusing stance can be explained with the labels of moral agency and moral patients; where we as rational human beings are the only ones that prescribe morals so *all who have the capability of rational self-determination (freedom, autonomy) are ascribed the right of self-determination,*[70] and all others lacking rational thought are mere patients or subjects in the system, but they are also the ones that originally project the value. Holmes Rolston III has stated something similar along these lines that "It is true that humans are the only valuators who can reflect about what is going on at this global scale, who can deliberate about what they ought to do conserving it. When humans do this, they must set up the scales; and humans are the measurers of things. Animals, organisms, species, ecosystems, Earth, cannot teach us how to do this evaluating. But they can display what it is that is to be valued."[71]

---

67   Source: (Næss 1972: 96).

68   Source: (Reed and Rothenberg 1993: 120), from Kvaløy's essay "Complexity and Time".

69   Source: (Galtung 1982: 234-235nn5).

70   Source: (Wetlesen 1993: 121).

71   Source: (Rolston 2003: 152).

Moderator: But who is to monitor that we are appropriate moral agents over the whole world as a patient?

Dammann: If you are alluding to God, I would rather we totally avoid the subject. Humans as the ultimate agent must regulate themselves, which is an underlying purpose of ecophilosophy, what we are creating here… somewhat of a dampening of our runaway agency.

Wetlesen: Exactly! Back to Rolston again, he also states that "there is something subjective, something philosophically naïve, and even something hazardous in a time of ecological crisis, about living in a reference frame where one species takes itself as absolute and value everything else in nature relative to its potential to produce value for itself."[72]

Næss: Well, I would like to refer the group to the first point of the 8-point Platform then: *The well-being and flourishing of human and non-human life have value in themselves (synonyms: intrinsic value, inherent value). These values are independent of the usefulness of the non-human world for human purposes.*[73]

Wetlesen: *If a person evaluates the natural environment, or parts of it, as intrinsically valuable, he or she will have a good reason to look after the environment and ensure its well-being rather than destroy or harm it. This attitude can be extended both towards individual living organisms [biocentric] and towards supraindividual wholes [ecocentric]… Morally right actions in relation to both humans and non-humans will be motivated by love, friendliness, or compassion, but not because of the pressure of moral duty. In the terminology of Kant this is called acting beautifully, not dutifully. In some sense, however, this kind of action is amoral since it is not considered to be morally binding.*[74] So, are we going to compose our framework for individuals to act beautifully or dutifully in respect to intrinsic value for the ecosystem?

Galtung: *Studying Gandhi, it may strike one that there is much more to it than the effort to make struggle compatible with goals…there is the element of optimism, and of innovation – love will win in the long run; coupled with imagination in devising new forms of struggle reducing the coercive element to a minimum, possibly even to zero, love is invincible.*[75]

---

72 Source: (Rolston 2003: 152).

73 Source: (Devall and Sessions 1985: 70).

74 Source: (Wetlesen 1993: 111).

75 Source: (Galtung 1982: 234).

Moderator: It would seem most natural for actions to be based on "beauty" than "moral obligation"; if an individual passionately adheres to the norms prescribed for biocentric intrinsic value and acts beautifully, then the individual's moral obligation is implied and included; if an individual does not adhere to the norms then they should not have moral obligation to do so, because it would be going against their will. A challenge of the will must be visited first, and this is a general approach of Norwegian ecophilosophy. An exception to this statement can be seen in point number 8 of the Deep Ecology 8-point Platform, where obligation is explicitly stated, although it is a totally unwarranted request.

Dammann: This point may be wandering into the deeper philosophical realm that we originally talked about avoiding [*motioning to moderator*]. Can we take it a step back from this point?

Næss: No, I must interrupt, this is important… *I have a somewhat extreme appreciation of what Kant calls "beautiful actions" (good actions based on inclination), in contrast with actions which are performed out of a sense of duty or obligation. The choice of the formulation "Self-realization!" is in part motivated by the belief that maturity in humans can be measured along a scale from selfishness to an increased realization of Self, that is, by broadening and deepening the self, rather than being measured by degrees of dutiful altruism.*[76] I would like to bring in this concept to our discussion, and how valuable it is to our proposed framework

Moderator: Self- realization is critical to our discussion, but Næss, as you have created in your own Deep Ecology apron diagram, self-realization is not a concept that can, or must, be included. Isn't it a more spontaneous mental level that can only be set accordingly by each individual? So, wouldn't it be incorrect to force it into the framework?

Næss: Yes of course, but I never said we need to force it, it can simply be stated as a mental state that can be desired for greater understanding if needed. So, still a part of the framework that is important to intrinsic value, but not a working condition.

Wetlesen: *Næss connects intrinsic value with self-realization, which, in turn, he bases on a Gestalt theory of the self. The self of a person is*

---

76   Source: (Næss 1986: 185).

constituted through a process of self-identification, and the scope of one's self will depend on what one identifies oneself with.[77]

Næss: *Roughly speaking, the term gestalt ontology is introduced to take better care of some important phenomena usually donated by terms such as holistic thinking. The usages of systems thinking are farther way, but not every use of that term... The gestalt character functions to widen and deepen the effect of identification. The concrete contents of experience become richer though the I/Thou relations with living beings.*[78] *Gestalt psychology imagines that the patterns of people's experiences are something going on in their heads... Get rid of the subject as a container of images and thoughts. It's all just as much out there as it is in you!*[79]

Kvaløy: Yes, I guess I can see Arne's use of Ecosophy in Deep Ecology as an individual's identity. This point is important because *identity for the individual means that person's history, an inherited total world view containing everything that is necessary to deal with 'survival-with-abundance' in her own place... Without identities reflecting the eco-social histories of the many different landscapes that Gaia presents to human beings, there would be no individuals or societies with sufficient moral strength and inspiration to counter difficulties as they arise, neither would there be alternative ways of doing things.*[80]

Moderator: Let's briefly put these ideas aside for now, I am sure they will come up in conversation again... Dammann has been patiently waiting to speak.

Dammann: I would like to introduce my approach, which is where an individual must start with himself or herself, as a start in time...

Kvaløy: Erik, before you begin, this "start with yourself" idea is minutely flawed.

It's something typically Western when some of the greens say that we can and should start by changing ourselves first, and through that get ready to change the sociopolitical system. That's still building on the view of man as a soul separated from his body and from his environment. In our world of passivity that's the worst kind

---

77   Source: (Wetlesen 1993: 110).

78   Source: (Næss 1989: 461, 466).

79   Source: (Rothenberg 1993: 153-154).

80   Source: (Kvaløy Setreng 1994: 36).

of recommendation, and ensures that nothing will happen… You have to step into the stream to be grabbed by something outside your private soul, something you do not control. It's then that you have a chance of being shaken so that you're changed, and through that already contributing to changing the system.[81]

Næss: Exactly, *It is not really a start in time but a kind of eternal starting point, that this idea of change must be your thought, not someone else's… you never thought that by introspection or meditation alone you could widen yourself in this Western society of ours. You widen yourself through getting into trouble, no, rather by cooperating with others in a social and political context, where the actions themselves require identification, where it is advantageous to have a large self.*[82]

Kvaløy: Excuse me Arne, but your praise of cooperation is admirable, your initial cooperative efforts in ecophilosophy *(snm)* and related actions) were less than fantastic, you inspired us and were there for philosophical support, but your direct participation was minimal. I will put this general misconception aside by commending and thanking you for your involvement today in our expanded endeavor. I just hope we can keep you at the table.

Næss: *First of all, I was then heavily engaged in theoretical work, and I would have liked to join them in some of the direct actions, but I have a very limited tolerance for meetings. And in order to really do the work there, you had to be in a really long series of meetings, talking and talking and talking, and that was impossible for me. I've never been able to do that. Never.*[83]

Group: [*all together*] Hmmm…

Næss: *I was a member of (snm), but I never took part in the real work to organize direct action on the great scale like Sigmund and half a dozen others, most of them not committed Marxists.*[84]

Kvaløy: OK, thanks for the credit there. But you were an *(snm)* member, just not an outspoken contributor or participator.

Næss: *I think I am to some extent a coward when it comes to fighting with people. Why did I never "raise hell"? Courageous among rocks, timid among men? I never slam my hand on the table. If I had done that,*

---

81   Source: (Reed and Rothenberg 1993: 128), from Kvaløy's essay "Complexity and Time".

82   Source: (Reed and Rothenberg 1993: 104), also in (Rothenberg 1993).

83   Source: (Rothenberg 1993: 133).

84   Source: (Rothenberg 1993: 132).

I'm sure they would have listened very attentively and I could have really accomplished something, but I was just resigned to my strange view, alone.[85]

Kvaløy: You did come at the last moment and surely helped us out at Mardøla by bringing greater attention to the cause. However, it was brief, but it was your first taste of direct environmental action as inspired by Gandhi, although how come you are always credited as the highlight of this action?[86]

Næss: *Yes, yes. That's right. That's unfortunate, because those who worked night and day organizing direct actions [Sigmund] were less well known, I am sorry to say, as well as believing in a nonhierarchical kind of organization without single leader. But the press wanted to identify leaders, and they decided that I was one of the major leaders.*[87]

Moderator: I understand that Professor Næss was going through a transition of his own in the early 1970s, and there was great mutual inspiration and influence between him all of the individuals and groups of the period dealing with ecophilosophy...but I am not sure of its great relevance in our forward-looking discussion today.

Næss: Yes, thank you, Gandhi summarizes this complex situation best by believing a *man can always change: "However debased or fallen he may be, [he] has in him the capacity of rising to the greatest height ever attained by any human being." How far he climbs depends on what people, and through them, what groups he come to be influenced by.*[88]

Moderator: Sure, and that "great man" is you Professor Næss. Anyways, I believe we have gotten a little off track, Dammann, what was your approach that began with "start with yourself"?

Dammann: *There are many of us who would like to go in for such a change in our own, personal way of life – if we thought it would be any use. It will be some use, if we act together. But we are too divided, belonging, as we do, to different parties and organizations. We lack the support of a larger group. We must unite, across the lines between parties, which have not as yet set their sights on these new goals.*[89]

---

85   Source: (Rothenberg 1993: 132).

86   Source: (series of phone conversations with Sigmund Kvaløy from 2006-2007).

87   Source: (Rothenberg 1993: 133).

88   Source: (Næss 1965: 88-89).

89   Source: (Dammann 1979: 170).

But this path to a holistic organization must all begin with each individual, starting with one 's self, and uniting... *That is why we inspire people to get together and support each other, in emancipation from the pressures of competition and consumerism, which are driving us all in the wrong direction.*[90]

Moderator: While the collective approach you explain is commendable, these pressures you mention are not the root cause that are driving us in the wrong direction, it is just a façade of our disconnect with our surroundings, you and FIOH may be inadvertently gathering people and leading them in the wrong direction.

Kvaløy: Back in *(snm)* and the Ecophilosophy Group, we were strong promoters of the idea that *"taking care of oneself" as a working member of a small farm community provides a more solid basis for expanding complexity, which also means getting nearer to a meaningful life.*[91] So, in order to improve the larger group for a better life, one must reflect upon their individual actions most importantly, instead of finding direct assistance with others as Dammann relies upon. We also believed that one's natural rural roots were the best places to experience this self-reflection.

Dammann: *I share the same dreams as Sigmund, but I disagree with his manner of presenting them.*[92] He has shown too much romanticism with a past that will never be the future, while this "closed" historic system can be examined as a reference system; we have to work with what we are dealt in order to truly be "practical". [93]

Moderator: Yes, there is a distinct romanticism within parts of ecophilosophy that adorns the perfect Norwegian (or Nepalese) farming village, and these are systems that Ecophilosophy views are in optimal working condition. But this is not nearly as extreme as many dogmatic environmental views such as in the U.S. that run primarily along the lines of wilderness preservation and conservation, with no concern regarding the human environment. [*unknown voice from behind open door*]: I fully agree, within ecophilosophy there is no talk about halting big industry and turning back to an idyllic pasture...

---

90   Source: (Reed and Rothenberg 1993: 221), from Dammann's essay "The Future in our Hands".
91   Source: (Kvaløy 1973: 152).
92   Source: (Reed and Rothenberg 1993: 212).
93   Reference: (Reed and Rothenberg 1993: 212).

Moderator: Excuse me, where did that come from? It sounds like Finn Alnæs.

Alnæs: *No talk about preventing technological research or to consider all cities as a cancer. A city, like an anthill, can be a natural part of the ecosystem. What we need to eradicate is... the building up and maintenance of an artificial existence that destroys nature and bases itself more on industry produced things than on the forests, seas, and growth of the soil; that lumps together humans in depressing cases.*[94]

Moderator: We understand your elaborative point (with exceptional references to both Hamsun and Nansen in the same sentence!); a complete fascination with wilderness (or just wild nature) should be avoided, as it is an extreme ecocentric position that alienates the human subject. You are more than welcome to stay Finn, but you shouldn't be sneaking around as such. Let's move on...

Næss: As Sigmund and Erik are aware, Niels Treschow was involved in something similar as this, while also going back to previous points: being holistic, but also individualistic. *There are two sorts of mysticism: in one of them you get completely absorbed in something much bigger than you, an organic whole or God, but on the other hand there is the mysticism you find in Spinoza, which tries to retain, after all has passed, the individual.*[95]

Moderator: This sounds somewhat contradictory; how does Deep Ecology solve this dilemma?

Næss: Through the passive utilization of self-realization – similarly to what Erik and Sigmund are alluding to, only that it starts with the individual thinking about the greater whole and acting upon it, but it does not stop there, the entire purpose is to come back to the individual with an even greater self- reflection of the greater circumstance contemplated, whereas Self can then be applied.

Moderator: Yes, Professor Næss, I also now recall how Niels Treschow elaborated upon something similar back in the late 1700s with his *Philosophy of Identity* which contained the three sources of truth: Reason, Experience, and Revelation. Treschow states that, "Moral, as well as physical fulfillment consists in the undisturbed

---

94   Source: (Alnæs 1976a: 14-15). Translated to English from Norwegian: "Det er ikke snakk om å stanse all storindustri og vende tilbake til en pastoral idyll, ikke snakk om å hindre den teknologiske forskning eller om å anse enhver by som en kreftsvulst. En by, likesom en maurtue, kan være en naturlig del av økosystemet. Det vi vil til livs er...oppbyggingen og opprettholdelsen av en kunstig tilværelse som raserer naturen og baserer seg mer på industriproduserte ting enn på skogenes, havens og markenes grøde; som klumper mennesker sammen i forstemmende bo-kasser" (Alnæs 1976a: 14–15).

95   Source: (Reed and Rothenberg 1993: 103), originally found in (Witoszek 1999: 460).

harmony or, in other words, achievement of complete individuality, where all parts are so connected that no one is less essential or necessary than the other and no chance intervenes".[96] Treschow's *Philosophy of Identity* is not too dissimilar from the Deep Ecology apron diagram where Level 1 and 2: Premises and Principles is Reason; Level 3 and 4: Views and Decisions is Experience; and Deep Questioning leading to Self-realization (traveling backwards from level 4 to level 1) is Revelation.

Næss: Sure, well put. Well I like to think that the concept of Self-realization comes from Gandhi where *usually we have no definite maximum in mind when we think of how far our relationships can go in this world, but for Gandhi there was such an ultimate basis of identification; he felt that the needs of his own self-expansion could only be satisfied by identifying himself with every living being. The 'set' of which he saw himself a part was the total class of all living creatures.*[97]

Moderator: The wide identification with all, that utilizes greater intrinsic value for all, opens the ports to self-realization.

Næss: To further explain, Gandhi believed that the *greater Self can be realized or cultivated maximally* this comes from the smaller self, the ego, *which should be and can be reduced towards zero... When the egotism-ego vanishes, something else grows, that ingredient of the person that tends to identify itself with God, with humanity, all that lives... I believe in the essential unity of man and for that matter of all that lives... One's own self-realization must therefore somehow include that of others. The requirement of helping the self-realization of others...*[98] This is the universality of the Self, oneness in all, total holistic thinking.

Moderator: Assisting in the self-realization of others is a delicate task, because in order for it to be genuine it must solely come from within. But I guess there are tasks which can encourage successful assistance, such as Deep Exposure leading to Deep Experience – these do not necessarily cross the line of intervention.

Næss: But before these tasks can be recommended, the individual must comprehend the value of Deep Questioning; which is a critical concept to the Pyrrhonian skeptical concepts that are overtly encouraged within earlier Deep Ecology.

---

96 Source: (Witoszek 1999: 460, 464n28), original source is: (Treschow 1807).

97 Source: (Næss 1965: 30).

98 Source: (Næss 1974: 38, 42). Quotation originally found in (LaChapelle 1978: 154).

Wetlesen: Yes, this is crucial. With Pyrrhonian skepticism, *its goal is practical, peace of mind, not theoretical, absolute truth. Nevertheless, the search for truth has an important function as a means to this end.*[99]

Næss: Only then leading to Deep Experience, which can be propagated through the help of Deep Exposure activities such as *friluftsliv,* where *understanding of anything in nature begins with direct experience, but this soon stimulates reflection.*[100]

Faarlund: Correct Arne, *friluftsliv* facilitates the path between philosophy and the opportunity for self-realization, *The Way Is the Goal. Encountering free nature is an experience of joy. There is no force stronger than joy. Joy is the way Home.*[101]

Moderator: *Friluftsliv* is an excellent modern Norwegian tactic to promote Deep Exposure. First recommended by Nansen at the beginning of the twentieth century as a response to his passionate disapproval of the severed Norwegian relationship with their true surrounds, he saw Norwegian too reliant upon their social constructions.

Faarlund: Even beyond that, *friluftsliv evokes such strong responses in Norwegian society because it evokes a national identity, as sense of really 'belonging' to the land…friluftsliv is a living tradition for recreating nature-consonant lifestyles. It implies making friends with nature and passionately recreating free nature's standing in our culture. It is an unselfish 'I-Thou' relationship that tries to come away from the anthropocentrism of a nature-dissonant society.*[102]

Moderator: So, not only is *friluftsliv* a contributor along the inner path of self-realization, but also along the outer path of identification. What a simple, but marvelous concept, that is uniquely Norwegian! Let begin to wrap it up.

Faarlund: I guess one advantage of going last is that I can give the closing remarks. *Changes of the type that our culture must go through are stuck so deep, that not even Espen Askeladd himself, with his innovative gang… will be able to snap his fingers and free us from the un-personified intellectual regime. Our societal machine is protected by control thinking and control functions. As long as the simplified mechanisms don't provoke catastrophes with uncontrollable*

---

99 Source: (Wetlesen 1982: 198).

100 Source: (Næss and Rothenberg 1989: 181).

101 Source: (Reed and Rothenberg 1993: 169), from Faarlund's essay "Touch the Earth".

102 Source: (Reed and Rothenberg 1993: 164), from Faarlund's essay "A Way Home".

dimensions (the greenhouse effect, changing of ocean currents, melting of polar regions), speaking in all probability, we can only wait to achieve a correction here or a correction there.[103]

Moderator: Well, we hope to alter the "machine" so there are eventually greater changes than mere corrections… and today we have compiled the basic ingredients; we just need to add some exotic spices, and most importantly, find the recipe…

Kvaløy: Well Nils, you really didn't think you would get the last word that easily, did you? One quick last comment, the task of philosophy is to look through the grid of conventional concepts; the task of ecophilosophy is to do that in a way that strengthens the observer's roots in the Earth. The grid to be penetrated now, more than at earlier turning points, is one that has grown dangerously abstract in relation to human needs: the urgent task now is to regain concreteness.[104]

Moderator: Yes, identification has been a central point in our discussion today at building a stronger relationship with nature. We have been going strong in discussion for a while now, it is best if we call it a day. What we have achieved today is a promising start towards the synthesis of Norwegian ecophilosophy. Much more discussion and work is needed to reach our ultimate goal, but we are certainly along the right path, headed in the right direction. *Tusen takk for i dag!*

References:

- Alnæs, Finn. (1976a): *Svart snø: Dokumentarbok fra en brytningstid.* Aschehoug: Oslo.
- Dammann, Erik. (1979): *The Future in Our Hands: What We Can All Do. Towards the Shaping of a Better World.* Pergamon Press: Oxford

---

103 Source: (Faarlund 2000: 5-6). Translated to English from Norwegian: "Endringer av det slag som vår kultur må gjennom, stikker så dypt, at selv ikke en Espen Askeladd med sitt leuge lag…ville være istand til i en håndvending å fri oss fra den avpersonifiserte forstands regime. Vårt samfunnsmaskineri er beskyttet av kontroll-tenkning og kontroll-funksjoner. Så lenge forenklingsmekanismene ikke utløser katastrofer med ukontrollerbare dimensjoner (drivhuseffekten, endring av de store havstrømmene, faretruende smelting av isen ved polene, osv.), taler sannsynligheten for at vi bare kan vente å oppnå en korreksjon her og en korreksjon der "(Faarlund 2000: 5-6).

104 Source: (Kvaløy Setreng 1994: 29).

- Devall, Bill and George Sessions. (1985): *Deep Ecology: Living as if Nature Mattered.* Peregrine Smith Books: Salt Lake City, Utah.
- Faarlund, Nils. (2000): "Natur-livsfilosofiske tanker i Per-og-Pål-tider" [online]. - URL: http://www.naturliv.no/faarlund/per_og_paal.htm
- Galtung, Johan. (1982): "Gandhian Themes" in *In Sceptical Wonder* edited by Ingemund Gullvåg and Jon Wetlesen, 1982, pages 220-236.
- Galtung, Johan and Daisaku Ikeda. (1995): *Choose Peace: A Dialogue between Johan Galtung and Daisaku Ikeda.* Richard L. Gage (ed.). Pluto Press: London.
- Kvaløy (Setreng), Sigmund. (1973): *Økokrise, Nature og Menneske: En Innføring i økofilosofi og økopolitikk (økofilosofisk fragment IV).* Oslo.
- Kvaløy Setreng, Sigmund. (1991): "Økokrisefilosofi - glimt fra det norske økofilosfiske forsøket" in *Den Uoverstigelige Grense* edited by Svein Gjerdåker, Lars Gule og Bernt Hagtvet, 1991, pages 102-116. Cappelen: Oslo.
- Kvaløy Setreng, Sigmund. (1994): "Inside Nature" in *Nature the True Home of Culture* edited by Børge Dahle, pages 29-37. Norges Iderettshøgskole, Oslo.
- Kvaløy Setreng, Sigmund. (2001b): "Gaia versus Servoglobe" in *Festskrift til Sverre Sløgedal*, NTNU Institute of Philosophy, 2001. Trondheim.
- Kvaløy Setreng, Sigmund. (2002):" To økofilosfier i Norge; deres begynnelse og en del til" in *Arne Næss: Festskrift til 90-årsdagen 27.1.2002.* Norsk filosofisk tidsskrift, nr 1-2, 2002 årgang 37, edited by Lars Svendsen. Universitetsforlaget: Oslo.
- Mysterud, Ivar. (1971): *Forurensning og Biologisk Miljøvern.* Universitetsforlaget: Oslo.
- Mysterud, Ivar. (1975): "Økologisk tenkning" in *Økologi, Økofilosofi* edited by Paul Hofseth and Arne Vinje, 1975, pages 14-49.
- Næss, Arne. (1965): *Gandhi and the Nuclear Age.* Bedminster Press: New Jersey.
- Næss, Arne. (1971b): *Økologi og Filosofi I.* 2nd edition. Institutt for filosofi: Oslo.
- Næss, Arne. (1974): *Gandhi and Group Conflict: An Exploration of Satyagraha: Theoretical Background.* Universitetsforlaget: Oslo.
- Næss, Arne. (1986): "The Deep Ecological Movement: Some Philosophical Aspects" in *Environmental Philosophy: From Animal Rights to Radical Ecology* (3rd edition) edited by Michael Zimmerman, J. Barid Callicott, George Sessions, Karen Warren and John Clark, 2001, pages 185-203. Prentice Hall: New Jersey.

- Næss, Arne. (1989): "Gestalt Ontology and Gestalt Thinking" in *SWAN* volume X, edited by Harold Glasser and Alan Drengson, 2005, pages 461-466.
- Næss, Arne and David Rothenberg. (1989): *Ecology, Community, and Lifestyle: An outline of an Ecosophy*. 6th edition. Cambridge University Press: Cambridge.
- Næss, Arne and Per Ingvar Haukeland. (2002): *Life's Philosophy: Reason and Feeling in a Deeper World*. University of Georgia Press: Athens.
- Reed, Peter and David Rothenberg. (1993): *Wisdom in the Open Air: The Norwegian Roots of Deep Ecology*. University of Minnesota Press: Minneapolis.
- Rothenberg, David. (1993): *Is it Painful to Think? Conversations with Arne Næss*. University of Minnesota Press: Minnesota.
- Rolston, Holmes III. (2003): "Value in Nature and the Nature of Value" in *Environmental Ethics: An Anthology* edited by Holmes Rolston III and Andrew Light, 2003, pages 143-153. Blackwell Publishers: Oxford.
- Wetlesen, Jon. (1982): "Næss on the Development of a Pyrrhonian Sceptic – Some Comments in the Light of Indian Scepticism" in *In Sceptical Wonder* edited by Ingemund Gullvåg and Jon Wetlesen, 1982, pages 185-199.
- Wetlesen, Jon. (1993): "Who has Moral Status in the Environment" in *Culture and Environment: Interdisciplinary Approaches* edited by Nina Witoszek, 1993, pages 98-129. Centre for Development and the Environment: Oslo.
- Witoszek, Nina. (1999): "Arne Næss and the Norwegian Nature Tradition" in *Philosophical Dialogues: Arne Næss and the Progress of Ecophilosophy* edited by Nina Witoszek and Andrew Brennan, 1999, pages 451-465. Rowman and Littlefield Publishers: Maryland. *Note*: Article also published in Norwegian in (Witoszek 1998: 153-166).

THE STETIND DECLARATION

Stetind in fog (1864), The National Museum, Oslo, Norway

We have gradually come to realize:

That our way of life has fateful consequences for nature and humankind, and thus for all life on Earth

The challenges we face as individuals and as a community are not merely of an economic and technological nature.

They concern our basic values and our fundamental conception of what it means to be human.

We acknowledge that:

Nature and humankind constitute a whole and share a common destiny. Nature is the home of culture.

Life is like a woven fabric of relations. To live is to be dependent.

The value of nature and human dignity are intrinsically linked. What we do to nature, we do to ourselves.

All life is vulnerable and therefore under threat.

Concern for nature implies a concern for greater justice: Our way of life affects in particular the poorest among us, indigenous peoples, and future generations.

We will:

Work to promote a renewed understanding of the relationship between nature and humankind.

Strive to base our choices, both as individuals and as a community, on this understanding.

Discover the joy of living in harmony with nature:

There is no path to harmony with nature. Harmony with nature is the path.

Humankind possesses great capacity both to create and to destroy.

At this crucial point in time we will take responsibility and commit ourselves to thinking and living in a way that promotes life.

I/we will work to fulfill the Stetind Declaration.

GOOD PLANETS ARE HARD TO FIND

Good planets are hard to find

ØYSTEIN DAHLE

The 2009 state-of-the-world (SOTW) report was introduced by a foreword written by the chairman of the Intergovernmental Panel on Climate Change, R.K. Pachauri. In his short introduction he claims that the SOTW report has evolved into a remarkable source of intellectual wealth that provides understanding and insight not only of the physical state of the planet, but on human systems as they are linked with ecosystems and natural resources around the world.

A later SOTW report moves one step further by analyzing and digesting the ultimate challenge why we do not seem to understand the systemic challenge, and that our collective efforts have been vastly insufficient to turn around the dramatic trends threatening to make our spaceship uninhabitable. It is remarkable that a number of outstanding scientists for a good number of years have claimed that our western consumption pattern is unsustainable, and furthermore that if the entire global population was consuming like us, we would require three to five planets to not exceed the ecological capacity. It is very few facts the entire global population could agree to, but this one is one of them: We do have only one planet!

The climate challenge is receiving a lot of attention these days. But the global temperature increase is not the real problem. The temperature increase is signaling that our living home in space has fever and the maximum temperature increase the planet can take is 2°C according to the collective judgment of leading scientists in the field. At the moment we are approaching

1°C increase. But just like human fever, we need to identify the disease to find the correct medication, rather than chewing aspirin to get the fever down it is overwhelming evidence that our fundamental challenge is consumption and exponential growth. And consumption is directly linked to purchasing capacity and pricing of irreplaceable resources. If we are not identifying the real problem of overconsumption, efficiency improvements are only postponing the crisis, and when we finally realize what needs to be done, it is even more demanding to adjust the global agenda.

In the Western world we have been warned many years ago of the challenge we are facing and it has become a meme saying that the civilization we have developed through our modern way of thinking has serious and fundamental problems, which cannot be solved by continuing to think as we have over a long time. This meme links our global problems to our way of living. The magazine *ECOLOGIST* had as early as in 1972 (*Ecologist*, 1972) a cover story with the title "A Blueprint for Survival".

In this magazine the challenge of exponential growth was discussed since the implications of this type of growth was not generally appreciated. As Professor Jay Forrester explains it (Forrester, 1970):

> *Pure exponential growth processes the characteristic of behaving*
> *according to a "doubling time". Each fixed time interval shows*
> *a doubling of the relevant system variable. Exponential growth*
> *is treacherous and misleading. A system variable can continue*
> *through many doubling intervals without seeming to reach*
> *significant size. But then in one or two more doubling periods, still*
> *following the same law of exponential growth, it suddenly seems to*
> *become overwhelming.*

This growth challenge can be illustrated by a biological experiment of bacteria growth. In a container with liquid supporting growth for a certain bacterium, previous experiments have shown that it takes fifty days to fill the surface of liquid when the colony of bacteria is doubling every day. It is a scary experience to realize that the surface is 50% covered with bacteria the forty-ninth day and hardly visible the forty-third day with only 0.7% of the surface covered.

An equally excellent illustration of the same dynamic expansion pattern is demonstrated very clearly when compressing the time from when life was introduced on our planet Earth to 1 year. Due to the absence of an ozone layer, life had to start subsurface water and it remained subsurface for more than half of the year life has existed. When our human predecessors entered the scene was a few minutes ahead of midnight, and during the very last second of this year of development people have become five times as many and ten times as rich. We are in other words in the middle of a biological explosion according to the exponential growth mechanism.

Unfortunately, the ecological capacity of our home in space is not expanding correspondingly. Global ecological capacity was according to a number of prominent ecologists used up more than thirty years ago. In other words, our overdeveloped circuit, Europe, US and Japan, has to release ecological capacity for those who desperately need to make a small step towards acceptable living conditions. The issue of global ecological capacity is critical and fundamental. If the global ecological capacity is used up or close to being used up, the challenge of global distribution is overwhelmingly important and the consuming world we belong to will be facing some very tough choices. There are unfortunately strong reasons to believe that our ever-expanding list of perceived needs is a dead-end route our Western world chose a long time ago.

The date of Earth Overshoot Day confirms this. The overshoot day is calculated by comparing humanity's total yearly consumption (Ecological Footprint) with Earth's capacity to regenerate renewable natural resources in that year (biocapacity).

Global Ecological Footprint and biocapacity metrics, in turn, are calculated each year with National Footprint Accounts. Using UN statistics, these accounts incorporate the latest data and the most updated accounting methodology (the National Footprint Accounts 2018 Edition feature 2014 data.) To estimate this year's Earth Overshoot Day, Ecological Footprint and biocapacity are "nowcasted" to the current year using the latest data from additional sources, such as the Global Carbon Project and others (Earth Overshoot Day, 2018).

In 2018 the Overshoot Day is estimated to be 1 August. When these calculations started in 1970 the Overshoot Day was estimated to 29 December. Twenty-five years later – in 1995 – the day was 5 October.

As interesting is to have a look a country's Overshoot Day which is the date on which Earth Overshoot Day would fall if all of humanity consumed like the people in this country. If all countries lived the way we do in Norway, the Earth Overshoot Day would be 12 April in 2018. If we all lived like people in the USA the day would be 15 March and Canada March 18. (Earth Overshoot Day, 2018)

Many economists, probably the majority of them, believe quite amazingly, that the world economy must continue to grow, and that a simple, low consumption life is a threat to our economic model. The founding father of modern capitalism, John Stuart Mill, cannot be counted as a supporter of that view (Mill, 1857). He realized that industrial society, by its very nature, could not last for long and that the stable society that must replace it would be a better place. It is scarcely necessary to remark, according to Mill, that the stationary condition of capital and population implies no stationary state of human improvement.

Ecologist Kenneth Boulding (1971) went even one more step further by suggesting that GNP be considered a measure of gross national cost, and that we devote ourselves to its minimization.

The need for a fundamental rethinking of modern economics was perhaps most eloquently recommended by Paul Hawken, Amory Lovins and Hunter Lovins in their book, *The Next Industrial Revolution* (Hawken et al., 1999) On this book, the *Financial Times* wrote in 2005: "An analysis of how capitalism would work if the world's 'natural capital' were properly valued, resulting in a drastic reduction in resource use by industrialized countries."

Finally, a special issue of *New Scientist* (2008) claimed on its cover page: "The folly of growth! How to stop the economy from killing the planet." In this magazine several important messages are presented. Herman Daly, one of the leading ecological economists in the world, admits that economists are still failing to grasp the simple message that earth's resources are finite, and until they do, we will never switch to a sustainable economy and avoid the ultimate crash.

Major conceptual changes in the way we think, are almost impossible to forecast, and it will require an open receiving system in the brain willing to accommodate the unexpected new paradigms. The two most well-known discontinuities in the history of mankind were received with skepticism and anger. The first was the revolutionary idea by people vastly ahead of their time, claiming that our home in space not was flat but rather a sphere. This was not a popular intervention in the general perception of their home in space, but rather a dramatic discontinuity in the prevailing way of thinking at the time.

The second shock came several hundred years later when our place in space was dramatically diminished. Rather than being in the center of the universe some brilliant and courageous astronomers claimed, and even proved, that our planetary system including the sun was positioned in the outskirts of a huge galaxy. It was time to feel lonesome. Not surprisingly, this new worldview was not at all received with enthusiasm, and the carriers of the new worldview became the opposite of heroes.

These days we are approaching shock number three: Our planet is small and our incredibly important life-supporting atmosphere is relatively as thin as the layer of varnish on a desk globe. Needless to say, this new worldview will not be welcomed with enthusiasm. The new worldview is also the transition from the "cowboy economy" to the "spaceman economy", another historic transition. The international space program contributed to the understanding of this reality, although not yet fully appreciated by everybody. When astronauts on historic space-walks circled gently their planet in approximately ninety minutes, it became evident that all of us in reality are astronauts on our spaceship Earth.

The question of never-ending growth in a closed system is pursuing us all the time. Nobody is suggesting or hoping that the human body should continue to grow over an entire lifetime. The growth period is approximately one quarter of a normal lifetime and everybody would agree that the end of the growth period not is the end of life, rather than opposite! It is the beginning of life. Continuous growth is the philosophy of the cancer cell.

But the challenge in a global growth culture is to get started on a new course. Obviously, nobody could expect the Chinese or the Indians to take the initiative to start non-growth thinking. At the moment it looks rather low probability that the US will start – or Russia. Could we find a very rich, well-educated corner of the world where the crucial turnaround process could start? What about Scandinavia? They could be challenged! When the former Norwegian prime minister Gro Harlem Brundtland, herself a brilliant politician with an outstanding ability to manage huge problems, delivered the conclusions from the World Commission on Environment and Development (WCED) in 1987, she concluded her presentation by saying that the planet's environment is seriously threatened, a fact nobody with a functioning brain could turn their back to.

Amazingly, the members of the WCED commission with representatives of all major nations of the world unanimously voted for the conclusions. That was a political masterpiece and a historical event. After 1987 we have come to realize that more than the environment was at stake, it was the health of the planet that was up for discussion. But a growing economy was never challenged. The incredible expansion of purchasing capacity in the western world is now spreading and a consuming culture is growing in dominance.

A person who has been trying to communicate the challenge and threat of exponential growth is Trygve Haavelmo, a Norwegian professor in economics who received the Nobel Memorial Prize in Economic Sciences in 1989. At the press conference after the award ceremony he was asked what he would tell the world's political leaders if he got fifteen minutes with them at one of their summits. Without hesitation he responded that he would have used the time to explain what exponential growth was and then asked for another thirty minutes to dig deeper into the challenge.

As the economy has been expanding, a number of unexpected problems have risen to the surface. One problem that surprisingly appeared to be unexpected for many people was the unexpected consequences of using cultivated land for biofuels for cars. With the best intentions to reduce oil use, the strategy resulted in significant price increases on grain because biofuel production "stole" agriculture land and reduced the available land for food production. Obviously – as usual – it is the poorest part of the population who will suffer most and go hungry to bed.

The strategy of reduced consumption obviously has an easily predictable consequence, unemployment. This is a problem that must be addressed since the social consequences are unmanageable. The win–win strategy is to reduce number of working days in a workweek, possibly as far down as one day per week. But even one-day-workweek is employment, and the priority jobs need to be decided on. Most probably, the farmer, the fisher and the teacher will be on the top of that list.

This new world, the post-industrial society, cannot be expected to be welcomed right away. The advantages are rather obvious, but the resistance to dramatic changes like those described is not difficult to foresee. In many ways the situation we would be facing has similarities to the famous and critical moment of the Second World War when Winston Churchill, even without television, told his country-men and women, that he could not promise anything but blood, sweat and tears. We will face a situation requiring real leadership, since we are the first generations being confronted with the "unpaid bills".

The two questions we have to answer are the following:

1. Will the planet have capacity to handle it if the entire global population were living like ourselves?
2. And can we solve the problems through efficiency improvements?

The answer on both questions is no even if efficiency improvements are a good start.

Our situation is quite similar to the *Titanic* event. All passengers were told that the ship could not sink, and so convincing was that assurance, that when in fact it started to sink, most passengers refused to accept what was actually happening.

Normally we are not expected to have positive comments on "ugly" graffiti, but the text on the white wall is really thought provoking. The first one:

GOOD PLANETS ARE HARD TO FIND,

and the second:

THE FUTURE IS CANCELLED
DUE TO THE LACK OF INTEREST.

The conclusion can be summarized in what could be called The Doctrine of Changed Circumstances

1. The objective of sustainability will require a fundamental reordering of global priorities
2. The Western world will have to develop a new culture including
    - a new intellectual culture
    - a new consumption culture
    - a new technology culture
    which will require ecological intelligence

3. Resource consumption in the industrial countries must be reduced to 10% of current levels over the next few decades to release resources for the developing world and signal to the rest of the world that we acknowledge our responsibility

4. How do we imagine our future when our commercial systems conflict with everything nature teaches us?

5. Spaceship EARTH is a closed system. The sustainability challenge is to recognize this obvious fact!

Reference:

- Boulding, K. E. (1971) Environmental Economics. *ENIVIRONMENT.* Sinauer Associates, Stanford, Conn.
- *Ecologist.* Vol.2, no 1, Jan 1972
- Forrester, J. (1970) *World Dynamics*, Cambridge, Mass: Wright – Allen Press.
- Hawken, P., Lovins, A. B. and Lovins, L. H. (1999) *Natural Capitalism The Next Industrial Revolution.* Boston. Little Brown & co.
- Mill, J. S. (1857) *Principles of Political Economy.* Vol. 11. London. J. W. Parker.
- *New Scientist* (2008) The folly of growth. How to stop the economy from killing the planet.
- Earth Overshoot Day (2018) Retrieved from: https://www.overshootday.org/newsroom/past-earth-overshoot-days/

Technology, encounter, and the dangers of abstraction[105]

ARNE JOHAN VETLESEN

Spending a day in the woods recently, two experiences stood out.

First, I saw an eagle. And that's all I can do, really: follow it with my eyes as it rides the sky, higher and higher, beyond my reach. Everything to do with my seeing the eagle and the significance it holds points beyond the utility calculus. I cannot lay hold of the eagle, cannot determine or predict its movements, cannot possess or control it. Riding the sky, the eagle is free. The best I can hope for is precisely this: seeing it. Whether I do or not, is not for me to decide. Getting to see it will be a pure gift. My day will be richer for it. I will feel grateful – not to the particular bird I happen to see, perhaps, but to the world of which I am part for containing such a creature.

Descartes' argument about animals being inferior to humans for lack of the ability to "join together different words" (1978a (1637): 45) appears ridiculous here. What an arbitrary criterion to use! How self-serving and question-begging is it not to take as the only valid yardstick a capacity – the linguistic one – found to be lacking in all nonhuman creatures! If anything, the eagle's brilliance at riding the sky puts my boundedness to the ground into sharp relief. Once the criterion is shifted – here, from linguistic capacities to the capacity for self-initiated motility – the roles of are reversed, the bird unequivocally being the superior one. Shift the perspective not only from one criterion to another, but from the human subject to the animal's, and what is widely regarded as a potent – and immensely influential – philosophical argument for human superiority emerges instead as a matter of envy – flying envy. Indeed, Freud, in concentrating on penis envy only, overlooked the entire *cross-* and *inter-species* dimension of this powerful feeling.

The second experience is of a different sort. I came across a vacant vehicle of the kind used for logging these days. Since there was no one around, I climbed on board and took the seat. Guess what commanded my attention?

---

105 Fragment from *The Denial of Nature*, Routledge, London 2015

The computer placed above the steering wheel did. Looking at the screen and pressing the appropriate keys (that is, doing exactly what I do right now, sitting in my home office), I would be able to direct the enormous grab toward the tree selected for felling, cut the tree, remove the branches, and place it onto the pile of timber on the plane. Of course, I didn't actually carry out any of these operations. But I have witnessed how it is done. It is a showcase of efficient, modern technology. What a generation ago would have taken hours to accomplish, is now effected in a matter of minutes. The selected tree may have taken more than hundred years to grow, it may be thirty or forty meters tall and weigh hundreds of kilos, thus requiring considerable physical effort and experience-based skill to be taken down by saw or by axe.

Felling trees when sitting inside a modern forestry vehicle makes for *abstraction*. My field of attention shrinks to keeping a keen eye on the computer in front of me, combined with the occasional look outside to check that the tree is indeed cut, the branches removed, and so forth; in a word, to check that the instructions I feed into the computer effect the prescribed machine operations and bring about the intended consequences in the outside world. The task at hand has lost – or overcome – the physical effort its distinct elements once called for: selecting the tree, deciding where and in what position to enter the appropriate saw, considering the optimal position for it to fall without mingling with other trees nearby, then doing the actual sawing, changing position, touching the tree to check how much more sawing is needed, looking around once more to make sure the tree is going to fall in the desired direction, completing the felling. Accomplishing this in the low-technology manner meant for the carpenter to engage in direct contact, indeed interaction, with the particular tree at hand, a contact of bodily-sensuous nature. Each tree would be different: different position in the landscape and vis-à-vis other trees and other kinds of trees, different height, different shape. Each would call for judgment concerning where, when and how. The felling of one tree would turn out to be faster and less laborious than expected; the felling of another the opposite. The physical effort required to complete the job, the time it would take, combined with the lack of complete predictability and calculability of each operation, would make each tree a *particular* challenge and a particular experience. No two trees are exactly alike. Nor are two carpenters. The trees only become alike, or eminently comparable, after the act of felling them, forming a pile of logs to be transported out of the woods, be it by horse and sledge or by tractor.

I propose that the principal shift involved in this example is from one sort of relationship and to an entirely different one. The parties to the relationship change: from one between the individual carpenter and the particular tree he is engaging with, saw and axe acting as direct physical extensions of his bodily movements, to one between the worker seated inside the vehicle and his computer screen. Whereas all the feedback in the former case would emanate from the tree, the locus of feedback to which the modern forestry worker's attention is directed, is the computer. The man–tree relationship has been substituted by a man–computer relationship.

It is important to see what is at issue here. The change that interests me is not primarily a matter of man's relating to the tree being mediated by a machine (computer) that literally is an in-between between subject and object. Rather, and more profoundly, it is a matter of the subject–outer reality relationship – a two-way affair, as we saw – being *replaced* by a man-machine (technology) one. The worker operates the computer which operates the machine that works on the tree. The machine – the computer directing the saw-machinery – works physically on the tree, the worker does not: he does not touch it, does not smell it, scarcely hears it falling, although he still needs to see it, at the distance provided by staying inside the vehicle while the whole process is being executed. The machine, in a comprehensive and multifunctional sense, stands between the man and the tree, the subject and his object, making a direct (physical-bodily-sensuous) interaction between them perfectly redundant. The tree felled is not a particular tree with a particular set of properties (location, age, shape, look) with which the worker interacts and to whose particularities he directs as well as adjusts his actions, as the carpenter did. Instead the tree has been transformed into an abstract entity, exchangeable not unique, operated upon via a technical device rather than being sensuously and physically experienced.

What counts as reality in present-day society is to an ever-growing extent made up of artifacts whose existence would be impossible without the workings of modern technology. Whereas wild nature is heterogeneous, involving the human person as a whole person, engaging not only the mind but the entire repertoire of faculties, virtually everything a human person, including children, now "sees, hears, smells, touches, and tastes is a human artifact," as John Livingston (1994: 135) observed twenty years ago. To be sure, one may consider this as aspect of humanity having entered the Anthropocene. But it points to a different dimension than that usually addressed in most environmental philosophy and politics alike, being concerned with the fact that today no part of the biosphere is beyond the range of anthropogenic influence. By contrast, my interest here is not so much in the ways in which changes in nature are increasingly *caused* by human activities, but in the ways in which virtually everything that physically makes up our world is of our making. In engaging with the outside world, modern man increasingly encounters only himself, either directly in the form of the products of his own technologically mediated activities, or indirectly in the form of the ways in which the nonhuman environment – what's left of it – is modified by those activities and their often unintended repercussions.

This then is the question I shall pursue in what follows: What happens when the "total environment" (Searles, Harold) changes from being predominantly a natural environment to becoming a predominantly human-made one?

Recall my fortune in seeing an eagle. Yes, fortune. I hold that eagle to have intrinsic value regardless of my, or any other human's, actually seeing it. My seeing or not seeing that eagle is a wholly contingent affair. That's one reason why I call seeing it a pure gift. To require, philosophically, the value of that creature to depend on my, or any other human's, experiencing it would be not only a case of folly: it would fail to qualify as valid argument. Berkeley's dictum that *esse est percipi* (being equals perception) cannot settle the issue of value in nature. Even in the case of the "last man" dying, the eagle surviving humanity's existence on earth would possess precisely the same value as when co-existing with humankind. In other words, the existence – contingent at that – of one species cannot be mandatory for the value of others. Value concerns *what resides in some specific entity – creature – in the world*, not in something to do with properties, be it most basically: the sheer existence, of some *other* entity (i.e., a human subject) that happens to relate to the entity in question and, moreover, without the existence of which that entity is fully able to be what it – species-distinctly – is.

I readily admit that this argument most probably will fail to make the philosophical opponents of value realism change their mind: the arguments pro and con have been rehearsed and refined for decades, yet consistently fail to convince the other side.

My claim, though, is that we don't have to leave it at that. Characteristically, the factor of technology is left outside of the purely philosophical debate over the value of – in – nature, thereby missing out on the truly dynamic dimension of the issue, namely the fact that its (theoretically construed) subject-matter is undergoing fundamental change.

For one thing, and to repeat what should by now be obvious, technology is presently instrumental in damaging and wiping out entire regions of what used to be wilderness – rainforests, pristine boreal forests – in addition to helping depleting various animal and fish stocks all around the world. As if this weren't enough, there is the growing momentum of what may soon prove to be runaway anthropogenic climate change, involving positive feedback loops such as the albedo effect, the melting of the tundra, releasing massive amounts of methane. There is no need to further list these developments here. The point is made: nature is not what it until relatively recently – throughout the Holocene and till the Anthropocene – used to be. As a result, the distinctive properties and qualities of the entity at the heart of the value discussion are a risk.

This leads to the second point about the relevance of technology for what has been discussed for so long as a philosophical issue *par excellence*, namely the value of things natural and other-than-human. In my view, this is where the insights of Heidegger, Anders and Catton converge: technology in the era of overshoot and enframing (leveling) is not only physically destructive of the nonhuman entities in the world; it is destructive of our chances to, and arenas for, coming to encounter them, sensuously experiencing them, as well. The two types of destruction are equally critical when it comes to the issue of value: they combine to alter the facts on the ground, in the air and in the oceans and seas. The reality domain within which the value originates phenomenally and where it experientially obtains – the "clearing" in which the nonhuman entities in question appear, to paraphrase Heidegger – is being ruined while we're busy discussing it, in seminar rooms and journals at far remove from the discussed entities' physical existence. The way I see it, one of the reasons for this happening, for it being permitted to go on happening, is that we – or too many of us, for too long a time – have answered the question in a wrong way: as a culture we have been so reluctant to grant these nonhuman entities value in their own right and protection from man-made destruction, that – on grounds of our *acting upon* that disvaluing, it *being a practice* and not merely a theory – they perish. Leaving aside the intellectual frustration generated by prolonged inconclusiveness in the value issue, its deadlock has been anything but inconsequential on a practical plane.

Given this situation, revitalizing focal practices and centering on focal events become an urgent task. It would allow for all types of nonhuman beings and life-forms to (re)appear in their separate existence, as having species-specific ends in their own right (Taylor 2011). Engaging in such revitalization will clearly be to our gain, however much we have come to fear it as a threat against progress, or to dismiss the whole idea as nostalgia or worse. But who can seriously dispute the Aristotelian insight that the more complex the faculties and skills to whose cultivation we are devoted, the more excellent our life? To engage fully instead of abstractly, bodily-sensuously instead of only cognitively with nonhuman life would mean to relate to it in a manner conducive to that complexity: the leveling visited on the outside world by way of standardization (Ritzer 2000, 2004) backfires and proves impoverishing to our human subjectivity. In other words, starting (or should we rather say resuming?) to see, hear, touch, smell and – last but not least – feel what we do because attentive and receptive to that (those) to whom we do it, would enhance our chances to halt senseless destruction of nonhuman life while there is still time.

If we are to take the lessons told about the impact of technology on the society-nature relationship seriously, the argument as developed so far comes up against a serious limit. The limit in question is not philosophical in nature: not logical, not conceptual. Of what kind is it then?

To be clear about what I have in mind, in what follows I shall speak in less general terms than above. Instead of "nonhuman beings or life-forms" I shall speak of animals, introducing a particular example.

Philosophers typically ask: "Is it morally right or morally wrong to inflict pain upon an animal – or to kill it?" "Do I as a human agent and a moral subject have a duty to protect animals from pain and death?" "If I have such a duty, how can it be justified? On grounds solely relating to me as a moral subject, or on grounds relating to the animal as a moral addressee?"

As is well known, anthropocentric ethical theories – especially in the Kantian tradition – hold that, for reasons to do with our status as moral agents, we have duties in relation to animals, but we do not have duties *toward* them, since animals are lacking in proper moral status. Such theories proceed on the assumption that moral responsibilities – hence rights, duties, and obligations – arise only within the circle of subjects capable of speech and action.

Advocates of virtue ethics or of utilitarianism (or consequentialism) or of contractualism would pose the question just the way Habermas (1993) does: "Is it morally right or morally wrong to inflict pain upon an animal – or to kill it?" "Would the act of killing it violate some moral duty or obligation on my part?"

To be sure, that is indeed how the question may be formulated in theory, to be followed by the answers to it known to be forthcoming from the various ethical theories. The problem, however – and I regard it as a huge one – is that this standard way of discussing the issue is at a loss to reflect on and to do justice to the standard way in which animals are generally treated these days, including how they are killed.

Let me make my argument by considering the case of the Eurasian eagle owl, being representative for my purposes here. When this owl (the biggest in northern Europe) was recently put on the list of endangered species in Norway, this was not a result of too many killings of eagle owls having been carried out, or more generally of too many people endorsing the attitude that it's morally all right to kill them. The precarious situation in which the eagle owl is placed today has quite simply nothing to do with either attitudes to this particular species, or instances of killings (for whatever motives) of individual exemplars. It has, that is, nothing to do with what may come to pass in a one-to-one relationship or encounter between a human individual and an individual eagle owl. This whole model, premised on the two parties – human and animal – taking part in a relationship, be it theorized as symmetric or not, reciprocal or not, does not apply to the empirical fact that the number of eagle owls in Norway is decreasing at a pace considered as critical.

So what is happening? Why – and how – is it that this owl species is now at risk?

The short answer is that if the eagle owl in the course of, say, the next two or three decades disappears from Norwegian fauna, it will be as the end result of a many-faceted process of *silent killing*: of what the Ministry of Environment technically calls "altered area use"; of industrial clear-cut logging using the superefficient vehicles I discussed at the start of this chapter; of area-intensive modern industrial agriculture; of the building of allegedly eco-friendly windmills along the Norwegian West coast; of the ever-growing expansion of human activities in general and establishment of new housing areas and expanded infrastructures in particular; of the concomitant loss of other species (prey) longer down the food chain; of climate change. All of these factors, individually and in concert, contribute causally to the fact that the eagle owl is now at risk. In other words, we are talking about a species that, like so many others these days, is at risk because the habitat it depends upon to reproduce and thrive as a species is becoming fragmented, is shrinking or is simply disappearing. All this is happening to the Norwegian population of eagle owls in near-complete absence of Norwegian individuals going about killing eagle owls, or for that matter, having the attitude that it would be morally all right to kill them even if one could not or would not personally do so. The point, then, is that the extinction of the eagle owl may come about without this being the intention of, or expressing the moral recommendation of, any individual human agent.

Since no intentional infliction of pain or suffering, and likewise no intentional killing, takes place here in the one-to-one context within which Habermas (representatively at that) conducts his entire discussion of the humans–animals relationship and the sort of morality that goes (or does not go) with it, the fact that today animals such as the eagle owl in certain regions are brought to the brink of extinction *without the one-to-one context obtaining at all* shows that Habermas and all those who subscribe to his perfectly conventional methodology in the matter run the risk of discussing it in a way that totally misses its actual *modus operandi*. In other words, the fate of a species such as the eagle owl in contemporary society is factually decided by entirely other factors than those involved in individual-to-individual encounters between human and animal, however philosophically intriguing and pedagogically instructive.

It is striking that Habermas (just like Kant, with his penchant for horse and dog examples) prefers to concentrate on the issue of the individual moral agent's responsibility for individual animals. In starting and concluding his argument within that setting Habermas misses out on the pivotal issue at the core of holistic theories, that of the ecological dynamics of biotopes, indeed of the whole biosphere. As holism acknowledges: when the whole (the system) is under threat, each individual (species or exemplar) is. Therefore, the moral questions – of status, of agency, of responsibility and rights – must address the habitat that every single exemplar is dependent upon. There is something atomistic and reductivist, and in that sense Hobbesian, in the way Habermas removes (abstracts) animals from their generic form of existence in a complex interplay with a large number of other species in nature, removes them, that is, from the whole of which there are part and outside which they cannot live, only to let them – one by one – become a concern of moral import the moment they come into contact with specifically *human* forms of life, as fully – or not so fully – partners in *our* networks of interaction. As Steven Vogel notes (approaching the issue in a different perspective than mine and taking it in a different direction), Habermas evades the difficulty posed for discourse ethics by anti-anthropocentric (I would rather say non-anthropocentric) environmental philosophy, namely the "problem of our ethical relation to entities in the *nonhuman* world, not to entities that have been redescribed as quasi-humans" (Vogel 1996: 159). In attempting, that is, to bring at least some of the natural world into the realm of the moral – namely by way of focusing on individual animals – Habermas starts talking about the "incomplete" and "quasi-moral" relationships with humans that the animal (in the singular) would qualify for, thereby solving the problem of a morality for nonhuman nature by defining it away.

From the perspective I am proposing here, the eagle owl is a particularly apt case in that it confronts us squarely with what Habermas bypasses: the responsibility of present-day society (as distinct from human agents considered *in abstracto*) for beings in the nonhuman world, including those among them who (as opposed to the domestic animals Habermas prefers to talk about) do *not* engage in interaction with us and so do not "quasi" participate in our human lifeworld. For there is no denying that a species with which we do not interact the way we do with dogs or horses puts the issues pertaining to environmental philosophy into much sharper focus than do domestic animals. Contrary to Habermas' approach, it is precisely the element of otherness exhibited in the eagle owl that commands our attention: the eagle owl's *absence* as partner in our interactions, and hence its non-assimilation to our current lifeform, increasingly urbanized and remote – mentally as well as geographically – from what remains of its natural habitat.

I indicated above that the case of the eagle owl's becoming extinct in parts of Norway will be a non-event and a non-experience for the large majority of Norwegians. Even in the case of the disappearance of eagle owls that used to live relatively close to people, there will be something abstract to their disappearance, abstract as far as the causes and the overall dynamics constituting and sustaining those causes are concerned. The eagle owl may disappear from my proximity-based *Merkwelt*; but the reasons for its doing so will refer me to the impacts from a *Wirkwelt* scarcely tangible. Why? Because the situation in which eagle owls disappear – currently disappear in a country like Norway – is one pervaded by the effects of ours being a globalized world relying on advanced technologies that have the capacity to split every piece of intention or action *here*, related to *that* agent, from the performed action's total consequences and repercussions *there*, far away from the spatiotemporal context in which they originate; far off not only in a geographical but also in a temporal sense. To say this is to recapitulate insights derived from Hans Jonas and Günther Anders to the effect that an ethics (in Habermas' terminology, morality) of proximity, focusing on individual-to-individual sequences of action and effect, of agent and addressee, is wholly inadequate to do justice to the mechanisms through which the issue we are discussing – the disappearance of a species such as the eagle owl, and numerous others – de facto comes to pass in our type of society.

Since the fate of the eagle owl is not, and will not, be decided by acts of killing – or of refraining from killing – as carried out by certain individuals, but will instead be sealed as a consequence of accumulated causes, not all of which are traceable to particular agents somewhere at some point pursuing this or that intention, the conclusion is inevitable that nothing less than our way of life, with all the technologies and the systemic mechanisms that go into sustaining it, is to be held accountable.

To be sure, ending on this note may seem overwhelming. It lands us in something extremely vague as far as everything to do with morality is concerned. Since this is deeply unsatisfying, not only in philosophical and intellectual terms, but in practical and political ones as well, one cannot help longing for the good old days and the good old moral philosophy, centering on easily identifiable agents in easily identifiable locations and situations, to be morally assessed for this or that action, easily identifiable as far as both intentions, motives, and consequences are concerned, these all being likewise localizable within a restricted spatiotemporal setting: that of the original action.

The deeper issue here is whether the assumption that *how we perceive something determines how we treat it, and thereby what happens to it* applies to the kind of environmental destruction that the fate of the eagle owl exemplifies. However tacit, this assumption is operative in everything from humanist approaches in environmental ethics to governmental and NGO campaigns to raise citizens' awareness about the importance of recycling and public transport. "Knowing is doing", "beliefs shape action", "attitudes determine behavior" – these are versions of the so-called belief-desire model holding that people's actions are determined by what they want to achieve and what they know, i.e., by values and facts. This model encourages the seemingly perfectly sensible notion that the more well-informed people are, the more they will be concerned with the ways in which their behavior impacts on the environment, thus providing a sense of ownership to the problems they are knowledgeable about and so a motivation to do something about them.

If this approach has failed to achieve the desired results, it is not for lack of faith. Al Gore got it wrong when he said, on accepting the Nobel Peace Prize in 2007, "Global warming is not a political problem, it's a moral one". Individualizing and moralizing the issue, wedding it to the cult of personal responsibility that has become part and parcel of neoliberalism, will not get us anywhere near solving the problem, sustained as it is on a systemic and structural level left untouched by appeals to the free will and moral resolve of isolated individuals (see Fisher 2009; Rogers 2012). To be sure, it is tempting to say that a problem such as air pollution is a consequence of the total number of acts committed by individual agents – such that in exhorting each of them to act more responsibly, the problem would be solved. But the decision whether to go to work by public transport or by car is ill-conceived as a purely individual choice. Rather, it is to a large extent a political one, determined by factors such as price, the organization of work, infrastructure facilities, distance and time. And as far as causal contribution is concerned, the part played by industry and commercial enterprises will far outweigh that of individual consumers. On the other hand, polls show that when politicians express confidence that new technologies will be developed to fix the problem, most citizens are passive, some feeling downright discouraged from being both part of the problem and – possibly – part of the solution: "technology" will sort out the mess. In a capitalist society thriving on consumerism, politicians much rather direct attention to technology development – greening the economy – than to the political roots of the problem: excessive consumption as driven by the twin imperatives of profit and growth. The core of the problem is tabooed, and the result is apathy in the population at large.

To return to my eagle owl example, it is one thing to get the facts of the situation right and so being able to frame the issue in what would seem an adequate manner – the issue, that is, of the human-animal relationship, with special regard to the question of responsibility, bearing in turn on the moral status of the animals in question. It is quite another to come up with proposals about how to proceed, given that the conventional individualist approach – concentrating on one-to-one relationships and interactions – today appears wholly inadequate to the task.

But if that is so, why have I devoted attention to the Crow people's hunting rituals, highlighting their respect for their animal prey? Well, a given culture's cosmology-based understanding of and stance toward animals *do* make a difference, practically as well as philosophically and morally. Native Americans denying animals the status accorded them by the Crow would probably, other things (including the technology at hand for hunting) being equal, kill more of them, perhaps driving to extinction species allowed to reproduce and thrive by the Crow. So clearly the culturally fostered attitudes in question, as adopted and acted upon by individuals, do make a difference when what we are up to is comparing two cultures whose levels and forms of technology are relatively similar. If they are not, comparison risks becoming merely an academic exercise – as would a direct comparison between Norwegians and Crow today. Among numerous other factors, the differences in technology in this case are so enormous as to make the fate of some specific species – say, an owl – in the respective societies a matter (a result) of completely different causal mechanisms – say, exaggerated hunting in the one case (*if* technologically possible), expanding infrastructure and real estate development, the methods of industrial logging and agribusiness, and climate change in the other. Whereas the former case is one of identifiable acts of hunting/killing within a one-to-one context restricted to a particular region, part of the year, and so on, the second is conspicuously lacking in such concrete, individuals- and act-related properties: working the causal mechanisms involved is who, exactly, where exactly, for what purposes exactly, and with what ideas about the end-effects?

True, there are and will continue to be will cases like Exxon Valdez or the Gulf oil spill; spectacular cases, followed by a media-led hunt to hold the responsible individuals (CEOs) and companies accountable, bringing the case to court, paying the directly affected parties economic compensation, and so on. But the disappearance of the eagle owl from Norway is not that sort of case: a matter of silent killing, and as such involving nothing hands-on, nothing one-to-one, its *modus operandi* also differs from that of accidents, be they technical in nature or caused by human mistake or incompetence. If this owl species becomes extinct, it will be as a result of business as usual, making the attempt to morally shame or legally bring to court specific individuals or "players" a futile one.

I grant that this conclusion appears overwhelmingly negative. Is this negativity compelling? Have I overlooked something?

Like many others working academically or politically or (preferably) both with environmental matters, I think that the crude "either/or" alternatives are false. The "both-and" approach is certainly more potent: concerned individuals will make a difference, as will structural and systemic changes. We need to "see the structural in the everyday", to quote Anna L. Peterson (2009: 106), and vice versa. Having said that, the structural does retain primacy in that it frames the context within which the individual agent tries to make a difference – with the structures more than the single individual deciding what, if any, concrete difference his or her action will in fact make. But again, structures do not change by themselves; for that to happen, change-intending individuals are required, be they placed inside or outside the structures in question. Individuals – at first, a few, eventually, a great many – brought down structural-institutional racism in South Africa, to pick an obvious example. But how do you get large numbers of people to take to the streets in order to halt the structural forces at work in the silent killing of some endangered animal species? Have people ever taken to the streets to demand what would amount to less money in their pockets, fewer products in the shopping malls? Or to demand more costly flights? Or the banning of SUVs? As well-off Westerners we may wish the millions of poor people in today's world to succeed in adopting our way of life, our level of material prosperity. Who am I to refuse to others the goods – the car, for example – I without question see myself as entitled to? But once you translate that (morally flawless) scenario into the increased carbon footprint it would imply for those involved, the result would be global ecological collapse. Mobilizing – philosophically, morally, politically – for a radically changed society–nature relationship is certainly much more difficult, for many different kinds of reasons, than mobilizing for, say, a less racist society, the latter being a case of conventional politics not challenging the anthropocentric–humanist paradigm (in fact expanding and universalizing it), whereas the former represents something very different.

With regard to the eagle owl example, the closest I come to end on a more constructive note is this: individualist methodologies and policies being demonstrably inadequate, any solution worthy of the name would have to be as *holistic* in kind as is the problem we are dealing with. This is very much in line with the plea for interdisciplinarity found in recent work in critical realism (see Bhaskar et al. 2010). Concretely, and to stick to my example, for protection of a species such as eagle owls to be secured, all the various human activities (listed above) helping cause the diminishing, fragmentation or downright destruction of the (large, coherent, and biodiversity rich) habitat it depends on will have to be either significantly reduced or completely stopped, and this by way of rigorous international as well as national legislation as opposed to voluntary measures. Environmentalists, politicians and legal scholars need to collaborate with ecologists, biologists, and other scientists to identify, as far as possible, the various factors that now threaten the habitats required for this species not only to survive but to thrive. In short, *the approach to be pursued must be as holistic as the problem itself,* given its factual features as set out here: it must, that is, focus on species, not individuals (they can only thrive provided the species does); on entire habitats and the ecosystems involved in the region; on the structural and systemic forces operative in the destruction and degradation of the habitat in question, inseparable as these forces are from the growth and profit motives intrinsic to capitalism as the entire world has now come to know it.

Bibliography

- Anders, Günther, 1956. *Die Antiquiertheit des Menschen, I –II*. München: C.H. Beck.
- Bhaskar, Roy, Cheryl Frank, Karl G. Høyer, Jenneth Parker and Petter Næss, eds,. 2010. *Interdisciplinarity and Climate Change*. London: Routledge.
- Catton, William R., Jr., 1982. *Overshoot: The Ecological Basis of Revolutionary Change*. Urbana: University of Illinois Press.
- Descartes, Rene, 1978a (1637). *A Discourse on Method*. London: Dent
- Fisher, Mark, 2009. *Capitalist Realism*. Hants: Zero Books.
- Habermas, Jürgen, 1993. *Justification and Application*. Oxford: Polity Press.
- Heidegger, Martin, 1977. *The Question Concerning Technology and Other Essays*. New York: Harper.
- Jonas, Hans, 1984 (1979). *The Imperative of Responsibility: In Search of an Ethics for the Technological Age*. Chicago: University of Chicago Press.
- Livingston, John, 1994. *The Rogue Primate: An Exploration of Human Domestification*. Toronto: Key Porter Books.
- Peterson, Anna L., 2001. *Being Human: Ethics, Environment, and Our Place in the World*. Berkley, CA: University of California Press.

- Ritzer, George, 2000. *The McDonaldization of Society.* London: Sage.
- Ritzer, George, 2004. *The Globalization of Nothing.* London: Sage.
- Rogers, Heather, 2010. *Green Gone Wrong: Dispatches from the Front Lines of Eco-Capitalism.* London: Verso.
- Searles, Harold, 1972 (1960). *The Nonhuman Environment in Normal Development and in Schizophrenia.* New York: International Universities Press.
- Taylor, Paul, 2011 (1986). *Respect for Nature: A Theory of Environmental Ethics.* Princeton: Princeton University Press.
- Vogel, Steven, 1996. *Against Nature: The Concept of Nature in Critical Theory.* Albany: SUNY

Writing poetry

HANS BØRLI

Not at all: it's not *difficult* to write poetry –
it's impossible.
Otherwise, do you think I'd have kept at it
for over 40 years?

Try, just try
to put wings on a stone, try
to follow the track of a bird
in the air.

(from Hans Børli, *Last Poems,* 1991)

A Declaration of dependence

FINN WAGLE

Introduction

And know that we are related to the earth, the wind and the white cloud, sing Aslaug Låstad Lygre and Geirr Tveitt. And we are happy to sing along with them. In this way we affirm our relationship with the earth and our interdependence with all living beings.

This beginning is meant to be a manifesto:

The time is ripe for declarations of dependence, not declarations of independence!

We need to renew our awareness that life is about fundamental relationships we are woven into: to each other, to nature and everything living, to the universe and the Lord of the universe – and to ourselves. All life is included in a great tapestry and has a common destiny.

This awareness was for many centuries part of humanity's collective consciousness. But after modernity came on the scene five hundred years ago, science and technology have waged war on organic nature, and human beings have not protested, since more and more of our desires have been fulfilled. An awareness of the mutual dependence of nature and humanity has been under pressure. Pope Francis puts it like this in his well-known encyclical from 2015: "An outsider looking at our world would be amazed at such behavior, which at times appears self-destructive" (Pope Francis. *Laudato Si',* *On Care for our Common Home,* the Holy See 2015). At the same time, the pope emphasizes that the world is not just a problem to be solved, "The world is a joyful mystery to be contemplated with gladness and praise". What we need here are diverse, eloquent voices proclaiming this alternative view. And that is what the Stetind Declaration is intended to be: In the Declaration's own words: "We will… discover the joy of living in harmony with nature."

The desert tradition

Personally, I find it natural to look for sources and roots in the Christian faith. Take for example the desert tradition, the monastic life and the lives of the hermits in the deserts of Egypt and the Sinai Peninsula. Here is a trail back to the first centuries of Christianity. And the trail from the fourth and fifth centuries can still be followed. It leads northwards over the European continent to the Irish-Celtic church in the west and the Orthodox Church in the east. Each in their own way, these express the spirituality of the desert tradition.

The desert movement was a reaction to what many saws as the secularization of the church. Thousands of people sought a life in the wilderness in order to find out what being the church really involved. Not surprisingly, *escape* is a theme that frequently appears in the desert literature. But they were not escaping from responsibility or relationships. They escaped in order to explore genuine, personal fellowship. Preserving silence was one way of strengthening fellowship. It was an *expectant* silence, the silence before sunrise, the silence that we only reluctantly break for fear of destroying what is opening itself for us when the light comes. (For more on the desert tradition, see the book *Silence and Honey Cakes* (2003), by the former Anglican Archbishop of Canterbury, Rowan Williams.)

Exploring genuine personal fellowship in the wilderness meant living close to nature and the continually shifting elements. But in spite of nature's inconstancy, the desert dwellers experienced being in deep harmony with God's creation. This understanding of nature springs from a view of reality where the triune God is concrete and perceptibly present in his creation, through both creation and incarnation. And since humans relate to a living and dynamic universe that they listen to, speak to and seek to live in harmony with, this relationship with nature is not only an idea in people's minds, but something that affects their whole being and is expressed in their faith and worldview.

In this way, nature was a source of knowledge and wisdom for the desert people. In the wilderness, the proximity to nature and the constant shifting of the elements created an awareness of the wholeness of God's creation, and of human beings as a part of this wholeness. Nature could therefore be read like a book about the Creator's intention and will. The desert pioneer Anthony is said to have replied to a philosopher in the following way, when the philosopher expressed surprise over how he managed without books in his lonely existence: *My book is the nature of created things, and every time I want to read words from God, I have this book right before my eyes.*

Hymnic life

For the desert people nature bears witness to the Creator. Even more than that: Nature sings an unceasing song of praise to the glory of God. Thus, life in the wilderness became a "hymnic life", where people participated with their voices in the great and unceasing chorus of adoration that can be heard throughout the cosmos. In fact, there is a line stretching all the way from the Old and New Testaments through the history of the church up to our own time, in which man and nature are united in common worship. As an example of this I include some verses from the patron saint of ecology Francis of Assisi's, "Canticle of the Sun". This hymn was written in the thirteenth century but is still sung all over the world. The pope has borrowed some words from it as the title of his ecological encyclical: "'LAUDATO SI', mi' Signore' – 'Praise be to you, my Lord'".

> All creatures of our God and King,
> Lift up your voice and with us sing,
> Alleluia, alleluia!
> Thou burning sun with golden beam,
> Thou silver moon with softer gleam:
> O praise him, O praise him,
> Alleluia, Alleluia, Alleluia.
> Thou rushing wind that art so strong,
> Ye clouds that sail in heaven along,
> O praise him, Alleluia!
> Thou rising morn, in praise rejoice,
> Ye lights of evening find a voice.
> O praise him, O praise him,
> Alleluia, Alleluia, Alleluia.
> Dear mother earth, who day by day
> Unfoldest blessings on our way,
> O praise him, Alleluia!
> The flowers and fruits that in thee grow,
> Let them his glory also show.
> O praise him, O praise him,
> Alleluia, Alleluia, Alleluia.

If we are to rediscover the joy of living in harmony with nature, we must rediscover how to sing, if we have not already done so! This applies whatever our faith or worldview. A wise man from the Far East might express it thus: *All the pine trees raise their branches towards heaven and worship the Compassionate One who sees them.* The song of creation never ceases! When this idea grips us, we will not be able to resist adding our voice to the song, because the bubbling delight at how life has been given to us bursts into our consciousness and demands to express itself.

The cry from a wounded planet

But creation is not only full of praise. It also contains a lament. Today we experience how the cry from our wounded planet earth is growing stronger, because the relationship between humans and nature is no longer what it once was. Today humans are strong and nature is weak, an easy prey for human beings' urge to conquer, for their pursuit of material growth and of the technological mastery of the natural world. In a previously unimaginable way, nature has become critically vulnerable to human violation and thoughtlessness. These new conditions encourage an "intransigence" towards nature that would have been inconceivable until just before our own time.

In today's Western way of thinking, a way of thinking that has gone from strength to strength all over the globe, nature is regarded more and more as being created for human beings and whatever human beings need. Behind this one-sided faith in growth is an arrogant urge to conquer the natural world, in which nature is reduced to raw materials that the consumer society demands, powered by an unstoppable craving for items we often have no use for. Today this attitude is affecting creation like a cancerous tumor. Consequently, it also affects us and first and foremost the weakest and poorest among us. If we really cared about the world, we would treat it with quite a different level of respect and tenderness than is the case today.

In this connection, it is striking to read how the relationship between nature and humanity is described for example in the Irish-Celtic tradition, a church with a direct link back to the desert people. A hymn attributed to Columba, a prominent church leader in the late sixth century, says this: *Although I fear death and hell, I will not deny that I fear more the sound of an axe in Derry.* In order to understand this, we must remember that the tree has always had a central place in Jewish-Christian tradition. (Cf. for example, the Tree of Life and the Tree of Knowledge in Genesis 2-3.) Many of the early Celtic monasteries were established in ancient oak groves. And special trees could be important pilgrimage sites, both in pagan and Christian times.

Before he left Ireland and went to Scotland, Columba had received an oak forest as a gift from the king so that he could found a monastery there. But to clear the site for the monastery was anything but easy for Columba. It is as though he perceives the lament of nature while the trees are felled. Therefore, what he feared most was *the sound of an axe in Derry*.

In the grip of growth

So far, I have tried to highlight what can be called ecological elements in the Christian tradition. But the picture must be elaborated, because the Christian tradition is ambiguous when it comes to the relationship between human beings and nature. It doesn't only contain ecological elements. There is also contempt for nature and depreciation of creation. Nature was often totally neglected in theology, not infrequently because nature was only thought to be connected with the transience of life.

But the ambiguity in the Christian tradition runs even more deeply. We discover this if we look at the significance of the biblical belief in creation for the emergence of modern science. One of the previous century's major philosophers, Karl Jaspers, says: *Belief in creation gives the world a dignity that no philosophy can give it. The world is neither devilish and therefore to be feared, nor divine and therefore to be worshiped in awe from a distance.* The biblical belief in creation allows us to observe the world with curiosity and confidence. What God has created is also worth learning about. And so Jaspers concludes with the following observation: *Perhaps the rise of modern science is unthinkable without the spiritual attitude and the impulses that have their basis in biblical religion.*

Here we have a key to understanding western culture in its ambiguity. The former Swedish Bishop Martin Lönnebo summed up this ambiguity in a lecture at the Synod of the Church of Norway in 2007: *Western culture is the first worldwide culture. It is the strongest and most commendable, but at the same time the most dangerous and the one that bears most blame.*

The characteristics of the Western way of thinking are technological dominance of nature and belief in increasing material wealth. Behind this thinking about growth are two basic assumptions.

1. In the first place: an economic system based on economic growth. Therefore, major crises occur when this growth ceases. We need economic growth, if only for the sake of the system itself. The comic strip *Wulffmorgenthaler* hits the nail on the head when it claims that

the greatest threat to the whole of Western civilization is to say: *I am completely satisfied with my life and have all I need. I'm not gonna buy one more thing ever.* It is a precise and concentrated rebellion against a culture that has dissatisfaction as its inner drive and requires an eternal craving for goods that we really do not need.

2. In the second place: The Western mindset itself, with its expansionist ideology and penchant for conquering others. Even today's scientific way of regarding the world represents one aspect of this conquest ideology. Science only views the world as something that humans can use for their own purposes. It measures the measurable and makes the non-measurable measurable. In this way we can gain control over nature by knowing its laws.

In the Stetind Declaration we point out that this mindset has disastrous consequences for nature and human beings and thereby for all life on earth. Our manic quest for growth and conquest is in the first place ecologically irresponsible, indeed catastrophic. *When the earth and its life are transformed into commodities, it rises up against humankind in the greatest slave rebellion in history,* says Martin Lönnebo. Moreover, growth thinking is inhuman, both in terms of today's flagrant gap between rich and poor, and when we think of the generations who will come after us.

But it is also false and unhealthy for ourselves. Being developed is not the same as growing and growing and growing… Our expansion in relation to other cultures and nature is not an expression of maturity but shows that we are prisoners of growth. In the midst of our aggressive obsession with growth we are deeply deficient and underdeveloped, restricted by a special form of spiritual poverty and stupidity. And this is affecting all other life forms. Our globe is filled with life forms with their own splendor and dignity. We are being aggressive and primitive when we, with eyes wide open, eradicate animal and plant species that have existed for millions of years.

There is a phrase that express our kinship with all these life forms, a phrase we are in danger of forgetting, and that we therefore need to make people aware of again: All these forms of life are our *fellow creatures*. Francis of Assisi, the patron saint of ecology, reminds us of this in his famous Canticle of the Sun, quoted earlier. In Francis' gratitude to God for life, our fellow creatures sing with us as our next of kin: *Brother Sun, Sister Moon, Sister Water, Brother Fire, Mother Earth, Sister Death…*

Without our fellow creatures, human beings cannot preserve their naturalness. Therefore, for our own sakes too, we must let the world around us in all its diversity be free to live its life. Previous generations, both in our own culture and among indigenous peoples, showed a form of restraint in relation to their fellow creatures which is foreign to us today. By showing restraint, the ecological balance was maintained. But there was more to this restraint: it was religious, it contained an element of taboo. It concerns that which is outside our own power: we are not here as a result of our own capability; the amazing thing is that we are here at all. Existence has given us life, without us asking for it, and it has given nature its complex and amazing forms of life, even though no one asked for that either. This existence is greater than humans, greater than our actions, activities, society and goods. Human beings were aware of this in former times. Therefore, they showed a restraint that we cannot understand today. This is our age's fatal secularization in a nutshell.

Reconciliation

I have previously stated that Christianity – as an impulse in the history of spirituality at a time when our culture was still very young – helped lay the foundation for our culture's ambiguity. This ambiguity has laid the world open to a way of thinking and to practices that have led us to a global ecological crisis. As an extension of this, I would claim that if the current crisis is to be overcome, we need a new impulse in our spiritual history. Therefore, the question of the future of the planet is not in my opinion a question of finding new technological solutions. It is a question of how we human beings understand ourselves and of maturity. It is ultimately a spiritual question. Can the Christian tradition – and the church as part of a community of religions and of all people of good will – still have a contribution to make? I am convinced that it has, not only in the form of practical cooperation, but precisely as an impulse in mankind's spiritual history. To explain the content of this impulse more closely, I will begin with the concept of reconciliation.

With all the resources at our disposal today, human beings are tempted as never before to live unreconciled lives. But if there is one thing that our relationship to nature and to life on earth requires today, it is reconciliation. Reconciliation. Sometimes this is a matter of crossing boundaries. There is a Norwegian saying: "No fence is permanent!" But on other occasions reconciliation means being aware of and respecting boundaries, the boundaries for life itself. It is here that our culture meets its own limits, driven by its unshaken belief that crossing a boundary is always progress. As though we never need to reconcile ourselves with the fact that there are some boundaries that can never be crossed.

Reconciliation is a key concept in the Christian faith. This is how Paul explains its content in his letter to the Colossians: "In him (Christ) all the fullness of God was pleased to dwell, and through him to reconcile to himself all things, whether on earth or in heaven, making peace by the blood of his cross." (Col. 1.19-20 ESV). God wants to reconcile *everything* to himself. *Everything* – nothing less. This means that both humans and nature are included in Christ's act of reconciliation. Our merciless treatment of creation shakes the very foundation of Christianity. In the Orthodox tradition it can be said: To destroy nature is the same as crucifying Christ afresh.

And the outcome of this all-embracing view of reconciliation is that the church's vocation is made clear: the church is to be a movement for reconciliation in contemporary history, characterized by what I would call *earth-focused piety*. If the church fails in its calling, this not only affects our efforts to heal our wounded planet; the church will also lose its credibility. If we take seriously the scriptural message of reconciliation, the fruit of reconciliation must not only be peace with God, but with the whole of creation. Perhaps the thought of reconciliation is the most important contribution the Church has to offer today. But note: Reconciliation is a calling for all humanity, because we are all part of a fellowship that has the power to destroy the very fabric of the earth. More urgently than ever before in the history of mankind we are being called to a life of reconciliation with everything that lives! Or, as it says in "House rules: The cry from a wounded planet" (Bishop of Nidaros, Church of Norway, 2001): *Sons and daughters of the Earth, you who have the power to destroy her tapestry, you are called to a life of reconciliation.*

The art of limitation – for the sake of life

Under this heading we shall examine the place and significance of self-denial as an ecological impulse. Self-denial is not merely a negatively charged word in our culture. It has become a foreign word. This is inevitable in a time when so much revolves around material growth, and where the form of restraint that characterized previous generations and other cultures is actually considered a threat to progress itself. Nevertheless, we cannot avoid the following questions: Who today is going to say no – for the sake of life itself? This concerns the place of self-denial in our lives, not as life-denial, but on the contrary: as a life force, as a necessary part of the very pulse of life itself. Without self-denial there can be no life.

Self-denial is a matter of deciding priorities. Something is set aside, not in order to gain some advantage, but because something else is more important.

It is a matter of learning the art of limitation. We must learn to set aside more things. In a time like ours, this is a difficult lesson to learn, but it cannot be avoided if we want to spread the joy of living in harmony with nature. That joy is spread by a desire full of love – the desire to love the earth for its own sake.

The mature human

Let us once again look for clues in the oldest Christian tradition! We turn to Irenaeus, one of the key figures of the early church and Bishop of Lyon in southern France from the middle of the second century. He describes the relationship between God and human beings thus: *God is, people become.* By this he means: just as it is the nature of God to *be*, it is the nature of humans to *become* through developing and maturing.

If we are to *rediscover the joy of living in harmony with nature,* I believe that we need to do just that: *become* through developing and maturing. This concerns not only our lives as individuals, but also the plans for life that we all share – as children of our time. There are good reasons to ask how much fertile ground for developing and maturing our own time provides – at least if it is to include such issues as reconciliation, the art of limitation and yes: self-denial.

But however, we consider the prospects for the future, it is possible to share the vision Martin Lönnebo draws in one of his books: *The development of the mature human being is the most important project of this millennium!* (Lönnebo: *Van Gogh's Rom,* 2005.)

How does Lönnebo explain his vision? *Humans die from bread alone. It is the nature of our species to bear responsibility and values, to be a spiritual person in the process of becoming, a Homo spiritus in embryo. A member of our species is called this because he/she is a steward of the most unique and valuable aspect of a human being: consciousness, knowledge, kindness, responsibility, humility, uprightness, honesty, empathy, humour, holiness.*

But the development of a mature human being does not happen automatically. Are we developing into a *Homo economicus* or a *Homo animalus*? Lönnebo asks. And he continues: *Such members of the genus require no conscience, and since there will be little hope left, the earth and all those who are weak will be plundered. Why must all other creatures be threatened by the worst predator evolution has produced, namely, human beings who are not human?* And so he finishes with the thesis I have already quoted: *The development of the mature human being is the most important project of this millennium!* And *this should be a goal for humankind's united efforts.*

147

Why is a human being's maturity – and humankind's maturity – so fundamentally important? Because power, responsibility and maturity belong together. If a human being's power becomes ten times greater, his/her responsibility will be equally greater. If his/her responsibility becomes ten times greater, the human being must become ten times more mature in order to be worthy of the responsibility he or she has been given. The technological capabilities humans possess today include a position of power on a previously unprecedented scale in relation to nature and to all living creatures. It is this power that must be balanced by responsibility and maturity.

With a background in such thoughts the German-American philosopher Hans Jonas has given the concept of responsibility a new dimension. It can no longer merely be "responsibility from proximity." Responsibility today must be a responsibility that crosses boundaries, as much in time as in space, a "responsibility from distance." This responsibility from distance embraces our responsibility for the poor among us, as well as responsibility for future generations and for all life on our blue planet in a cosmos moving into an unknown future. From this, Jonas formulates the following categorical imperative: *Behave in such a way that the effects of your actions are consistent with an enduring, authentic human life on planet Earth.* This is the challenge for the mature human being and a mature humanity!

A final observation: The lilies of the field...

The time has come for a concluding observation. I choose to ally myself with the Norwegian author André Bjerke and his little poem about "The Lilies of the Field". It is to be found in a collection of fifteen poems to which Bjerke gave the following heading: "Those who saw him". All the poems in this collection are about people and other creatures that have one thing in common: They experienced Jesus at close range. Bjerke's approach is in reality close to ours in the Stetind Declaration: To work for a renewed understanding of the relationship between nature and human beings.

One of the poems is put into the mouth of the donkey that carried Jesus into Jerusalem, when he was met with palm branches at the end of his journey. In another poem, the words come from the lilies of the field, to whom Jesus referred when he spoke about not being worried and said: *Consider the lilies of the field, how they grow! They neither toil nor spin, yet I tell you: Even Solomon in all his glory was not arrayed like one of these.* (Matt 6:28-29 ESV). We do not think about this so often: But most of what Jesus said and did, was done outdoors. He was an outdoor person, and he used nature in his teaching. The text about the lilies of the field is not an exception. It is the outdoor man Jesus who is speaking and acting here, and in a very similar way André Bjerke allows nature itself to provide answers.

The lilies of the field experience what it is like to be observed with sensitivity by the Master himself. André Bjerke makes this experience the starting point for a little, complete poem. In its own way, it is about how humans and nature are mutually dependent on each other and may be a blessing for each other. We may consider the following little poem as a declaration of dependence – this time from nature itself!

> *We stand here despite the Easter cold*
> *testifying summer shines in Lebanon.*
> *He saw our beauty. He blessed us,*
> *and therefore, we bloom when he comes.*
>
> (André Bjerke 1966,
> from the collection "En skrifter rundt oss"
> [A sacred writing surrounds us])

A Prayer for our Earth

When Pope Francis sums up his ecological encyclical, he says that "this lengthy reflection… has been both joyful and troubling." But after the reflection it is natural for the pope to include prayer. This is necessary since the encyclical borrows words from St Francis: "Laudato si' – Praise to you, my Lord!" And in the pope's prayer, praise is present as an undertone, just as it is for ecology's patron saint. But today life itself is under threat, as never before in human history. The cry from our wounded earth is heard clearer and clearer. And the prayer must therefore contain both praise and lament – and a call to take responsibility. This is the pope's prayer, a prayer for our earth:

> All-powerful God, you are present in the whole universe
> and in the smallest of your creatures.
> You embrace with your tenderness all that exists.
> Pour out upon us the power of your love,
> that we may protect life and beauty.
> Fill us with peace, that we may live
> as brothers and sisters, harming no one.

O God of the poor,
help us to rescue the abandoned and forgotten of this earth,
so precious in your eyes.
Bring healing to our lives,
that we may protect the world and not prey on it,
that we may sow beauty, not pollution and destruction.
Touch the hearts
of those who look only for gain
at the expense of the poor and the earth.
Teach us to discover the worth of each thing,
to be filled with awe and contemplation,
to recognize that we are profoundly united
with every creature
as we journey towards your infinite light.
We thank you for being with us each day.
Encourage us, we pray, in our struggle
for justice, love and peace.

The deep joy of being at home in nature

PER INGVAR HAUKELAND

*"The path to eternity goes passed
the farmyard at home."*

(Norwegian poet Hans Børli)

Genus loci – the spirit of place

It is October in Breskelia, a small hamlet at the foothill of Lifjell mountain outside of Bø in Telemark, Norway. From the window of my study, I see directly into a forest dressed in all colors. In between the tree trunks, I catch a glimpse of the small stream that runs near our house. The kids are placing bark-boats in the stream, running down the stream to see how far they sail. The trees sway softly in the autumn wind, the sun paints the landscape yellowish and crisp, and behind it all, the majestic mountaintop of Bryggefjell rises above the magical treeline. A small bird comes up to the window and pokes at the glass with its beak a clear message: "There is no food left!" As I walk out to give them more, I hear a song of spring from the treetops. The song awakens in me a feeling of the mysterious and magical unity of all life. It makes me deeply joyous and grateful to be alive.

Our place is a former farm called Myrvang, but the home stretches beyond the buildings and the borders to our property. In fact, the room in our home that I am most proud of is a special place up by the stream where there is a beautiful waterfall. Sometimes my kids and I bring our hammocks up there to sleep next to it. We fall asleep from the soft and deep tunes of the water falling into the small pond below, just like a beautiful lullaby. When we get visitors, I ask if they would like to stay in the best guestroom we have, and if they say "yes", I take them up to this special room. Some stay, others just shake their head, but I often hear they speak of the special spirit that is in that room. Places we feel at home can often influence who we are, what we think, our identity and way of life. The influence can also be negative, as we witness when

151

people see their homes desolate and overgrown. If you do not feel you have a say in what happens to your home, it can cause an alienation to home as self.

For the founder of the Deep Ecology movement, the Norwegian philosopher Arne Naess (1912–2009), it was his cabin named Tvergastein that was his Home with a capital H. He writes:

> *The loss of belonging to a place is noticeable, the longing is still there, and this emphasizes the need to express what it means to belong to a place. It strengthens the tendency to develop a home-feeling, to re-awaken the inner relationship between one self and the environment. This is of great significance for the motives to participate in the Deep Ecology movement* (Naess, 1993, 102–103).

On his last trip to Tvergastein in May 2008, Arne Naess, who was 95 years old, he had been tired and weak at the elder home in Oslo. We had to carry him from the car onto the trailer behind the snowmobile. He also needed help in getting into the cabin, but after a while inside the cabin, something happened. He got his energy back and ended up hustling from room to room with deep joy and enthusiasm. We who witnessed this was in deep awe for what the sense of coming home to one's place can do. A place can in this way both empower and disempower.

A useful concept in this regard is *genus loci*, used in ancient Rome to describe the protective spirit of a place. Today it is used more to describe the uniqueness of place, its atmosphere. As we speak of the spirit of time, we can speak of the spirit of place. The Norwegian architect Christian Norberg-Schulz (1980) is known to use the concept in architecture, inspired by the phenomenology of Martin Heidegger where time and place fuse into being (Dasein). It demands of us, not only in architecture, but also in natural and cultural heritage management that we are attentive to what is "in place" and what is "out of place". We can often be "home-blind" to the qualities in our place. When we moved to Breskelia, there was a rusty old plow just on the other side of our entrance, totally dominating the landscape. When I asked neighbors about it, they said it had come there after a neighbor quarrel in the 1970s. Now both the people who were in the quarrel are long gone, but the plow remains, as a taken for granted scene to our everyday life. When I asked if I could remove it, they were all very happy about that, and the day after it was gone to the recycling business in town. We may need to de-learn what is taken for granted and re-learn the sensitivity to what is *in place* and the genus loci. Changes need to *take* place; we need to be that change.

The sense of wonder

Naess used to say that philosophy starts with wonder and ends with wonder. Rachel Carson, who Naess called the mother of the Deep Ecology movement, writes in *The Sense of Wonder* "It is a wholesome and necessary thing for us to turn again to the earth and in the contemplation of her beauties to know of wonder and humility." (Carson, 1965).

Both Naess and Carson encouraged us to live more integral lives, between deeper values and concrete decisions, so to realize peaceful, just and ecological sustainable changes wherever we are. Many associate the prefix *eco* in *ecophilosophy* and *ecosophy*, perhaps too narrowly, with nature protection, but there is a need for a stronger life-orientation and an integral approach to nature, culture, community, economy and spirituality in places where we live.

The word *eco* comes from the Greek *oikos*, usually translated as *household*, but it can also be translated as *home* and interpreted as our *home in life*. In this view ecophilosophy or ecosophy can be understood as life philosophy, and ecocrisis as life crisis and ecocentrism as life-centered. A personal life philosophy is something we all need to develop, inspired by a sense of wonder and a love of wisdom into all related aspects of our home in life and of the home to all life on this wonderful planet. Such deepened and widened sense of wonder can enhance the necessary humility and reverence that makes us act in awe toward the web of life.

The Stetind seminar in 1966 brought ecology and philosophy together in between the climbing, framed in deep joy, friendship and a sense of wonder in nature. Stetind is a symbol of the greatness in nature, and even though we all should travel to this beautiful mountain in Northern Norway at some point in our lives, it is in accordance to the eco-philosophical heritage to discover the symbolic *Stetind* where you live, something that awakens respect and awe. For me, it is Bryggefjell.

The mountains have been central in the development of eco-philosophy and Deep Ecology in Norway and elsewhere. To climb mountains is not only an activity, it is an activeness – a way of being in nature – where one is fully present with one's self. Naess used the term "fjelling" (mountaining) to describe being *in* the mountain, not *on* it. The magnificent mountain, Hallingskarvet, which his cabin is placed in, is described by Naess in a mythopoetic language as a father-figure. He called it "the good, long life's father," inspired by his journey to Nepal and the mountain Tseringma, which the Sherpas called "The good, long life's mother."

Life seen as an open landscape

In *Life's Philosophy* (2003), Naess and I wanted to challenge people to reassess the direction in their life, to go deeper into the relationship between what they value and what they do. I used the following metaphor: "To live is like traveling through a landscape with both easy and broken terrain, light and dark places, all concealing the unexpected... to feel at home in life requires both moving toward a goal and simply being" (p. 1–2). The metaphor can help us understand better the relationships between: 1) map and territory and 2) traveling and resting. The relationship between map and territory is like the relationship between the world of thought (mental maps) and the world of concrete things (reality). A map is not the territory, as the name is not the thing named, but it says something about its abstract structures.

In the forest behind our house, there is a rock known *Bakstekjerringa* (*Old baker woman*) in our place-based culture. Someone put up a sign in front of the rock telling three stories. The first story is about an old woman who had to climb the rock in order to escape from an angry bear. The second is about an old baker woman who refused to give some bread to a poor beggar and immediately was turned into the rock. The third story tells us that the rock is a rock that came with the ice over 10,000 years ago. Which story is the real one? If we view the life of the rock with only one map, or tell only one story, would we not make the rock less than what it is and impoverish our world of experience?

We need to be critically aware of the maps we use. Some are more dominant than others, such as the Cartesian map of mechanism, objectivism and dualism. Alfred North Whitehead warns us of "the fallacy of misplaced concreteness," where we take something abstract as the concrete. If we think of nature as "out there", as a machine for human purposes, and we act upon this conception while we in reality are an integral part of nature, we have not only an ecological problem, but also an existential problem.

Naess makes a distinction between *abstract structures of reality* (mapped world) and *concrete content of reality* (experienced world). Science can tell you how fast you fall from a ladder, but not how it feels to fall, nor how fast you fall when you fall in love. We have access to the concrete content of reality through direct, spontaneous experiences, which is a world of wonder and magic where everything is alive and speaks. The Norwegian poet Hans Børli tells of an early morning walk when something suddenly happens:

A clear bellflower-morning, you may experience one of these seldom moments when you, in a way, rise out of yourself and into all-life.

In these moments of revelation, you sense all things directly – no name, no shadowing word-image stands between you and the naked, own-life of things. Nothing is "as something", you can erase the comparisons, analogies – the things are what they are under the sun, and you converse with them on a silent language of fragrance and premonition. You are within the wordless poetic sphere, where the word-poem never can follow you. But it lasts so short, it passes by like a dream, and you wake up again in a world where the impressions always strive after an "as" – an image to be registered in the archive of experience (Børli 1992, p. 161; my translation).

Naess would say we rise into our *ecological Self* in such spontaneous experiences. Through a process of identification, we expand our understanding of our Self (with capital S). When I was a kid, there was a beautiful fir tree in the nearby forest that I loved very much. It was the chief of all trees, and the first tree I had a deep relation to. Under its protection we build our teepee, and we loved to climb it and it loved to be climbed. After several years abroad, I went back to honor the old chief. As I came to the area, I was shocked – it was all clear-cut. I searched and found the tree stump of the old chief, sat down and cried. A part of my Self had died. When we expand our Selves to encompass others, we would care for them as we would care for our Self.

We can speak of three ways of traveling in life's landscape: 1) traveling by map (thinking); 2) traveling by the territory (feeling and sensing); 3) traveling by compass (intuiting). We need to include all three to best orient ourselves. This can be illustrated with the metaphor of a sailboat. The boat is our Self. Feelings are the sail. No sail, no movement. The source of movement is the wind (spirit). Our thinking is the map we navigate after. Reason is the rudder that sets out the course, but there are two kinds of reason. A shallow reason that says something is reasonable, like building a new parking lot in the city-center, when it is the logical thing to do given there are so many more cars and since there is a political will to do it, it is technically feasible and it is financed. A deep reason that says something is reasonable if it coincides with our deeper values in life. We related this deeper reason in *Life's Philosophy* to the term *ratio* in Spinoza's philosophy. It is also related to what Blaise Pascal (1623–1662) said in *Le Pensées*: "The heart has its reasons of which reason knows nothing." With this deep reason a new parking lot may not be that reasonable. We need to question the reason behind the direction we individually and as a society are heading in.

Finally, it is important to rest in life's landscape, to regain our breath (spirit). To rest means different things for different people – a walk in the forest, family, friends, a concert, a good book or simply dwelling in life's many intrinsic values. You have to find out what makes you rest, and then seek that as often as you can, since it gives you the power to move.

Into the depths of Deep Ecology

Fritjof Capra says in the book *Web of Life* (1996) that Deep Ecology is the new paradigm he sees arise in our society. Arne Naess coined the term Deep Ecology in the early seventies to describe an approach that went deeper into the problems as well as into the solutions of the ecological crisis. People adhering to this approach did so from various total views (ecosophies), inspired by philosophy or religion, and they shared certain values and visions, for example seeing all life as having intrinsic value and the need for a nonviolent revolution of how we think and act in all areas of life. Naess described also a *shallow ecology movement,* known as office-desk environmentalism, where it makes sense to protect nature in so far as it has value for humans, and where the solutions to the ecocrisis come from technological fixes.

There is a similar shallow and deep approach to the current economic crisis. Instead of going to the roots of the problems, governments have poured billions of dollars into the same institutions that in many ways are the problem. Is that a long-term solution? Why we do not change seems to do with a consumer-addiction to global economic systems that are themselves addicted to our addictions: "Got to have it, just got to have it!" We are in a double-bind. On the one hand we are told to reduce our consumption to solve the ecological crisis, while on the other hand, we are told to increase our consumption to solve the economic crisis. There are alternatives, as we see in transition towns, bioregional movements and voluntary simplicity, where we consume lesser, smaller, simpler, slower and smarter, but these alternatives can only be realizes, it seems, by breaking the pattern of addiction.

The cultural ecologist David Abram, the initiator and co-founder of the Alliance for Wild Ethics (AWE), together with Stephan Harding, Per Espen Stoknes and myself, uses the term *depth ecology* to avoid the dichotomy between the deep and the shallow, and to emphasize what he finds inspiring with Deep Ecology writings, namely how we are an integral part of nature. We have in AWE explored this in our various work (see bibliography), especially related to the enchanted world of wonder and magic.

We can speak of four depths to depth ecology of place: 1) depth of immersion, which goes deeper into the soil of experience, to those deep, mystical experiences that spontaneously mark our soul and alters us in some way, which also at how we are deeply rooted in place we call home; 2) depth of consciousness, which entails the coming together in awareness, individually and collectively, through a process deep inquiry into our values and visions, which is also for home-places that many are blind to; 3) depth of consequence, which addresses consequences of our awareness through various plans of actions in the different areas we are at, including how to overcome that which inhibits profound changes and how to promote that which enhances such changes; this also relate to place-based planning, seeing places as *glocal* in the sense that they unite the local and the global; 4) depth of emersion, which addresses how we realize our Self through what we do in concrete situations; this also relate to how we our lives in the place and participate in its development. There is a natural sequence to how these depths co-evolve, but they are also depths that keep on taking place in parallel and interrelated processes.

A renewed sense of the sacred

The life philosophy I seek to express is inspired by being a Quaker (earthQuaker), and I find that there is in my life, my soul, a unique and personal pattern interconnected with the greater spirit and the greater body of God. In the book *Himmeljorden* (2009), I describe what I see as the unity between heaven and earth that we have direct access to through our spontaneous experiences. It awakens in us the mysterious unity in life; where there is no distinction between subject and object, map and territory, between me and the other. It is a spiritual or mystical experience of oneness with the world. We delve deep into the sacred and holy ground of being where our soul and the soul of God unite. It is closer to us than we think. The first Quaker, George Fox (1624–1691), writes in 1648 after his revelation: "Everything in creation gave another smell to me before, more so than words can express." And the Quaker William Penn, who founded Pennsylvania, writes in 1693: "How can humans find the conscience to misuse the Creation, while the Creator looks them directly in the face, in all and every part of it?"

I advocate a *panentheistic* view, where we answer to that of God in all living beings. I see an inner light, a creative, vital force – soul – in all that lives and moves. This inner light is related to what Spinoza, who had Quakers in his close circle of friends, calls *ratio*, the deeper voice of reason. This inner light would bring about a very different kind of Enlightenment of mind than that which was based on encyclopedic reason in Western culture.

157

The term *Heavenearth* is similar to what Abram, in *Becoming Animal* (2010), calls *Eairth*. Bringing the letter "i" in the center of the word *earth*, the word *air* appears. The word *eairth* gets at how I am immersed in the air which is immersed in the earth. It is an expression that brings the spirit and body together in a sensuous whole. The air we breathe is the spirit that upholds our body like the atmosphere is the greater spirit that upholds the body of God.

I use the metaphor of *Tree of life* as an image of realizing the unity between our soul and the soul of God. The tree has four interrelated parts: roots, trunk, branches and fruits, which I see as soul-awakening, soul-awareness, soul-consequence and soul-realization. The roots of the tree are the mystical experiences of awakening to the unity of our soul with the soul of God. The trunk of the tree brings soul-awareness, where we become aware of the values and visions of the soul, our true Self. The branches show us the consequences the soul puts on our way of living in the various places we are at. The fruits of the tree are the realizations of the soul, which takes place when we live our lives in unity of spirit-body, heaven-earth, Self-God. Soul-realization is when we live according to the inner light, *ratio*, the deeper reason, inner compass or the voice of God within.

A renewed sense of the sacred is born in the good, dark soil of being and the inner light helps it grow into existence as soul-realization. We realize the unity of all beings, which will widen our understanding of the saying: "Love thy neighbor as thy self," since the neighbor you share the place with, human and non-human, are ultimately part of your Self. A renewed sense of the sacred should furthermore be expressed in how we speak. If I speak of a tree as an object "out there", I will relate to it very differently than if I speak to and with the tree as a unique, living being. It has to do with humility and awe to the unity that the tree and I share.

Sources of change

We have the knowledge and the technology to make fundamental changes in a green, just and peaceful direction, but still the changes are not taking place in our lives. I will here look at three sources that I see strong enough to help people make profound changes in their lives: fear, love and joy.

Fear is based on felt threat or crisis. Many will then change, but many will continue to live in denial and hope all goes well. It is as if our society is a large cruise ship that has just hit an iceberg and is taking in water. Some try to close the hole. Others yell to the captain to turn the direction the boat is heading in, if not it may hit more icebergs. Others are sitting in the restaurant, drinking wine while the water is reaching their knees, saying: "Don't worry! The boat cannot sink!" Today many find ignorance to be bliss. Felt fear may get people to react quickly, but fear is a negative force we seek to avoid, and arguments intended to scare people, may lead to the opposite.

The other source is love. When two people fall in love, they are willing to do everything to care for one another. This is a positive force of attraction, which makes everything and everyone come into that light of love. But how can people fall in love and care for other living beings when research shows that people in the modern society use almost ninety percent of their time indoors. It is difficult to love our neighbors, both humans and non-humans, when we never meet them.

Finally, there is deep joy. When I gathered texts by Naess on Deep Ecology over the last forty years, I was struck by the deep joy underlying it all. To live more in tune with our deeper values, following the inner light that enlightens our mind to our true Self, brings about a deep joy in us. We need to find our way into the changes where we are, what Naess called *sva marga* (*your way*, in Sanskrit), but at the same time, we are relational beings who are dependent on others to walk the way. Some would argue that profound changes will cause forsaking goods and going back in time, but a change of focus from standard of living to quality of life can be joyful and make us feel happier. Wealth is not in what you have, but in how you feel – you may have everything, but feel poor, or you may be poor, but feel rich. The deep joy of being immersed in this wonderful world, of living according to what one values, and of coming together with others, is the sustaining force that makes changes we seek to be wherever we are lasting.

Bibliography

- Abram, David (2010) *Becoming Animal: An Earthly Cosmology*, Pantheon Books, New York.
- Bowers, C. A. (1995) *Educating for an Ecologically Sustainable Culture*, SUNY, New York.
- Børli, Hans (1992) *Med Øks og Lyre*, Achehoug books, Oslo.
- Capra, Fritjof (1996) *The Web of Life*, Anchor books, New York.
- Carson, Rachel (1965) *The Sense of Wonder*, Harper and Row, New York.
- Glasser, H. & Drengson, A. (red.). 2005. *The selected works of Arne Naess*. Dordrecht: Springer.

- Harding, Stephan (2006) *Animate Earth: Science, Intuition and Gaia*, Green books, Devon.
- Haukeland, P. I. (ed.) *Dyp Glede: Inn i Dypøkologien* (*Deep Joy: Into Deep Ecology*), Flux   books, Oslo.
- Haukeland, P.I. (2009) *Himmeljorden: Om det av Gud i naturen* (*Heavenearth: On that of   God in Nature*), Kvekerforlaget, Stavanger.
- Naess, Arne with Haukeland, Per Ingvar (2003) Life's *Philosophy: Reason and Feeling in a   Deeper World*, University of Georgia Press, Athens, Georgia.
- Næss, Arne. 1985. *Det gode lange livs far: Hallingskarvet sett fra Tvergastein*. Oslo: Damm.
- Stoknes, Per Espen (2009) *Money and Soul*, Green Books, Devon.

My friend the mountain

GRO DAHLE

Hallo?

I greet the mountain:
Hallo, you grim gloomy face!
You scary old man,
your steep and solemn forehead,
that familiar scowl,
those sunken-in cheeks!

Hallo, you black and bleached wall.
I'm not afraid of you, I say,
even if I am,
I can outrun you
down the road and back,
I can jump the fence
and hide
in the hassel bush brush.
The mountain can't do any of this.
Why should I be scared?

This deaf and mute being.
Can you even hear me?
I raise my voice to the mountain,
but the mountain doesn't seem to listen,
has nothing more to say,
stands sullen, silent, still
head held high
and doesn't answer me.
Will not answer? Cannot answer?
Or maybe it speaks in another frequency?

Stetind at night with Northern Light or Aurora Borealis

Telling tales,
singing songs
I cannot hear?
Small songs about streams and creeks,
a poetry of trails?
Great songs about rivers and waterfalls,
stories about distant moors,
the whispers of blue gossamer hills,
the telling of forests?

Perhaps the voice of the mountain

lies within its rocks,
a mouthful of stones,
a voice of highland flowers,
bog bean, mountain queen, heather?
The words of sedge and cottongrass
so quiet so quiet
not even the mice
can hear it.

Hallo, I greet the mountain.
That famous blue coat of yours, that shine of your shoes!
You bright and beautiful being,
waiting patiently for next winter, next spring, summer.
Is that a new hat?
A cap of snow?

He's just standing there, smiling down at me,
beaming, listening,
lending me an ear,
no matter what I've said,
no matter what I've done,
he won't leave me behind,
doesn't scorn me.
I always know where to find him
in that same place as before,
this fatherly figure.

Hallo, old friend, I say,
the mountain gives me a nod,
waving me on
with the wind.
A friend standing by
with the whole sky upon his shoulders.
I'm so lucky with friends like this!

PRACTICAL CONSEQUENCES – A CHANGE EMPOWERED BY JOY!

The good society? Can we measure it?

SIRI NÆSS

Are there any societies that are better than others? Yes, I mean some societies are better than others; the communities that take care of nature are better than those who do not care for nature.

But if we are to say that a society is better than any another, we have to do a kind of measurement. We must be able to measure the goodness of a society. It is not enough to say that some of us think some societies are good and others bad. Maybe we need an index? Many indexes have been suggested that suggest something about the goodness of society.

Within several professional traditions, one has approached this issue. We can say that the different subjects have chosen keywords for which they have linked to concepts, operationalization and measurements.

For example, economists have chosen words as gross national product per capita, GNP, and in other contexts, words such as purchasing power, utility and others are used to compare communities. The sociologists have been interested in social indicators, often living conditions variables, as goals for the good society. Within this tradition, the Human Development Index, HDI, measures illiteracy and the proportion of children attending school, average life expectancy and gross national product. Psychologists have proposed gross national happiness, BNL, while physicians are focused on health.

But then, there have recently been some eco-philosophers on the track who are not just talking about people, but also about other creatures and the whole planet. They propose the index HPI, Happy Planet Index. In their opinion, a society is good when it contributes to the well-being of the whole planet, not just people living today, but also future generations of people and other creatures. This sounds promising!

Let's take a closer look at this index. But first some words about the precursors, the first indexes that were proposed to measure the goodness of a society.

Gross national product

The first ones who tried were the economists. Gross national product (GNP), tries to measure the overall economic activity in a country. There is broad consensus that there are many disadvantages by using this unit of measurement if one wants to measure the goodness of a society. It includes activities that we believe are not good (including combating criminal activity), and it does not include other activities that we believe are good (including non-registered activities in the homes and in voluntary work). Another theme is that it is based on an assumption that economic activity is a very effective instrument for realizing other goods. Economists do not claim that economic activity is a good in itself. But they believe it is an important means that gives society members the opportunity to realize goods that have intrinsic value. It has been assumed that the richer a country is, the more self-realized, happy, etc. are those who live in the country. And the more they are able to pass on wealth to future generations.

Human Development Index, Human Poverty Index

Whether economic activity is an effective tool, or how effective it is, is constantly being discussed. GNP is not rejected as a mean of promoting the goodness of a society, but it is agreed that there are other means too. It is argued that it should be supplemented with other measurement units, as the sociologists do. In the Human Development Index (HDI), in addition to gross national product, attempts have been made to measure society's level of knowledge and average life expectancy.

This is the index that for several years has named Norway as "The world's best country to live in." An assessment of the index has concluded that it provides useful information on the development level, but not on future development opportunities.

Another less-known index, the Human Poverty Index (HPI), assumes that it is easier to measure a society's poorness than its goodness. This index, in addition to life expectancy and illiteracy, also reports the number of unemployed and the proportion of people below the poverty line (50% below the median household income).

Health

When life expectancy is included as part of a society's goodness, we are in the arena of medicine, namely health. Attempts have been made to measure health in different ways, for example by recording infant mortality and the number of doctors per capita. Some have suggested that people are asked how good their health is, they call it "subjective health" or "self-reported health". One then bases on the individual's experience of well-being. But many are skeptical of such "soft" goals on how well people have it. Life expectancy, infant mortality and the number of doctors per capita are easy to measure. It provides "hard" data. Average life expectancy is perhaps the goal that is most used to measure health, and which many accept as a measure of the goodness of a society.

Happiness

Not everyone is skeptical of "soft" variables, on the contrary, some believe that these variables are the best, because they represent what people want. Dalai Lama (2000) believes that seeking happiness "lies in our nature":

The desire or need to be happy knows no bounds.
It is something that lies in our nature. As such, it needs no
grounds and it is justified by the simple fact that
it is something we rightly want out of our nature.

We want income, job and a partner, if this makes us happy, not because it has value in itself. Some propose gross national happiness (GNH), as a measure of a community's goodness. It will be based on answers to questions about whether one experiences life as good, is satisfied or if one is often happy, and rarely unhappy.

A widely shared, old experience (we got it from Asia!) :
- Everybody are participating, and the project is complex and continuous, producing local invulnerability

Work a home community: Same!

Work = home!

Norwegian water mill

Nepalese water mill

RIVER

- A few experts' applied science (all get it from Euro-America)
- The community served is non-participating, and the project is complicated and often short-lived, producing local vulnerability

Home and employment: Two different worlds!

- During construction, employment rate is high above normal — after completion negligible

"IIIrd Alternative": Learn from both experiences, - to develop a "Middle Way"!
- Think! - Feel! - Try! - Accomplish! (4)

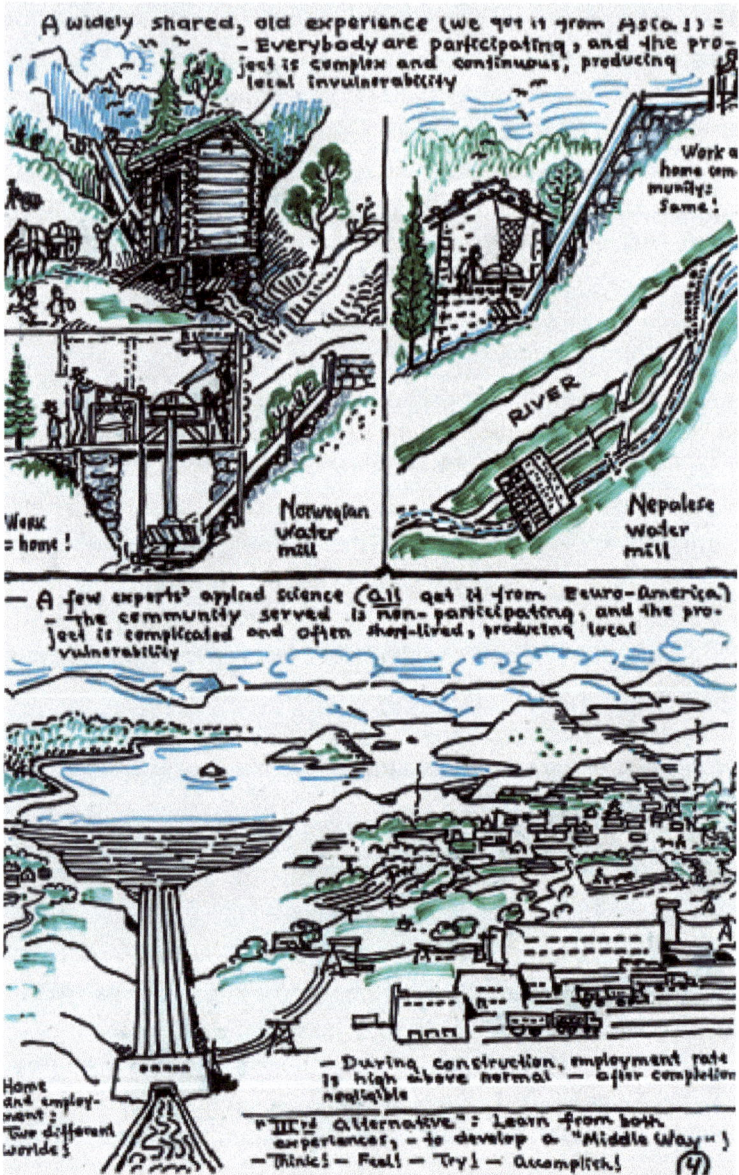

To compare countries with regard to Happiness is difficult. One of the problems is language. Is "happiness" ("lykke") in Norwegian the same as "happiness" in English? Or is it perhaps something more extreme, something stronger? Language studies have been conducted in multilingual countries such as Canada, China and Switzerland. The conclusions have been predominantly positive, but with a good portion of uncertainty (Diener and Oishi, 2000; Veenhoven 2009).

One has also asked if happiness is as important in all cultures. The answer is that happiness is at the top of the wish-list in every country; It is more important than wealth and to come to heaven, and as important as love (Diener and Biswas-Diener, 2008).

Furthermore, one has pointed out differences in cultural norms that encourage modesty, or sobriety, and which inhibit tendencies to use positive descriptions of themselves. Modesty seems to be more prevalent in East Asian cultures and less prevalent in Western cultures. The opposite tendency to "positivity", desire and willingness to present themselves and their own in a beautiful light can be understood as a personality trait that contributes to real life satisfaction, but it can also be understood as a source of error. If this trait varies with culture (it seems more prevalent in South American countries than in North American), differences in results may be difficult to interpret (Diener and Biswas-Diener, 2008; Diener and Oishi, 2004; Diener & Suh, 1999).

Another issue that makes international comparisons to be interpreted with caution is that the statistical analyzes become uncertain when the number of survey units is low (few countries) (Diener and Oishi, 2004). Moreover, it is difficult to get a representative sample in poor communities where not everyone has attended school, and where those with low education often fall out in questionnaire surveys (Veenhoven, 2000). If the poor, who often say they are less happy than the rich, will fall out (not participate in the surveys) in poor countries, poor countries will come out with higher happiness scores than they would have if the entire population had participated.

All of these methodological problems must necessarily slow down the optimists who believe that gross national happiness is the best measure of a society's goodness. But it should not lead to the idea being rejected. I want to remind about the story of the man who was searching for his key under the street light, even though he knew he had lost it further up the street – he thought it was impossible to look for the key there, because it was so dark. More street lights are needed! More method research is needed!

The relationship between the indicators

Happiness measurements, measurements of subjectivity and other positive experiences, do not necessarily stand in contrast to other goals of the good life. Those who respond that they are very happy have consistently better health than those who answer that they are less happy. Not only do they have better subjective health ("soft" data), which one can expect, but they also live longer ("hard" data). They are less often unemployed, and they are less poor. They are more tolerant, nicer (more generous, more helpful), believe in god, and have greater confidence in their fellow human beings. (Tov and Diener, 2008).

In terms of economic indicators, the relationship becomes more complicated. Norwegians who earn a lot have higher happiness-scores than Norwegians who earn less. (Hellevik, 2008). Admittedly, this does not only have to do with material goods. It also has to do with success in the workplace (interesting jobs are better paid). Moreover, the connection between happiness and personal income is stronger in poor countries than in rich countries. It must be agreed, some studies in some poor countries, especially in Latin America, have a relatively high average level of self-reported mental well-being. But all countries with high GDP are high on the happiness scale (Diener and Biswas-Diener, 2008).

Nevertheless, it has been found that the average self-reported happiness in many rich countries has not risen in recent decades, although wealth has multiplied. This may mean that the happiness curve has flattened. We have got a diminishing border benefit. But it is not necessarily so that increasing wealth does not help, that we have reached the maximum level. This may mean that what makes us richer has been costly. The wealth, or what has been the prerequisite for wealth, has reduced a quieter life, close and stable relationships, we are moving apart. A materialistic lifestyle has a negative connection with happiness (Hellevik, 2003).

Happy Planet Index, ecological footprint, sustainable wellness

Despite many reservations, the conclusion must be that economic development has given many people a longer life, better health and more happiness. Will continued economic development give even more people better health, longer lives and more happiness? Is economic development a good one for future generations as well? Is it a good thing for the planet?

It is more doubtful, as the situation is today. The ever-increasing material advancement in the rich part of the world is based on the fact that rich people provide a disproportionate amount of non-renewable resources. And polluting. A warmer climate is the result of overuse in the rich part of the world. It has, first and foremost, harmful consequences for those who are now poor. But in the longer term, the whole world is threatened.

We need a simple goal for sustainable well-being. This need has produced a proposal to measure the goodness of a society with an extended happiness index, which is called Happy Planet Index (NEF, 2009). The index will direct attention to conditions that degrade the quality of life of other creatures, and ultimately threaten the survival of humanity. It is about the use of non-renewable resources and partly about pollution. Use of non-renewable resources, e.g. food production based on resource-intensive raw materials, exhausts the Earth's arable land. Emissions of greenhouse gases, which are a consequence of our way of life, threaten the environment.

The Happy Planet Index was launched by the New Economics Foundation (NEF) in 2006 as a measure of a community's progress and an alternative to economic growth. The index is an attempt to measure "what really matters to us," a long, happy life, and "what matters to the planet – our resource use." It is based on both "hard" data and "soft" data.

The Happy Planet Index 2016 is explained in the methods paper (NEF, 2016)

> *In essence, to calculate HPI scores we begin by multiplying the mean life expectancy of residents of a given country by mean experienced wellbeing of residents in the same country. Unlike in previous releases, in the 2016 release we have adjusted the main results to reflect inequalities in the distribution of experienced wellbeing and life expectancy within the population of each country. This gives us the number of inequality-adjusted Happy Life Years experienced by a typical resident in each country.1 We then divide the average number of inequality-adjusted Happy Life Years achieved in each country by that country's Ecological Footprint per capita, to reveal the average number of inequality-adjusted Happy Life Years produced per unit of demand on the natural environment from the country's residents.*

The formula is

$$\text{Happy Planet Index} = \frac{((\text{Life expectancy} \times \text{Experienced wellbeing}) \times \text{Inequality of outcomes})}{\text{Ecological footprints}}$$

The purpose of the index is, to put it briefly, to increase our happiness and longevity and to reduce our ecological footprints. Or even shorter:

Live better, spend less

Maybe we will be less happy if we impose on ourselves less driving a car, eat less steak and go less often in the sauna. Maybe not. Maybe we live shorter if we change to a more sober diet? Probably not. Perhaps we have to do it anyway to survive as a species and for other species to have a chance to survive.

NEF (2016) has calculated values on Happy Planet Index for 140 countries. Highest ranks Costa Rica and a number of other countries in Latin America. The population of Costa Rica has high values for happiness and longevity, and they have low values of ecological footprints. Norway has very high values of happiness and longevity, but also of footprints. In total, Norway is ranked twelfth and therefore highest among European countries, but closely followed by Albania. The United Kingdom is at thirty-fourth place, Canada number 85 and the United States number 108.

In most countries, NEF finds a slight improvement in the score on the index, but this does not apply to the three largest countries in the world, namely India, China and the USA. NEF (2009) points out that there is great variation in ecological footprints between countries with the same score on happiness and life expectancy. High score on happiness and high life expectancy do not indicate large ecological footprints.

One can doubt one of these measurements, perhaps especially happiness measurements in poor countries. Some engage in ecological footprints, but are skeptical of "soft" variables. happiness measurements. They can choose to use other indices as a measure of a community's goodness, such as the Human Poverty Index, and adjust for ecological footprints. Future in medical and social science research can provide other perspectives.

A future perspective like this, is to elaborate on the concept of ecological footprint. What is a "happy planet"? Is nature's intrinsic value sufficiently taken care of when the footprints are measured? Or is it just the people who are in focus? The happy planet may not necessarily be the planet where happy people live. People are not the only creatures on the planet, perhaps not the most important. Or are they?

Summary

Let's go back to the question we asked in the beginning: Are some societies better than others? The answers we have found provide all answers on behalf of humans. Economists respond with GNP, the sociologists with HDI and HPI, the physicians suggest different goals on health, among other things. Life expectancy; all are human-related goals. But then comes HPI, Happy

Planet Index. Does it require an answer on behalf of the planet? Yes, it says we must measure the footprints that humans put on the earth. It does mean that the interest in the rest of the world is also considered? It depends on how the index is interpreted. Choosing goals can easily be justified by the need to protect the earth's resources on behalf of people who come after us.

It is usual to say that there is no contradiction between human protection and nature conservation – what is good for nature is good for humans. This is a standpoint we like to believe in but it is not easy to defend. It requires careful thought and exploration. We must strengthen research on the theme of "nature-joy".

An exploration of this relationship may indicate that contact with nature is essential to the quality of life of some people, but not to everyone.

For some, this is irrelevant, or at least not crucial. In the deep ecological movement, it is a basic principle that all forms of life in principle have intrinsic value and therefore the right to unfold (Haukeland, 2008). People are part of nature, but do not necessarily have a special position. Nature has intrinsic value, regardless of the utility it has for humans.

References

- Barstad, A. (2006). Norge verdens beste? *Tidsskrift for velferdsforskning*, 9, s. 39–43
- Dalai Lama. (2000). *Tanker for et nytt* årtusen. Oslo: Cappelen
- Diener, E & Biswas-Diener, R. (2002). Will money increase subjective well-being? A literature review and guide to needed research. *Social Indicators Research*, 57, s. 119–169.
- Diener, E. & Oishi, S. (2000) Money and happiness: Income and subjective well-being across nations. I: E. Diener & E.M. Suh, *Culture and Subjective Well-Being*, s. 185–218. Cambridge: The MIT Press.
- Diener, E & Oishi, S. (2004). Are Scandinavians happier than Asians? I:F. Columbus (red.), *Politics and Economics of Asia* N.Y.: Nova Science Publishers.
- Diener, E. & Suh, E.M. (1999). National differences in subjective well-being. I: D. Kahneman, E. Diener & N. Schwarz (red.), *Well-being: The foundations of hedonic psychology*, s. 434–450. New York: Russel Sage Foundation.
- Diener, E. & Tov, W. (2007). Culture and subjective well-being. I: S. Kitamaya & D. Cohen (red.), *Handbook of cultural psychology*, s. 691–714. New York: Guilford

- Haukeland, P.I. (2008). Dyp glede. Med Arne Næss inn i dypøkologien. Oslo: Flux Forlag
- Hellevik, O. (2003). Economy, values and happiness in Norway. *Journal of Happiness Studies*, 4, s. 243–283
- Hellevik, O. (2008). *Jakten på den norske lykken.* Oslo: Universitetsforlaget
- NEF (New Economics Foundation). (2009). Happy Planet Index. Lastet ned fra http://www.happy-planetindex.org/public-data/files/happy-planet-index-2-0.pdf
- NEF (New Economics Foundation). (2016) Happy Planet Index. Lastet ned fra: https://static1.squarespace.com/static/5735c421e321402778ee0ce9/t/578dec7837c58157b929b3d6/1468918904805/Methods+paper_2016.pdf
- Tov, W. & Diener, E. (2008). The well-being of nations. Linking together trust, cooperation, and democracy. I: B.A. Sullivan, M. Snyder & J.L. Sullivan (red), *Cooperation* Malden: Blackwell.
- Veenhoven, R. (1996). Happy life-expectancies. *Social Indicators Research*, 39, s. 1–58.
- Veenhoven, R. (2000). The four qualities of life: ordering concepts and measures of the good life. *Journal of Happiness Studies*, 1, s. 1–39.
- Veenhoven, R. (2009). The international scale interval study: Improving the comparability of responses to survey questions about happiness. I: V. Møller & D. Huschka (red.), *Quality of Life and the Millennium Challenge* (s. 45-58). New York: Springer.

On eternity's tablets

HANS BØRLI

Nothing vanishes. Everything
gets indelibly engraved
on eternity's tablets.
If but a bird flies through the sunset,
two people exchange some friendly word
at the postbox one morning, or
a track snows up slowly by the woods,
then will these very little things
be saved in the universal consciousness
as long as the days dawn in the east,
the nights let fall their mercy over Earth.

There is a memory in space,
An all-embracing cosmic memory
That cancels Time
and joins all things
in a single star-white *Now*

(from Hans Børli, *On a Harmonica,* 1991)

Love for urban nature

HANNE HERMANN

This contribution to the memorial volume on Nature was written ten years ago. Since then many things have changed in our relationship to our surrounding world, in our relationship to the animals and the nature with which we share the planet. Our perception of nature and climate are changing as well as where and how we meet it and enjoy it. The last years people living in urban areas and cities have started to use their balconies and roofs for cultivating plants and enjoying nature. Research studies have shown that nature in itself has a positive effect on human health and that access to parks, beaches, green lungs, and walking areas in the city are important contributions to a better health. The motivation behind this shift is manifold and various, but three major trends are perceptible: the reduction of carbon emissions by nature, the wish to live in a nature-friendly way and a growing and more acute understanding of the challenges we face with the ongoing changing climate – and thus the acknowledgment of that there is no necessary barrier between urban life and nature. Still there is a long way to go in practice, mentality, respect and knowledge of our surrounding world in order to adopt a nature-friendly way of living as the foundation of all our activities.

The motivation behind this memorial volume to Nature is the urge to make people live in a nature-friendly way no matter where they live. In order to choose to live in such a way we must have access to knowledge, information, dare to speak our own mind, and be in possession of the love and will to act accordingly. The joy, which here is connected to the experience of the heritage from nature, might generate more joy for more people by increasing the extension and intensity of it, by taking care of it and give it a living space. Perhaps the enjoyment of nature is the best starting point for a nature-friendly life style to be developed in urban areas? In order to realize that, I believe we should stop chasing nature out of our cities and urban areas, and instead invite nature to join us – to be around us and realize that we are ourselves part of nature.

Meeting urban nature

When I enter Frognerparken in Oslo my body is grounded – I imagine almost like the plant roots itself in the soil, and my soul becomes calm. The connection between nature in the park and me is spontaneous. The long alleys between the tall trees, the big lawns stretching out and covering the varied topography of the park landscape. All over the park there are the sculptures by Gustav Vigeland (Norwegian sculptor,1869–1943); the park's official name is Vigelandsparken, and is dedicated to Vigelands sculptural works. It was he who conceived of the plan and presented it to the municipality of Oslo, and Oslo in turn offered him to use the area, which since the start of the works in 1928 has been an important place of recreation and beauty for people; inhabitants and visitors alike. Inside the park life is in a way put outside down compared to the busy city life outside of it. The continuity into which one enters is not measured in time but in duration. In nature duration is visible. Duration is a non-measurable entity between two points of time. Duration is attached to every form of life and has a qualitative character, neither can it be reduced to parts or be subject to analysis. It is continuous development that excludes repetition – here understood as a one to one copy of the previous. The duration opens up the possibility for a rhythmically rebirth (here our ability to recognize patterns appears). In nature duration is present in the changing seasons where an ongoing life process ensures a preservation and rejuvenation of the nature. To me meeting nature is a reminder of the origins of life – my own nature. This is a place where silence might reign, and the calm sound scape might offer a space for afterthought and a peace of mind.

The role and place of Nature in future cities and urban areas

Historically cities were established as a defense against intruders, and as political centers (i.e. the Greek *polis*). Time has taught us that enemies do not only arrive from the outside, but might as well be nurtured in ourselves. We know that an enemy is not necessarily the result of hatred or lack of friendship, but might as well be the result of a lack of knowledge and of understanding.

Today about 80% of the Norwegian population lives in cities. In the years to come an increasing number of us will continue to establish ourselves in cities – mostly in the eastern part of Norway. Of Norway's population of 4.8 million, nearly 2.7 million live in the eastern part (July 2009, Statistics Norway). Why is that? Most people prefer to live in the cities because of the job and education possibilities, the access to subcultures, a better and more diversified offer than in the countryside and in general a higher degree of possibilities. Due to the fact that there will be many more people in the cities in the years to come, that far more children will pass their childhood there and a high number of grownups will become old people there, it is very important that we have good outdoor areas, parks, playing grounds and green lungs. Tall and obscure buildings standing side by side on tight places, the lack of possibility for an outdoor life in natural conditions in the cities are not a good way of planning for the life of future generations. This is because nature by itself is good for the common health and because the presence of nature teaches us how to respect, enjoy and take care of it.

An increasing population in the cities in the years to come raises some very important issues that must be handled by the politicians, and these issues demand a strong vision combined with knowledge of and respect for nature while planning for the development of infrastructure, housing and service areas. The fact is that the areas at hand are under a strong pressure. How we want to plan and construct our cities must be based on demands supporting a sustainable and nature-friendly policy. The green areas in the cities ought to have the same political status as the policy for the open air/outdoor life. Since 2010 several action groups appeared in Norway, as in Bodø with the group Preserve Rønnvikjordene, in Oslo with the Network for green lungs, or in Arendal where people are engaged in getting a park in the city etc.

Urban nature has seen a dramatic reduction in the last years and people are fighting to stop this trend. The dismantling of urban nature should be seen in connection with the political goal of offering a place in a kindergarten to every child under school age in Norway as well as the overall goal of densification from the early 1990s onwards. This started as an effort to limit the expansion of cities because it would lead to an increased need for transport, higher emissions of CO_2, and the dismantling of cultivated land and forests outside of the cities. Still cities represent a more sustainable way of living than life the countryside. In the cities it is easier to develop public and common solutions than in the countryside where people live further apart from each other and are dependent of cars to get around. Still it is of great importance that the planning of the cities has a clear vision of what a good life in the city should be like. Further it is important to invite inhabitants to participate in the development of their own living areas. People today are well informed and educated and they want to take an active part in the shaping of their living environment. An important part of that is the maintaining of the green areas and parks in order to ensure that people have an access to urban nature. The challenge is to establish a nationwide and compulsory dedication to this work over time.

Together

Our reflections about the origins of life, its meaning and development do not take place in a void. We are here together with other creatures. The knowledge of and understanding that we are part of a complex life system whose climatic and nutritional conditions are undergoing major changes opens up the possibility of an eco-philosophical approach to life in general and to our fellow creatures. Such an approach might enable us to meet and solve the challenges – not with fear but with a joyous love and respect for life.

In general, culture is defined in opposition to nature. Culture represents something human made: be it agriculture, a piece of art, architecture, urbanization, the planning of cities and societies. Nature is not made by any human being; it is original, it is present around us and within us, it is the very foundation of life. Still the distinction between the two is not unambiguously. Partly thanks to technological developments, but also because cultural and natural elements might live side by side. And we need to combine them in our lives. Cities and villages are such places where high-tech solutions and "primitive" nature should, could and ought to live side by side…

A nature-friendly life

What does it mean to live in nature-friendly way? To be clever in handling your own waste, to bike and walk instead of driving your car, to let your shopping habits be led by what you need and not your impulses? Does a nature-friendly lifestyle imply a series of environmental correctly deeds, or an attitude and recognition of the life cycle of which we are a part? I believe we need both: we need to act according to knowledge about our world and we need to change and develop our attitudes towards the living world around us.

Today we are forced to rethink our way of living because of the big climate changes taking place all over the world. A reassessment that also sheds a light over the fact that other life forms are threatened by our way of organizing our lives. Slowly we are getting aware of our lack of understanding for and evaluation of life forms such as animals and plants. And slowly we are accepting that the traditional hierarchy where we are on the top of the food chain is in for change. Nature does not exist for our sake. Nature exists for its own sake. Nature has its own intrinsic value which is of great importance to us, to our life quality and our survival. It is an established truth that we, the human beings are without importance to Nature.

A love and understanding for everything

When you love something or somebody, you love the entity not the single parts. Love is feeling, insight, recognition and a will to act. Love might be directed towards oneself, other people, animals and nature. Love is a source of joy bringing forth the qualities of the beloved and in one self.

The eco-philosophy represents a will to consider the entirety we are a part of, using emotions and empathy, and to make this a basis for the development of the society. In an article for the weekly newspaper *Dag og Tid* in 2004, Sigmund Kvaløy Setreng (Norwegian philosopher and farmer) called for the committed amateur wanting to alter the society as a counterpart to the ruling specialists, both as a defense for democracy and for the nature. In our context this attitude makes sense. An amateur (of Latin *amare* – to love) is someone who loves. In order to get rid of the utilitarian way of thinking and the expert ruling's perspective on nature, Setreng is looking for a super amateur, that is a committed citizen with the necessary amount of knowledge, courage and empathy to resist any form of enforced silence by the experts in private and public sector. This engagement is kept alive by the wish to find a way out of the problems:

> *Today we are facing a total "systemic crisis", it means a crisis where we are witnessing attacks on everything, from attacks on the body and soul of the individual, to the civil system and the nature within which everything is functioning. The task of the eco-philosophy is to try and understand this critical development, above all in its entirety, and with this approach as our starting point to present alternative ways to get out of this situation and into something new and more expedient.*

Setreng presented an important reminder about the limits of the natural sciences:

> *These are sciences that can offer us useful knowledge, but no counsel in value questions. We must ourselves clarify the assumptions and values we stand for. We also need empathy, because without it we*

will hardly be able to act. Emotions are within the limits of our
task, and have a right to be taken into account. The eco-philosophy
is an overall commitment. It ought to be just as embracing as the
attacks we are witnessing on human society and ecosystems to day.
Overconsumption, destruction of the nature and the unfortunate
effects on society and culture are threatening our civilization. The
academic tradition is the true child of the competitive and industrial
system, and is unfortunately imposing limitations we have to criticize
and even oppose. The sciences have a long tradition for separating
and dividing in order to gain knowledge and insight; the part has
been central. This particle-founded knowledge is imposed on the an-
organic and organic nature as well as on human society alike. (Dag
og Tid, issue number 18, Friday 30. April 2004.)

A good sound environment

Since 1963 the Norwegian Association against Noise (NFMS) has worked
for a nature where natural sounds dominate, and a society with good sound
environments because this is of vital importance to people's health and life
quality; people's health deteriorate from being exposed to a continuous noise.
The noise pollution is met with the particle-based understanding Setreng is
talking about. Noise is treated as an unimportant secondary effect of pollution,
and is standing far behind in the queue of urgent environmental tasks; one
seldom hears about noise in the environmental debate. The perception of
noise is protected by people's understanding of it as something you have to
live with and accept when you live in urban areas. Then you have to tolerate
noise, and you get used to it. You never get used to noise, even you believe
you don't pay attention to it, your body does. Cardiovascular diseases are
connected with a permanent exposure to noise. Adding to this, the politician's
lack of will to implement their own goals for reducing noise levels on a local
and national level, there is no wonder that noise leads a silent existence in the
individual and collective conscience.

Noise is a type of pollution to be equaled with, for instance, local air pollution,
and since the 1970s onwards both politicians and health professionals have
been aware of the negative health effects of noise. The increasing offer and
use of noisy items ought to bring forward a considerate use of them because
what is sound to the user might be noise for the involuntary listener. Also
living close together demands a considerate way of living, when playing music

or restoring your flat you have to take into account that your neighbors are involuntary participants listening to your activities. Therefore, house rules and statues are important ways of preventing problems among neighbors, and should be regarded as such.

The biggest source to noise pollution is the transport sector, and above all the cars and trucks. Therefor it is important to see a reduction in air pollution in connection with a reduction in noise pollution. Since 2000 noise from the transport sector has risen by 9% according to Statistics Norway. That is the opposite development of what has been stated in the national environmental policy, goals, projects and statements in Norway. Traditionally outdoor life and nature enjoy a greater protection than life in the cities. That might be due to the long traditions for a life outside and for searching peace and quiet in nature. In a survey done by the Norwegian Trekking Association in 1999, 90% of the participants answered that silence was their main reason to be in the nature. That's is why it is important to preserve the sound environment in nature through, among other things, a restrictive legislation.

As most people live in the cities and living means passing the majority of your time there, planning for a good sound environment should be just as evident as planning for a good public transport system. Nils Faarlund has for years been offering "sound walks" in urban areas to make people aware of the permanent sounds and the different qualities of them that surround them. Together with Faarlund, NFMS has offered sound walks to politicians in order to raise their knowledge and awareness of the importance of sound and noise in areas where many people live together, and to connect this issue to the planning and regulation of dwelling areas.

Consciousness and noise

In his essay "Consciousness and noise", the philosopher Hans Kolstad talks about the effects of noise on our consciousness and the fact that today's approach to the problem is insufficient:

> It is typical of today's debate that the noise phenomenon is related
> to two main factors, the administrative/political and the physical/
> bodily or the health aspects of it. In the first case one satisfies oneself
> by considering the phenomenon by measuring it and by categorizing
> it in relation to a given level. In the second case one points to the
> health-related effects and dangers due to the phenomenon. What

one doesn't do is to assess the phenomenon in relation to perhaps the
most important factor of them all, namely the consciousness; or said
in another way: to the living human being whose consciousness lives
and unfolds itself within a framework of noise. Noise paralyzes the
consciousness whose creative and dynamic expression is prevented
by the noise. Since this is the essential part of the human existence,
noise is actually preventing people from being human. And here
we are at the very core of today's environmental debate: We need
an environment that enforces the human, and not destroy it. Noise
makes the society inhuman.

Thus, our cities must be developed and constructed with the human needs at its center. That means by ensuring that urban nature and sound environment have an obvious status in our societies, that the cars must give way to parks and green areas. It is the organic life in nature and the changing seasons that is the basic for our humanity – not traffic machines.

The motivation behind this memorial is to make people chose to live in a nature-friendly way. Choosing presupposes knowledge, love and action. A joyous life is attached to the heritage from nature, and might increase by taking care of it and cultivating it. I started this article by saying that perhaps joy is the best starting point to develop an urban nature in the cities. So let us stop chasing nature out of our cities and instead invite it into them – to be around us and with us. We need it so much.

Happy the man whose pleasures are simple

GJERMUND ANDERSEN

Early morning in January in the cabin in the forest. Freezing cold indoors. I slip out of my sleeping bag to light the fire in the wood stove, then lie back and enjoy how the flames crackle while the yellow light from the air hole dances on the wall. Feel the heat penetrate the room. Ready for a new day in the forest.

Skis glide over the glittering snow-crystals. I hear a faint tinkle when the ski-tips score the white blanket of snow. Cold blue light over the forest. The February full moon illuminates the clearings. But where the trees are dense: a mysterious darkness. The night invites me to make my journey a long one.

Soaring summits, snowdrifts hanging over sheer cliff faces. The last rays of the sun turn the western slopes to gold. Our ski tracks meander across the landscape behind us. It's almost evening; time to set up camp for the night. Everyone knows the routine. Before the tent is pitched, water is already boiling on the primus. Dry woolen singlets next to the skin, the wet ones over them to dry out. Ready for another relaxing evening in the tent, another winter night in the mountains.

What was that? Pitch black night in the shelter. Half past four. Sounded like…? Yes! I hear it again – the capercaillie's ancient display call, slow at first, then faster and faster and ending with a sound like a reluctant cork leaving the neck of a wine bottle, and then a scraping sound like a blunt bow saw cutting a frozen log. Outside, we catch a glimpse of the primeval bird, posing with its tail spread – ready to defend its territory. Ready for the spring's greatest theatrical performance.

Early morning in May. An icy crust makes the snow as hard as iron. We pull down the tent and now we are ready. Cold and stiff in our limbs after the night. We eat breakfast quickly; we need to go before the sun melts the snow and makes it rotten and prevents us from continuing. We are lucky, we get five or six hours enjoying ourselves on our skis on the vast mountain plateau, before we have to find a bare patch to pitch the tent again.

A night in June, long and light. We cycle to the end of the road, and from there on we have virgin forest. The daylight won't yield; even in the middle of the night it's light enough for us to find our way. Down to the edge of the water, under a towering pine. We light an illegal campfire, make a toasted cheese sandwich and a hot dog. And since it's midsummer, we treat ourselves to a bottle of beer with the food. Coffee and a slice of cake for dessert. Then we go further, to the viewpoint where the rising sun is at its most impressive. Here it's good to be alive.

The heat persists. All the lakes are lukewarm. It's fine in the forest, but hot walking when the ground is uneven. It's not so hard to overcome my childhood fear of water; a cool, bracing dip in a lake provides the relief I need. I lie naked on the rocks to dry myself in the sun and wind. A bird swims nearer, oblivious of the presence of a human intruder. It's a black-throated diver – and sure enough, it dives and then surfaces again. Gathering food for its chicks? It'll get a shock when I stand up!

Abundance! We have enough golden cloudberries to guarantee our supply of homemade liqueur. Now the time has come for blueberries. Not only for pancakes, as the husband of Mrs Pepperpot might have said. We are lucky: just pop out into the woods and we can pluck as many berries as we want. Not fair, some will say, since most of the berries will have no one to pluck them.

What colors! September in the mountains! Enough said.

Scary? No, magical! The mist descends wistfully on the skirts of the fir trees and covers the cones on the pine trees. A majestic dead pine stands like a black monument in the grey landscape. Everything is damp; the branches of the fir trees have got their own shade of green. The birches have shed their leaves and the forest floor emerges covered with moss and heather. A time for melancholy, but also for getting to know the soul of the forest. No need to travel to the other side of the world if you have learnt to be friends with the seasons. The forest is awesome, also in the autumn.

The first snow in November. The marshes are frozen, cranberries are red-grey in the peat moss. And then the snow comes drifting, cautiously at first, turning the world grey. The trees turn grey, the heather turns grey, the ice on the pools turns white. Winter is on its way, but we can still wander around in the woods without skis. enjoying the shortening days in a fairy-tale world.

It will soon be Christmas. In the shopping centers the chaos is complete, but for those who know better there are other pleasures. Try an evening in December with good friends, make a campfire with a couple of logs. It gets dark around four o'clock, plenty of time to discuss what's on your minds before creeping into your sleeping bags around midnight. Nothing can compare with sitting round a campfire, feeling the warmth and the friendship, watching the sparks and enjoying simply being alive.

Spring comes on nicely

KNUD HAMSUN

Spring comes on nicely in the fields,
the animals awakening to giggle and flirt,
the fir trees all cracking with resin,
that life's elixir dripping into the dirt.
The stars above silent and pale as comes the day,
The birds below now beginning to play.

It brightens everywhere
as one by one the stars homeward return,
and from beyond the world's edge
a vast fire breaks forth to burn.
The sun, the sun, God's flaming eye,
resting upon a river on high.

By what sorcery is the Earth aroused?
All its bosoms heaving,
all its limbs stirring,
and all hearts hard beating.
Morning mist rises from the river along,
to much howling and brawling, a tumult in song.

Behold, spring comes to the valley.
The lean bear awakens from sleep to roar,
and high over the western mountains
the royal eagle does soar.
In all houses is preparation on for the youth
to wed in chastity and truth.

Let spring sound out over the Earth!
And within this music of nature so vast
comes a humming from my heart,
of thanks for each spring gone past.
My chest throbs to its hoof beats and cheers,
and my eyes well up with tears.

The taste of water

BEA REUTER AND ULRIKE SCHENK

Summer

Karl plunges the paddle into the water again and again. It is a beautiful summer day. He sits in his canoe, and is on the way down the river. What a great silence! He is alone, all alone in the Norwegian wilderness. Karl is strong. He keeps on paddling the whole day. He proposed himself to reach the entire river down towards the sea. For sure, there are more extreme adventures like a hiking trip across Norway, or a skiing trip to the South Pole. But for Karl, this is extremely enough. He is German and comes from a big city. There are no rivers like this in his hometown. Karl is a doctor and 42 years old. He likes his job and works like a madman. Sometimes, of course, it is getting too much and he needs a break. He has never been to Norway before, but he has seen lots of pictures of the beautiful landscape there. Now, he finally arrived in this wonderful nature. The river is in his sight.

The only thing he has to do, is to paddle. All he needs for the next ten days is stowed in his canoe: food, a camp stove, clothes, a tent, a sleeping bag and a roll mat. Didn't he forget anything? This is the first trip, where he has not to carry drinking water in heavy bottles. In a travel guide, he has been reading that it is possible to drink the water directly out of streams and lakes in Norway. And now the time has come to taste it. He puts the paddle into the boat, and bends over the edge of the canoe. With his hands, he takes some water out of the river and drinks. "What a taste! That's great! I can get fresh and clear water at any time I want." He is leaning back, drifting down the river and looking at the blue sky.

In the evening, he sets up his tent right on the riverbank, cooks some food on the camp stove and says to himself, "That's wonderful. No stress. I'm all alone. And nobody is asking stupid questions." Soon after, he crawls into his sleeping bag and falls into deep sleep. The following days are pretty much the same: Karl paddles 25 to 35 kilometres a day, passes the beautiful landscape, sets up his tent in the evening, eats and sleeps. Then the last day has come. Karl enjoys the beautiful landscape for the last time. While he is gazing into some buttercups, which are in full bloom, Karl saddens. He realizes, that the journey draws to a close. Soon he will reach the town by the sea, from where he will return home.

Back in Germany, the alarm clock rings at six o'clock the next morning. Karl has to hurry out of bed. While he is searching after his jacket, he takes a sip of his coffee. Out of the house, down to the subway and right at work. Doctor Karl takes the morning visit. Five hours without a break. He is tired. Nevertheless, both body and brain work well at work. He cares for his patients as much as possible. When he sits down in the break room with another cup of coffee, he notices that his thoughts are still somewhere in between Norway and Germany. "The time in Norway passed all too fast," he thinks, daydreaming about the experiences from the paddle trip. Suddenly, he is interrupted by colleagues entering the break room. "Hey Karl, tell about your Norwegian expedition! Did you paddle right up to the Arctic Circle?" "Eh, what?" Karl replies, as he wakes from his daydreams. "Well, your expedition! Do you deserve a gold medal? He-he-he!" "No, maybe not that, but I had a great time in Norway, you know. Just imagine, Stefan, the water was so clean up there that I could drink right out of the river. It was amazing." "Okay? That was all you experienced? Didn't you plan a giant adventure down the river through white water rapids? Once, I saw an adventure report on TV, where some people paddled through rapids, it was awesome. They screamed and were completely hyper when they returned to the shore." "You know, I paddled through many rapids as well, and the boat almost overturned, but I managed to keep balance. I kept on paddling, until I was completely exhausted. It was fun!" "Cool, and you did that just in a normal canoe? Maybe we should conquer a peak on foot together next time! May I join you?" "Of course!" Karl says, while being a little scared of thinking about such a trip. Was that what he really wanted? Before he thinks through to the end, he is called into the emergency room. Here one must act quickly. He starts running. And so it goes in the following weeks: Little time for reflection, lots of time at work. And the summit ascent has never been mentioned again.

One day at the hospital, Christine says, "Karl, you are looking bad. You need a break! Otherwise, you can soon find yourself in one of these beds, and be treated by us." "That's true! But what should I do?" Karl asks. "I guess, we are enough people here at the hospital, and overtime you have more than enough. Take a week off!"

Autumn

No sooner said than done. In autumn, Karl travels to Norway again. This time without canoe. He has decided to do a hiking trip from cabin to cabin in the Norwegian mountains. His backpack is heavy, but it is not as heavy as the work pressure at home. He is in a good mood. Surrounded by a great landscape dressed in autumn colours, he whistles a song. The heather blossoms purple, the leaves of the dwarf birch have a deep red colour. Karl collects blueberries, and can't almost stop eating. In the evening, he reaches the first cabin. He lights a fire in the stove, and fetches a pail of water from the stream, which babbles nearby. He cooks a meal. Candles must be lit, for there is no electricity inside. "It's so cosy in here!" he says to himself. It was a long day. He cannot keep his eyes open anymore and falls asleep.

The next morning, it is pouring with rain. Karl is having breakfast and is in a bad mood. "It was so lovely with the sun yesterday," Karl thinks. He leaves the table to get another cup of coffee. As he rises, he bumps into a shelf. A book falls down. Karl picks it up to put it back in place. Then he discovers the title, "Walden; or, Life in the Woods". He has never heard of it. With the coffee cup in his hand, he returns to the sofa. The rain drums on the roof. He opens the book. It starts like this:

I do not propose to write an ode to dejection, but to brag as lustily as chanticleer in the morning, standing on his roost, if only to wake my neighbours up.[106]

It is the journal of Henry David Thoreau, who moved into the woods. There he lived for two years and two months in a cabin that he built with his own hands. After a while, Karl is completely lost in the book, and is preoccupied in thought. He forgot the time. Suddenly, he gets up, just like waking up from a dream. "Oh no! What time is it?" he shouts out loud. "12 o'clock!" He has no chance to reach the next cabin before it gets dark, and decides to stay one more night. It is still raining. He lights a fire in the stove, makes some coffee, and immerses himself in the book again.

Every morning was a cheerful invitation to make my life of equal simplicity, and I may say innocence, with Nature herself. [...] I got up early and bathed in the pond; that was a religious exercise, and one of the best things which I did.[107]

---

106 Henry David Thoreau (1854), *Walden; or, Life in the Woods*, p. 92. Boston: Ticknor And Fields

107 Henry David Thoreau (1854), *Walden; or, Life in the Woods*, p. 96. Boston: Ticknor And Fields.

He looks up from the book and stares into space. The next morning, he gets up early and goes down to the lake nearby. He takes off his clothes and jumps into the cold water. He gets out of the water again and stands stark naked by the lake. He admires the sunrise. "Great!" It will be a fine autumn day. Not a cloud in the sky. The wind strokes his skin, which dries slowly by itself. Karl takes a deep breath. While the early sunbeams rise over the mountains, he looks at the beautiful landscape. On the way back to the cabin, he gets the idea to pick some blueberries for breakfast. There are plenty of blueberries around the cabin, which he picks up in a small bucket. He is completely absorbed in harvesting. Time is standing still. After two hours, he starts up. The sun is already in the south, when he realizes, that it is too late again to reach the next hut. "Never mind!" he thinks, while cooking a lovely blueberry soup, which he will eat in the sun in front of the hut.

In the afternoon, he sits down by the stream and continues to read the book "Walden". "If Thoreau managed to stay for over two years at one place, well, than I can for sure stay at this cabin for four days." In the next two days, he goes on a few hikes near the cottage. Sitting dwelling upon a stream, his thoughts are flowing freely, and Karl loses the sense of space and time. However, the time passes, and in the morning of the last day of his trip, he has to leave the cabin to get back to the starting point. From there he travels home to Germany.

This time he went back on a Saturday, so he has one extra day off, before he has to start working again. Karl is sitting on his sofa staring out of the window. It is raining. The big city appears oppressively drab and grey. In his mind's eye, the whole trip to Norway recalls the past. And of course, he is thinking about Thoreau's life in the middle of the woods. "It must be wonderful to have so much time for yourself and your thoughts. I am glad to have experienced at least a touch of this feeling." And so, the day goes by with daydreaming, and he falls into deep sleep until the alarm clock is ringing on Monday morning. Karl can't be bothered to work. He'd love nothing better than to return to Norway.

But for all that, the reality catches up with him. He gets up, has breakfast, puts on his shoes, grabs his jacket and runs to the subway. In a professional and seasoned way, he gets his job done at the hospital. There is not much contact with colleagues this day. He is just running from patient to patient. Actually, he is quite happy that nobody is asking a question about his trip. Only with colleague Christine, he bandies a few words. "What happened to you, Karl? You're talking so slowly!" she remarks. "Oh, do you think so?" Karl replies on the go down the hallway. He is wondering, "What did she mean by that? Am I appearing so sluggish?"

Next evening, he meets some friends in the pub: Holger, Michael and his wife Claudia. Holger starts the conversation with, "Karl, tell me, how was your hiking trip? Did you summit some mountain peaks? Did you follow in Reinhold Messner's footsteps?" "And what about the weather?" Claudia tosses in. "How many kilometres did you manage to walk? Did you see some elks or bears?" Michael asks in a breath. Karl faces the barrage of questions, and tries to find some answers. The weather, yes, that's easiest to answer. "On the first days, it was a lot of rain," he starts to tell. "So, I decided not to go all the way from cabin to cabin as I had planned. I stayed at the first cabin for four days." "Four days at one and the same cabin?" Claudia asks. "Were there many people?" "No! I was all alone." "Oh my God! Poor you! All alone at a mountain cabin in the rain?" Michael notes. "It was actually fine. At the beginning, I was saddish about the rain, but now I'm really glad, that it happened. It was totally relaxing. I've been reading a book, which I've found in the hut. It was about a man, who lived round about two years alone in a cabin in the middle of the woods, and he describes his life in this book." "Oh, how exciting!" Holger says with an ironic undertone. "Karl, the hermit! Well, that wasn't the aim of your trip, was it?" "You're right, Holger, it went to be totally different than originally planned. But what I got out of it, is the experience of a great silence and of being free." Speaking those words, the longing for the mountains is written all over his face. "If only I could, I would like to live like that in my everyday life from time to time." "Then you have to move to your aunt's allotment! He-he-he!" Holger comments. Michael and Claudia are laughing as well. "You don't understand anything!" Karl thinks, and decides not to tell more about his trip. The evening at the pub continues with some beers and lots of talk about this and that. On the way home, Karl thinks, "Not even my friends understand, what I'm trying to express! Maybe I'm a little weird?" At home, he is lying awake almost until the alarm clock rings, to remind him that the daily routines will continue. He drags himself out of bed, struggles to go to work, and regrets the last beer he took in the pub. He has a headache.

Days and weeks are going by as usual. One day, Karl is sitting in the break room, thinking, "It's not yet three weeks ago, since I left my oasis in the Norwegian mountains. It feels like an eternity. It's a pity that the noise, the stress and the dull routine of everyday life has taken over again, so that I can hardly remember the silence." This evening, he does not join the pub crawl. Karl is not in the mood to meet people. However, at home on the sofa, he feels tired, lonely, and misunderstood by the whole world. "Everything goes so fast in everyday life. It's almost impossible to follow without being completely burnt out. How did I manage that for all these years? And why did everything feel so easy and simple up in the mountains?" He is puzzled about his own thoughts. There is chaos in his mind, and he does not know, how to handle this condition. He has always been so sovereign, brilliant at work, and he never had problems to deal with the people around him. He was everybody's darling. "Did I really become a hermit, as Holger called me?"

A few weeks later, Karl gets an offer from his colleagues. "Will you join us on our trip to St. Moritz? Alpine skiing and après-ski with lots of beer. Sounds great, doesn't it? Just think about it! The whole clique will come along!" "Hm, sounds good, I'll think about it," he replies, noncommittal. "Come on, Karl, it will be fun!" He just answers with a tormented smile, says goodbye and leaves the hospital. "Pull yourself up, Karl! Maybe I should just do that, it'll be fun in St. Moritz," he says to himself, while waiting for the subway. "And it's nice, that they organize this trip." Suddenly, the loudspeaker comes on and announces a one-hour delay of the subway. Karl is tired from work. It is cold and dark. "That's the last thing I needed!" he scolds. Out of sheer rage, he kicks at a dustbin. Everything is going wrong right now. He does not want to wait for an hour, and decides to go home by foot. Karl has never done that before. Surrounded by beautiful old buildings, he walks through narrow streets in the old town. There is a bit of snow on the roofs and in the streets. He takes a deep breath. The air is cold. Out of some of the apartments, warm candlelight is shining. Karl puts one foot in front of the other. Suddenly, the image of the cabin in Norway appears in his mind. He looks around. There is nothing that reminds him of the Norwegian mountains. But then, he notices the fireplace smell coming from the chimneys. "It was that smell – calling up the memories in my mind!" he thinks, moved by deep longing for the freedom, he had experienced in the mountains. "I have to get back to the cabin in Norway in the winter holidays," he concludes, walking on with a smile on his face. Now, it is easy to make a decision – against St. Moritz. When he arrives at home, he feels recovered and balanced. He did not even notice that it took one hour to walk all the way home from the hospital. A few days later Karl is taking a look around in a second-hand bookshop. There he gets hold of a book entitled "A Winter Idyll" by Karl Stieler. "Well, that fits perfectly!" he thinks. "I'll take it with me to Norway."

Winter

In Norway, he finds a winter wonderland, a white landscape just like in a fairy tale. Karl puts his new skis on, and enters the snow paradise towards the cabin. Almost without effort, he glides over the snow, impressed by the fact that he can just cross the lakes he knows from the summer and the autumn, which are frozen and covered by snow now. After almost three hours on skis three hours walk on the skis, he takes a break. He is sitting on a resting pad in the snow, taking lunch and drinking tea from the thermos flask. "Wow, it's so silent and peaceful out here," he considers before he continues his trip. After two more hours he reaches the small cabin. To get inside, he has to shovel the snow in front of the door. Inside the cabin it is so cold that he can see his breath. "I have to start the fire in the stove," is his first thought while looking for firewood and matches. After he got the fire burning, he squats in front of the stove. However, he has to go out again to get some snow to melt. On the stove, it takes quite a while before the snow turns into water. He brews up a cup of tea and cooks some food, and then he is sitting on the sofa covered by a woollen blanket. He feels happy to get some warmth inside his body. Eventually, it gets really warm and cosy in the cabin. "Finally, I'm here again," he mumbles before he falls into deep sleep, as always here in the mountains.

The next morning, he takes a look out of the window. It is snowing and the wind is blowing outside. But still he feels the urge to get out. After breakfast, he puts on his skis and enters the white wilderness. It is not as easy as it was the day before, when the sun was shining. He must constantly be aware not to get lost. The tracks he is dragging in the snow are all blown away just after a short while. His hands are cold as ice. "I have to get back," he resolves. Fortunately, he has following wind on his way back to the cabin. Inside there it is still warm and cosy. After a while holding them near the stove, he can feel his fingertips again. Outside the wind is still howling. With a cup of hot chocolate in his hands, Karl is leaning back on the sofa. The stove crackles. It feels marvellous to be inside here.

The next day, the storm has stopped and a light blue sky is waiting outside, inviting him for one more tour on the skis. Today he can see the nature in all its glory. It looks completely different than in the autumn. But he still recognizes some details. There is the ledge, where he was seeking a refuge, when it was starting to rain. And there is the brook, where he was sitting reading the book.

Karl takes off his skis, lies down on the roll mat that he took with him, and closes his eyes. Without any movement, he is lying there, just listening to the sounds of nature. But there is no sound to hear. It is completely quiet. No brook, no bird, no wind. Absolutely nothing. The only thing he can hear is his own heart beating. He never experienced such a peace and quietness before. On his face, he feels the delightful warmth of the sunrays. Completely intoxicated by this great silence, he can do nothing but remain lying there. After about one hour he gets up, a little dazed, and continues the skiing trip until he reaches a plateau. Standing up there, in the middle of nowhere, it hits him, "Here I'm feeling free. Free to be myself, nothing and no one disturbing me."

In the evening, when he is back in the cabin, he takes the book he had bought in Germany out of his backpack. "A Winter Idyll", written by the German poet Karl Stieler. It is an old book from 1885 with a beautiful cover. He opens the book, and already after some verses he has been reading, he recognizes that there is something familiar with the scenery which is described there and his own perception of these days in Norway. It is about the great silence in the winter mountains. Karl continues reading. The poem describes a way of life in nature – out of the poet's perspective. Naturally, there is also another lifestyle existing on the other hand. Life in sociability, with partying and amusement all night long. A lifestyle the poet opted out of – to rather find happiness in solitude. Deliberating about whether the life in solitude or the life in sociability is to prefer, the poet wonders:

> *Who got the best part?*
> *I knew it well, but I must not say it.*
> *My room was silent and my way snowbound,*
> *But lonesome not was my loneliness,*
> *As I listened to my heart as a quiet scout*
> *And bonded this life*
> *Into the context of the age-old life,*
> *It may sound simple. – Who stood humans closer?*[108]

While reading these lines suddenly his colleagues – who he has not thought about a single second in the last few days – appear on Karl's mind. "Yes, they are for sure having fun at the après ski in St. Moritz at this moment." "*Who got the best part? I knew it well, but I must not say it.*" He is filled with satisfaction

---

108 Karl Stieler (1885), "Ein Winteridyll", p. 36. Leipzig: Insel-Verlag.
German original text:
Wer hat das beßre Teil davongetragen?
Ich wüßt es wohl, doch darf ich es nicht sagen.
Stumm war mein Zimmer und mein Weg verschneit,
Doch einsam nicht war meine Einsamkeit,
Da ich mein Herz belauscht als stiller Späher
Und eingefügt in den Zusammenhang
Uralten Lebens diesen Lebensgang,
So schlicht es ist. – Wer stand den Menschen näher?

while wondering about these lines. The end of the six days in the mountains is near. The winter idyll is over. Karl has to travel back to Germany again.

Out of solitude right into amusement: It is the boss' birthday. All employees are gathered in the staff canteen. The whole clique just came back home from St. Moritz, and around the buffet there is a lot of talk about all the adventures from their skiing trip. Karl is standing there in the middle of the crowded canteen without being particularly affected by what they are talking about. But of course, he is questioned about his trip to Norway as well. "It was fine, thanks," he replies friendly and briefly. As he is listening to his own words, he reminds the last lines in the book he has been reading in the cabin.

When I'm back home, they will surely ask me,
What I have experienced? – But then I remain silent.
What I have experienced? ... Nothing. – Just idyll.[109]

"Oh, it was fine! And that's all you have to tell about your winter expedition, Karl?" responds Stefan in an ironic tone. "You should have joined us; it was great fun!" "Yes, maybe," Karl answers. The conversation is finished as both concentrate on the buffet again while Karl wonders, "Maybe it is sometimes best to keep things for yourself. They will never understand the depth of what I experienced. It just cannot be described with words."

Karl leaves the hospital after a long working day. It is a cold and clear winter evening. The air is fresh, and he decides to walk home instead of taking the subway. He is happy that the working day is over, and that he can walk alone for a while, without being surrounded by people. He still can feel the inner tranquillity he brought with him from the Norwegian mountains. Moving through the streets of the city, he is thinking, "I don't want to lose this feeling again. Is it possible to keep it in everyday life? What has actually happened to me, since I came back from the paddling trip last summer? It must have been something that really affected me, otherwise it would not have provoked such a chaos inside myself."

The next Saturday, he walks around in the crowded pedestrian street to do some errands. Out of a sudden, he recognizes what it was, that knocked him out of the everyday routines that he has been following for years without

---

109 Karl Stieler (1885), "Ein Winteridyll", p. 36. Leipzig: Insel-Verlag.
German original text:
Wenn ich daheim bin, werden sie wohl fragen,
Was ich erlebte? – Doch dann schweig ich still.
Was ich erlebte?... Nichts. – Nur ein Idyll.

putting them into question: He experienced an alternative. The simple life in a secluded cabin surrounded by nature. A life merely concerning the basic human needs like motion, keeping warm, sleeping, eating and drinking. The only thing he had to do up there in the mountains was to follow the rhythm of nature shown up in the shifting weather, without having control over it. "If I look at myself as a natural being, then it is not that strange that I felt more like being home in this 'natural' rhythm than here in the city, where most of the people are rushing around as they were on the run. Here I miss the silence, the tranquillity and the feeling of having time at leisure. There I experienced the outflow of thoughts and dreams, based on this indescribable feeling of freedom, when I was moving freely in the natural terrain. It was magnificent. Drinking water directly from the stream. That felt like in paradise. Even in the winter it was possible to get fresh water, just melting the snow. Those were moments which felt like pure luxury," he reminisces in a trace of melancholy. Karl remembers that the water in the winter tasted differently than in the summer, "It really tasted a little like snow."

Immersed in his own thoughts, he bumps into a man in the pedestrian zone. "Oh, I'm sorry," Karl says. But the man does not hear and just moves on. This clash tears Karl abruptly out of his thoughts. "Oh my God, now I really start to ponder about the taste of water. If I tell that to any of my friends or colleagues, they will for sure think I am going slightly mad." That is what he is considering on the way out of the pedestrian street towards a park. He already can see the trees. They are still bare. Arriving in the park, he pauses for a moment and watches the ducks swimming in the pond. "Somehow I am stuck in a dilemma now," he continues to ponder. "I have been touched by the great silence and the freedom in the Norwegian mountains, but my everyday life is here in the city. And it has its advantages. I like my job and here I have friends. I enjoy going to the cinema, the theatre and concerts. Here in the park, I can take a walk. That's nice. Nevertheless, there is the danger of getting caught up in the stream of hectic bustle, which is difficult to get out of. Anyhow, I have no plans of getting out of civilization and living in the wilderness instead. That cannot be the solution. It must be something else I have to change, in order to find new orientation in life."

Karl is moved by such thoughts now and then in the next time. One evening he is sitting and reading in the book "Fatu Hiva" by Thor Heyerdahl. There he finds a hint of what he has been poring over all the time. Described is the way of life of a man. He was no nature child or illiterate. His world was neither a cave in the wilderness nor a castle in a city. Surrounded by books the man lived in a small cabin with a garden around. There he had created his own form of civilization. The essence, which can be extracted out of the encounter with this man, is as follows:

He carried his own paradise with him – inside himself. As a persistent attendant resource. If the surroundings had helped him to get there, than just by means of all that, which could be summarised in one word: simplicity. Simplicity had given him what millions of others had been searching for by pursuing progress, by complicating everything around them.[110]

"That's what it's all about," Karl agrees with. "It is not about a binary choice in between extreme external lifestyle. The man here finds joy in his own soul. And if my own soul leads the way to happiness, and nature with its simplicity is just the trigger to find it, then it must in principle be possible to find confidence anywhere. Of course, there are many commitments here in everyday life. And inside the stream of bustle it is not easy to step aside and take a bird's eyes view on the man-made complications of everyday life's struggle. However, at last it is me who can take choices. The encounter with a simple way of life helped me to regain freedom. Now the confusion in my mind finally turns into a new point of view. Even in the middle of the city, I can find nature. My own nature. I will take the time for things which are important in my life now." He calls Stefan. "Hello?" "Hey, it's Karl calling." "Karl!" "Stefan, do you want to eat out with me?" "Yes, why not. When?" "In one hour, in the little restaurant at the corner?" "Okay, see you."

In the city, life is in full swing. The music is roaring out of the pubs. In front of the restaurant at the corner, a torch flickers to welcome the guests. Stefan is already waiting for Karl. It has been a long time since they talked to each other. Just some sentences in between work at the hospital. Stefan starts the conversation in his typical sloppy way. After they are finished with dinner, their conversation has come as far as talking about the old days, warming up a lot of funny episodes from the time, when they were studying together. At once Stefan remarks, "It is good to see you laughing again. I've been worried about you, because you've been so serious and quiet in the last time. Now you seem to be happy and lively again." "You know, it has not been that easy

---

110 Thor Heyerdal (2002), "Fatuhiva", p. 237-238. Oslo: Gyldendal.
Norwegian original text:
Han bar sitt eget paradis med seg – inne i seg selv. Som en stadig nærværende ressurs. Hvis hjulpet ham å finne det, kunne det uttrykkes med ett eneste ord: enkelhet. Enkelheten hadde gitt ham hva millioner andre hadde lett etter ved å hige etter fremskritt, ved å komplisere alt rundt seg.

for me in the last few months. Now things are looking up. I'm starting to understand what actually has happened to me after I went to Norway for the first time last summer." "Tell me." "Well, in the meantime I really thought that I can't bear this life here anymore. Nothing was running smoothly as it did before. I didn't recognize myself anymore and questioned my whole life. But I think it was not about starting a new life. No, what I found on my trips to Norway is a new awareness of life. And this awareness can also be preserved while staying here. Just a little walk for example can evoke a hint of this indescribable feeling of freedom." "I see. Now I can understand why you were behaving so unusually. The others at work began to talk about you as well, because it looked like you were living in a completely different world. You actually seemed arrogant, and we felt somehow like idiots. Just as if you had no truck with us anymore." "You are right. I also noticed that I was no longer the old and funny Karl. I could hardly answer, when I was asked about my trips. When I tried to tell something about Norway, I was upset afterwards. I had the feeling that I could neither reach out nor belong to the rest of the world any more. But I didn't care about it. I thought the best thing was to shut up and keep it for myself. Now I see that this behaviour seemed arrogant to you." It occurs to Stefan that Christine was the first one who noticed that Karl had changed. He remembers that she once remarked, "Something happened to Karl. He needs no longer to play the role of the cool and sovereign fellow, always saying 'yes' even if it is screaming 'no' inside himself. He has somehow become more tranquil." Stefan continues to tell, "She was the only one who regarded this change in a positive way. She felt it was much more convenient to associate with you now than before." "For sure?" Karl is surprised while he wonders for himself, "Was it that she meant when she once noticed that I was talking so slowly? It was not meant as a reproach from her side?"

"It was good to talk to you, Stefan. Now I have the feeling that the world got me again." "Hold on now, Karl, or I'll start crying. But I hope that I may join you the next time you are going to your cabin." And so the two friends went on talking far into the night – in a way they never did before. On his way back home through the calm darkness of the night, Karl is filled with a deep sense of joy and the feeling of 'being home'.

It is easy in the world to live after the world's opinion; it is easy in solitude to live after our own; but the great man is he who in the midst of the crowd keeps with perfect sweetness the independence of solitude.[111]

---

111 Emerson, R.W. (1968). Essays and Journals. I: R.W. Emerson, Self reliance, p. 93. Nelson Doubleday.

Early one Sunday morning in March, Karl is stepping on the balcony of his apartment. The big windows are wide open. He breathes the cold air, which is surprisingly clear in order to be in the middle of the city. Down there on the pavement, a man takes his dog for a walk. Some cars are already driving out there. On the other side of the street, the postman comes along with the Sunday paper. Karl glances over the roofs of the city. On a ridge nearby a blackbird is singing its song. He cannot remember that he has ever heard a bird singing as beautiful as this one.

Insects: 1 Ladybird

HANS BØRLI

On a flower's leaf in the evening sun
a shining ladybird.
As I stand looking
it opens itself like
a tiny red-lacquered box
with a curved lid,
elegantly unpacks a flight
like antique silk.

The ladybird acts
in the midst of the human world
as if nothing existed

(from Hans Børli, *When Evening Stands Red over
Hesteknatten*, 1979)

The eco-crisis and local food

OLE-JACOB CHRISTENSEN

The food and us

At a nearby gas station, a large poster says: "Have you remembered to fill your stomach too?" Food is fuel, but is there anything more to it? Can this poster at a gas station in a Norwegian village say something about – not just our attitude to food – but also our relationship with nature in general? Can the poster explain why we are on the brink of destroying nature and becoming enemies of our fellow creatures in addition to strangers in the world we are born into?

The food we buy in the stores may not remind much of nature, and modern shopping centers have an environment that is as far as possible from nature. Plastic wrapped, thermostatically controlled, antiseptic, odorless and dipped into low background music, still food is a piece of nature that we digest when the wrapping is removed. Nevertheless; when the packing is removed, the food we eat is a piece of nature that we put in the mouth.

Industrially processed food from industrial agriculture has indeed moved away from real nature. Animals that the meat comes from may never have seen daylight, and they are fed with food that is far from what they are created to digest. In many cases, animal feed is transported from the other side of the globe and composed and transformed as much as the sausages or breads you put into the basket. However, all food still has a starting point in nature. Even the finished pizza with all its dyes, flavors, and thickeners consists mainly of flour, tomatoes and cheese. The hamburger is still meat, even though it can originate from hundreds of different bulls and cows and looks like someone has jumped on it.

No wonder many people today have an ambivalent relationship to food. We look forward to it – and fear it. We rejoice the taste, but fear it can make us sick. More and more people avoid more and more types of food. Serving a meal for friends has become a slalom course between intolerances, diets, preferences and principles. After hours in the kitchen, you find that most of the ingredients are left uneaten. Leaving something on the plate is an expression of disgust at your own appetite and at the physical food. "To honor the food" collides with a widespread aversion to food as a physical, biological phenomenon, such as smell, taste and consistency. Perhaps certain types of bulimia and anorexia are the ultimate consequences of these feelings?

Estranged from nature

Our feeling of alienation to our food may reflect our feeling of alienation to both nature and our own body. Already almost forty years ago, the French author Michel Tournier wrote a chronicle in *Le Monde* about how we had displaced the scents of society. The fishmonger, butcher, shoemaker, baker, and sausage maker – all filled the towns and villages with smells. What an experience it would have been to experience the Halls of Paris as Emile Zola describes them in the novel *Le ventre de Paris*! A strong experience, most probably, but perhaps today's people had turned up their noses at the smell?

I still remember from my early childhood the mind-blowing smell of carrots at a local gardener. She had a tiny outlet in a basement, and the carrots mixed their sweet smell with the moisture from soil, onions and celery. The vegetable counter at the supermarket cannot compete.

Dr. Bergljot Børresen describes in one of her books how man has become *The Lonely Monkey* (2006). We have become the animal that will no longer be animal, and defined us out of nature, placed us above and beyond. Hence our ruthless exploitation of it. The whole thing, Børresen argues, began when people switched from being hunters to shepherds holding large animal flocks. The killing of animals changed from being something done occasionally, to a daily routine. The mental shutdown of the empathy with animals that had to be mobilized during the hunt became an almost permanent state. The animals went from being fellow creatures to becoming pure utility articles.

A similar development has taken place in agriculture. Two to three generations ago, most European farmers held a few livestock. Some of them were literally livestock. In several places it was common for cows, goats and sheep to have their barn as an extension of the housing, without a wall between them. Calves, kids and lambs were playmates for children. Hens and other poultry were free-range, and pigs strolled in the farmer wife's heels when she came out with the garbage bucket. The horse was, at least in Northern Europe, so highly respected that it was buried rather than eaten when it could no longer carry out the farm work. The number of animals was small in most farms, and related work was manual. The contact between animals and humans had to be close. If you have brushed a cow, seen it rolling with its eyes and heard the friends lowing jealously, you understand.

Today's dominant industrial livestock with hundreds – sometimes thousands of animals in one herd – has many parallels to the large livestock flocks that herdsmen had in the past. The relationship to animals is impersonal, and slaughtering takes place on a large scale. At the same time, the proportion of farmers has dropped to around 2–3% in most industrialized countries. Few have direct contact with livestock anymore. Most displace the idea of where the meat comes from. Few things are less popular if, for example, you are served chicken, rather than fussing about the farming conditions these poor birds are exposed to in their lives of just over a month. The mechanism that Børresen calls hunter insensitiveness is always turned on.

Agriculture at the focal point

I believe this alienation, or even the fear of nature, is one of the reasons we have problems to act when we see that our existence is threatened because we destroy our livelihood. When we lose contact with nature, we also lose the ability to act rationally towards it. Remarkably many of the measures proposed to mitigate climate change, move the problem more than solve it. If we try to replace fossil energy with bioenergy, we open up for ruthless exploitation on forests and cultivated land. Increased focus on electricity will require ever-harder mining for increasingly poorer deposits with enormous nature interventions and toxic waste as a result. This does not mean that bioenergy, electric cars, solar and wind energy must be important parts of the green shift – only that they can hardly give us the abundance of energy that oil, gas and coal have given us. Thus, this is the second lesson a closer contact with nature can give us: no trees grow into the sky.

Looking closer, it is the biology, the renewable energy and the renewable resources that will increasingly set the limits for our existence. Agriculture, i.e., land and forestry will again be the "mother industries".

Our century faces great challenges. Can agriculture play a role in solving these, creating a better world both for us and for future generations? If we are to highlight some of the greatest challenges that are urgently needed to solve, the following issues stand out.

Hunger. Almost one billion people are chronically malnourished, and another one billion have deficient nutrition (enough calories lacking essential minerals and vitamins in the diet).

Climate: Little indicates that the world will reach the goals of the Paris Agreement. This can, according to a report from "The Future in Our Hands" from 2015, send one to two billion people fleeing from hunger and lack of water.

Biodiversity. According to a UN report, we can lose over 40% of today's species within 2050. In Germany, 75% of flying insects have disappeared over the last thirty years. In Norway, between a third and a quarter of the threatened species (red list species) are linked to the agricultural landscape.

The groundwater is drained below many of the world's most important agricultural areas and is polluted by runoff of pesticides and fertilizers.

The world's oceans are heavily polluted and filled with plastic. In a few years we can risk having more plastic than fish!

Erosion and deterioration of soil. Behind a Norwegian average menu there is an annual loss of around five tons of soil!

More and more disease-causing bacteria become resistant to antibiotics, and we risk that infectious diseases such as pneumonia can no longer be treated with antibiotics, and that surgical procedures become more dangerous since subsequent infections cannot be treated.

All these challenges are related to agriculture and food production. Hunger can only be eradicated through better agriculture and more equitable distribution of land, market access and purchasing power. It is obvious that agriculture is essential for biodiversity. Both in agriculture (plant varieties and livestock breeds) and around (insects, soil organisms, flora and fauna in peripheral zones and grazing areas). The causes of descending and contaminated groundwater are, of course, agriculture – and are closely linked to deterioration of soil and loss of organic matter that keep moisture and nutrients. Half of the antibiotic use in the world occurs in animal husbandry, and food production is a large consumer of plastic – from grass conservation to packaging and the carrier bag.

Agriculture's influence on climate is often underestimated (about 10% is a number that is often used in Norwegian agricultural debate). However, counting from soil to table, food production stands for far greater emissions. Increasing Norwegian food production, and at the same time reducing greenhouse gas emissions by increasing the import of feed, is a widespread agricultural policy trick.

About 13% of our total emissions come from livestock. In addition, approx. 18% from new cultivation, including cutting down forests. For this, we must add CO_2 and nitrous oxide from the production and use of fertilizers, CO_2 from plowing, as well as CO_2 from transport and processing of food products. In other words, we do not reach the 1.5- or 2-degree target without changing agriculture as a system.

Everything is related to everything – and very much related to agriculture. Intensive livestock farming is based on waste of resources. If the situation seems bleak, it is a bright spot that it can be improved. However, it requires recognition of agriculture being that we realize that agriculture is a crossroads for the major challenges we face, and taking agricultural policy, both nationally and internationally, seriously. Agriculture is not a marginal mining industry, but a basic human activity that shapes both society and our relationship with nature around us.

Enlightenment philosophers, the so-called physiocrats, understood this when they claimed that all production originated from agriculture. Today, when we see that we can no longer use fossil energy, but must rely on energy from the sun, this point of view has gained new relevance. Agriculture is precisely the only industry that utilizes solar energy directly in the production of plants.

The world needs a new agricultural policy, and there seems to be an understanding of the need for a radical change. Organic farming is increasing; many poor countries focus on agro-ecology, which are a combination of organic farming methods and more equitable distribution of land.

More and more agronomists argue that agriculture can help to solve the major problems that it has created. Hans R. Herren, agronomist and super-development specialist, president of the Millennium Institute, argues in the book *So ernähren wir die Welt* (2016) for a multifunctional agriculture, an agriculture that through good agronomy, fair trade and land distribution solves our major challenges. This multifunctional agriculture is based on local resources, and not long-distance transported raw materials and chemicals. Such agriculture will be able to bind carbon rather than emit, as a number of countries have backed up through the so-called four-per-minute agreement.

What can we do? Specific changes need to be made, not just airy visions and general talk. Bring more hands into agriculture in rich countries, improve capital access in the poor, and favor easy but effective mechanization everywhere. Adapt agriculture to local conditions. In Norway, this will mean both securing the small farm structure and favoring feed intake on outdoor grazing rather than import concentrates (soybeans and corn).

Base livestock production on meadows and pastures. Open fields, which lead to erosion and CO_2 emissions, must be reserved for human food (grains, potatoes, vegetables). Moreover, open fields must enter a shift that maintains soil fertility, thereby increasing its water retention capability and minimizing the need for pesticides.

Reduce meat consumption in rich countries, especially feed-based meat consumption. Increased feed price is the most effective method to achieve this goal.

Stop the dumping of food prices on the world market and ensure well-functioning local markets with access also for small farmers on fair terms. A more natural animal husbandry can also reduce the use of antibiotics.

Develop a coordinated food and agricultural policy for healthy food for everyone as the main goal. The fight against food waste and the use of grain for feed will be important tools (grains that we use today for animal feed could have given enough food to over three billion people...).

Conduct a (land) reform that gives the world more than one billion smallholders with access to land, grazing, necessary capital and local markets.

Stop the rich countries' dumping of food on the world market.

Stop land grabbing.

Build up food stores nationally and internationally to prevent price speculation and hunger.

These measures will allow us to provide enough food for all residents of the world, while making agriculture a zero-carbon emission and with sustainably conserving resources.

Back to food

This detour of the great, global challenges of our time thus brings us back to our food, i.e. the right to food for everyone, the respect for food, and the joy of food. These things are connected. Around the table the good conversations are found. The food we share can remind us both of the necessity to share and the knowledge of how we can produce what is to be shared.

Food reminds us that the world we live in is physical and alive. Banal? I do not believe that Abstract economic calculations govern the world, and politicians believe that eternal growth is possible. Moreover, they believe that all depleted resources can be replaced. However, what happens is that the biological world disappears and is replaced by the digital.

Politicians and economists say that poverty is about to be eradicated in the world – while the number of malnourished people is stable around one billion and the number of people living with a deficient diet is double. Maybe these people have a little more money than before. But they lack the essentials for living: food.

A rediscovery of the living biological world we live in is necessary. If we are to restore an empathetic and sympathetic relationship with the planet we live in, we need a positive counterbalance to the consumer culture and belief in eternal economic growth. As the philosopher Baruch Spinoza has already emphasized, a negative feeling can only be countered by a positive.

Contact and work with nature is such a positive feeling. A visit to the beach or the mountain, a fishing trip or a berry hike, a morning in the vegetable garden, a visit to a farm picking apples or strawberries, or a voluntary work in a city street to set up plant boxes in the parking lots, are examples of empathetic pleasures, pleasures interacting with nature. Or something as common as a good meal, or a walk in the square. The food – on its entire way from soil to table – can be one of the hyphens we need to live in harmony with nature again.

Many seek a closer contact with nature and the living by cultivating their own food. In a parcel garden, in a communal garden, in boxes of soil or in the windowsill. The work with plants and soil provides another, and perhaps closer contact with nature than the one we can get by just using it for recreation. There is an interaction, a sympathy that covers a need in our otherwise artificial world. Many participate in different types of cooperative farming or purchasing cooperatives. In this way, the consumer connects with the manufacturer – and the manufacturer with the consumer. Here too, a mutual sympathy – or perhaps we should use the word solidarity, is essential. In this way, the long chain from soil to table where the farmer is grossly underpaid, and the consumer gets a powerful and processed product that has lost many of its original qualities, is broken.

Sharing bread is an old symbolic act. It reminds us of our responsibility to create a sustainable world. In addition, it reminds us of what is the real basis for human existence, i.e. to produce food. Or as Voltaire's Candide concluded after experiencing the misery of the world: "We must cultivate our garden."

References:

- Herren. H.O.: *So ernähren wir die Welt"* 2016. rüffer & rub Sachbuchverlag GmbH, Zürich
- Børresen, B.: *Den ensomme apen* 2006. Koloritt forlag. Oslo.

Rowing under Stetind

FRANK A. JENSEN

In the beginning, I believe, they hear a reverberating drone from somewhere. An omen that an even newer time is coming; that boathouses will be demolished, rowboats be burned; that while Sirius still shines over the Vaisa mountains and Stetind, more and finer houses will be built. That Seljenes will be changed forever; every pine-covered hilltop will be crushed, every woodland pool be drained until only dry heaps of gravel remain, and where the black grouse now calls, roads will be carved out and deep pits be dug to feed the iron jaw. Therefore, this sound from somewhere in the middle of the fjord. A drone that they know comes from seven thousand horses, reverberating from here to Garvaluokta, a noise so penetrating that no one can catch the sore undertone warning that the day can come when the mountain has been emptied.

But in this night hour where I will begin, there is only a man and the phosphorescent glow in the water. And the oars in the rowlocks. The oars, with their straps from Narvik. The oars that chafe the copper mountings sparking blue lights between the thole pins. And hands that don't seem to belong to a priest's daily life: calloused hands with remains of soil in the palm lines and under the fingernails. How they grip and drag, these hands! Drag and push back. And the echo from their rowing gets louder here under the cliffs.

Those who saw the priest row into the fjord that evening knew why he was coming. Therefore, many of them sit and watch through their windows; and foreboding deep inside some poor creatures makes them peer out at the still water while trying not to be seen themselves. But there is no mistaking the smoke from the chimneys: they are watching and waiting. The night sky is not yet just a milky-blue sheen over the Vaisa mountains, so the boat can be seen from the weather-beaten houses huddling inland on Seljenes. The extra high prow and the broad, white gunwale over the tarred planks make it easy to distinguish this boat from other rowboats on the fjord. And when the breaking dawn takes over and he begins the return journey, it will be easy to recognize the man: the way he rows, that he often turns to face the towering mountains. They can imagine him: the black, curly hair, so black that it almost looks blue, the straight nose, the broad chin and the narrow lips.

To row like this is unusual, also for a man like the priest Arthur Sander. And it is unusual to speak of it; that he rows quietly under the moon that shines over Hallaluokta. The moon that is cold and clear and makes him lay the oar shafts on his knees while the boat glides through the water. The moon that makes him rest his elbows on his knees and his head gently in his hands, while he stares at the phosphorescence, mareel, the sparkling drops sliding from the oar blades and falling into the blackness. Do his parishioners know what this light is? he maybe thinks, out there in the darkness. That it is myriads of tiny living creatures, as numerous as stardust? They can plant potatoes, pull fish out of the fjord, collect firewood in the forest and stop bleeding – some of them. But wait for the mareel, close their eyes in the warmth from their own hands? Feel like a mountain peak?

The oars dry out, and I imagine that he dips them into the water again in order to sit and see the rain of light once more. To sit on this seat in the boat just as his father had done, the very same seat. Painted white at the ends, worn smooth in the middle. But not only his father. Wives and children, locals and Sea Sami, have worn down the same piece of wood. It has taken many years to make it so smooth, the seat in the priest's rowboat.

And when he digs his heels in and puts his weight on the oars it's because he manages without a boatman. These days a priest must roll his sleeves up, people always have an excuse. Not just that they are afraid of the dark, in the winter they had to work on the new road, before that it was the quay that had to be built. But he is as good as any other boatman, a boatman who can go home, tired and satisfied after doing his job, and sleep in his own bed.

After a while he is hidden from view as the boat glides along the coast by blacksmith Einar's land. Before the houses appear from behind the headland, he can smell the smoke, and I imagine that he thinks about the boundless darkness surrounding the sturdy smith, who constantly complains that there is something in soil and cellar, something that makes the fields themselves moan. So the smith will be awake, waiting. But not his wife Magda, he imagines. She will be asleep under the turf roof, and perhaps the chains will rattle when the boy stirs. Magda is unaware of the powers. Magda has no need of them.

And his journey will soon be over.

Frank A. Jensen: From *Lengselens* år (Nordbook AS, Skien, 2005)

THE FUTURE – CHILDREN'S PERSPECTIVE

The future belongs to our children

BØRGE DAHLE

Our children will bring forward our heritage to nature and culture. The child has a unique ability to adapt to the nature in which they are born. In this understanding, man's destiny lies, but also hopes for the future. Children grow into a culture that has become more and more strained for nature, but of course children are also able to adapt to a culture that develops in a nature-friendly direction. The child relates to the nature and culture in which it grows

Brox (2009) concludes in his book:

> *If those who take over after us are affected by the catastrophe in*
> *a hundred years, it will be because our mental picture of relationships*
> *in the world now. It is the map we construct and manage now, that*
> *will determine the terrain that our descendants must adapt to 2110.*

This understanding means that we as parents today have great challenges if our descendants are to have a safe future. We must admit the critical situation our planet is as a result of our nature-threatening ways of living. We must be willing to change our way of life and thus stand up as good models for our children on a path towards a nature-friendly society.

But this is a change that must apply to everyone and thus it also becomes a political issue. It must apply to everyone and it must happen at the same time for everyone. The problem is so simple that our consumption culture needs to be changed – and that applies to most of us. This must be the simple and understandable message our politicians have to decide.

In order to succeed in this important "educational task" we must also have an idea of what opportunities and limitations the "nature-friendly leisure society" opens up for. It is about raising children to a life in a society that give our descendants opportunities for a diverse life-style, but also limitations seen in relation to today's consumer society.

The child's most important "learning room" is the living nature and culture of which the child is a part. In this learning room, the child is formed and educated and builds its values. Our orientation of values is a prerequisite for our choice of ways of living and will and ability to change our behavior.

We know that positive attitudes to nature do not necessarily lead to nature-friendly behavior. We are all, more or less, "bound" by the ways of living in our time. Many find that the values they represent are difficult to transform into actions, they are forced into unwanted ways of life – scarcity of time and a hunt for material goods. Positive attitudes, based on understanding, provide an increased readiness to change behavior. In this educational context, action is preferable to exhortations. Through nature-friendly actions, the child's opportunities to live a more nature-friendly life increase.

Children have perceived the global climate threat and are unsure of what will happen in the future. Faced with children, one must not focus on crisis scenarios, but build up "hope for the future". Children must learn to live nature-friendly through concrete actions, and as stated in the Stetind Declaration: "Children must find the joy of living nature-friendly".

Leisure time as an arena for the development of nature-friendly ways of living

The ever-increasing leisure time in the western world offers great opportunities for processes to change lifestyle and behavior patterns. We can largely decide for ourselves how we want to spend our leisure time. Here we have a real choice as opposed to occupations where one to a much greater extent is limited by workplace and working hours. There are, of course, various obstacles that limit our pursuit of leisure time. They may be of an economic nature, due to lack of physical skills, lack of time or social reasons.

Leisure time should ideally be used to raise our quality of life and give us surplus energy. What you do in your leisure time is therefore of great importance for your experience of quality of life. In this context, the leisure time we spend with our children will be very important. We must strive to socialize our children into nature-friendly ways of life to reduce our burden on nature, and it is possible to do so with joy!

Calculations show that much of a family's greenhouse gas production is linked to leisure time. In the consumer society, shopping has become a leisure activity for children and young people. It is therefore important to focus on how we use leisure time to reduce our greenhouse gas emissions and most importantly – leisure time is a suitable arena for the development of nature-friendly ways of life.

A good way would be for the family to sit together and reflect on how they could enjoy their leisure time without burdening nature. It is important to find forms of leisure activities that give everyone rich experiences in safe and good social contexts. "A rich life with simple means," as the Norwegian philosopher Arne Næss expressed it.

We remind about the Stetind Declaration:

We must work to promote a renewed understanding of
the relationship
between nature and human beings.

References:

– Brox, O. (2009). *Klimakrisen – Hva kan vi gjøre?* Oslo: Aschehoug.

About money

ARNE GARBORG

Money has no value in itself. You cannot eat them, drink them, dress in them. You could have your pocket full of them, and be hungry, thirsty and freeze if there were no food, drink and clothes to buy. For money you can have everything it is said. No, that is not true. You can buy food, but not appetite; medicine, but not health; soft beds, but not sleep; knowledge but not intelligence; glitter, but not comfort; fun, but not pleasure; acquaintances, but not friendship; servants, but not faithfulness; grey hair, but not honor; quiet days, but not peace. The shell of all things you can get for money. But not the kernel. That cannot be bought for money.

CONTRIBUTORS

Andersen, Gjermund: Born in 1956. Daily manager of the Norwegian Conservation Association in Oslo and Akershus. Works especially with questions related to forestry, diversity, outdoor life and nature experience. Forest worker for seven years. Education in forestry.

Børli, Hans: Born in 1918. He worked his entire working life as a logger and was a writer as well, and got the label "the poet of the forest". Børli's starting point was the forest and life there; in the poetry he was also concerned with politics and increasingly existential problems such as anxiety, faith and death. He is primarily known as a poet, but he also wrote novels, short stories and plays. He died in 1989

Christensen, Ole-Jakob: Born in 1960. He has worked as a teacher, environmental worker, interpreter and since 1986 has run small farms with his wife. He has worked as a French teacher at his own expense. The farm is organic, and processes all milk even for cheese, butter and sour cream for direct sale.

Education: Master of Science, with subjects French, Sociology and History of Ideas. Master of French Area Studies from the University of Oslo. The title of the master's thesis: La décroissance ou écologie humaniste. He is active in the Green Party, and has previously held positions of trust in the Norwegian Farmer and Small Farmers' Union. He has also served on the central board of Oikos, now Organic Norway

Dahle, Børge: Born in 1947. Growing up in close proximity to nature. Living on a Norwegian mountain farm. Educated in pedagogy, biology and sports. MA in Friluftsliv. Worked as a teacher in upper secondary school and as Associated Professor at the Norwegian School of Sport Sciences.

Dahle, Gro: Born in 1962 in Oslo. Author of poems, prose, picture books, theater and opera. Raised with great love for mountains, rocks, heather, reindeers and grouse.

Dahle, Øystein: Born in 1938. For twenty years, chairman of the board of Worldwatch Nordic and chairman of the Worldwatch research center in the USA. Ten years chairman of the Norwegian Tourist Association and six years as chair of the board of Friluftslivets Fellesorganisasjon (The Norwegian Outdoor Council). Until 1995 he was affiliated with ESSO. The last ten years as Vice President with responsibility for land and coastal activities. His great interest has been nature and outdoor life first as a climber and glacier-guide, later as a forest and mountain hiker. During most of his life he has dedicated himself to protection of the environment and a commitment to reduced consumption.

Faarlund, Nils: Born in 1937. MSc biochemistry/microbiology NTH 1961. Founder Norwegian School of Mountaineering 1967. Took *friluftsliv* to University level at Norwegian School of Sport Science 1968. MA level 1975. Honorary member International Federation of Mountain Guides Associations 2000 for development of values-oriented guiding. Knight 1st class Royal Norwegian Order of Saint Olav for services for nature and humanity, 2008.

Garborg, Arne: Born in 1851. Norwegian writer. His novels are profound and gripping while his essays are clear and insightful. He was never inclined to steer clear of controversy. His works tackled the issues of the day, conflict between national and European identity, and the ability of common people to participate in political processes and decisions. He had a strong feeling for nature and a great ability to write about nature. He died in 1924.

Hamsun, Knut: Born in 1859. He was a Norwegian writer who was awarded the Nobel Prize in Literature in 1920. Hamsun's works spans more than seventy years and shows variation with regard to the subject, perspective and environment. He published more than twenty novels, a collection of poetry, some short stories and plays, a travelogue and some essays. He died in 1952.

Haukeland, Per Ingvar: Born in 1966. He has an MA from Oregon and a PhD from Berkeley combining eco-philosophy, place and education. He has collaborated with Arne Naess for many years, including two books: *Life's Philosophy* (2003) and *Dyp Glede* (*Deep Joy: Into Deep Ecology*) (2008). From a Quaker perspective, he wrote the book *Himmeljorden* (*Heavenearth*) (Kvekerforlaget, 2010). Currently Haukeland is Professor at University of South-East Norway in the fields of eco-philosophy, ecopedagogy and *friluftsliv*. He lives with his family, including Luna, an Alaska huskey, in a mixed community of all beings at the foot of majestic Bryggefjell mountain in Bø in Telemark.

Herrman, Hanne: Born in 1958. She was the Secretary General of the Norwegian Association Against Noise from 2007 to 2015. Her formal background is academic and from the fields of arts and culture. She studied art in Norway and France, and has made several expositions in Norway and abroad with sculpture. She has a master in French, a bachelor in international cultural and civil studies with the subjects political science, folklore, West-European-history (from 1870 onwards).

Hanne Herrman works with art and cultural issues, and literary translation. She has an engagement for questions related to society, philosophy and eco-philosophy; the understanding of (human) life and society as well as the possibility of influencing our conceptions of our surrounding world

Kvaløy Setreng, Sigmund: Born in 1934. Norwegian philosopher, writer and farmer. He was central to the development of Norwegian eco-philosophy. Setreng grew up in Lom and gained a close relationship with nature through walks in Jotunheimen. In the 1950s, he served in the Air Force. In 1958 he began to study philosophy at the University of Oslo. He was Professor Arne Næs's assistant from 1961. In 1965 he took the magister's degree in philosophy. Setreng visited Nepal a number of times. The Sherpa's form of Buddhism aroused Setreng's interest in Buddhist philosophy which he saw as compatible with ecological thinking. He planned and participated in the Mardøla campaign in 1970, the Alta campaign in 1980, and was involved in No to the EU. He died in 2014.

Naess, Arne/Næss, Arne: Born in 1912 was Norway's leading philosopher. Through his books and lectures in many countries, Naess taught that ecology should not be concerned with man's place in nature but with every part of nature on an equal basis, because the natural order has intrinsic value that transcends human values. Indeed, humans could only attain "realization of the Self" as part of an entire ecosphere. He died in 2008.

Næss, Siri: Born in 1927. Worked at Institute of Applied Social Research. She is now researcher emerita at Nova Research unit at Oslo Metropolitan University

Randall, Scott: Born in 1975. He became passionate about nature as BA student at Gettysburg College and his MA at Johns Hopkins University. Became engulfed in Norwegian inspired eco-philosophy at the Center for Development and Environment at UiO, Norway, 2003, discovering that Norwegian eco-philosophy could be used as a tool for global (social) change. MA thesis on compiling the various facets of Norwegian eco-philosophy for this purpose.

Reuter, Bea: Born in 1979 in Germany. Learned Norwegian culture and friluftsliv to know through schooling in Norway. Studied sports, art and pedagogy at the University of Hamburg. Started together with Ulrike Schenk in 2008 "Friluftsliv – Leben draussen" which evolved into "Friluftsliv & Livskunst" in 2012. Since then she has been in Bortelid (a small place in southern Norway) most of the time, living and working to spread the idea of "A rich life with simple means" (Professor Arne Naess).

David Rothenberg: Born in 1962. He is a distinguished professor of philosophy and music at the New Jersey Institute of Technology, author of *Is It Painful to Think? Wisdom in the Open Air, Survival of the Beautiful, Nightingales in Berlin* and many other books. The musician and philosopher wrote *Why Birds Sing, Bug Music, Survival of the Beautiful* and many other books, published in at least eleven languages. He has more than twenty CDs out, including *One Dark Night I Left My Silent House* which came out on ECM, and most recently *Berlin Bülbul* and *Cool Spring*. He has performed or recorded with Pauline Oliveros, Peter Gabriel, Ray Phiri, Suzanne Vega, Scanner, Elliot Sharp, Iva Bittová, and the Karnataka College of Percussion. He worked on eco-philosophy with Arne Naess in the 1980s, and wrote a book about him called *Is It Painful to Think?* and also a collection of essays by the founders of Norwegian environmental thinking, *Wisdom in the Open Air. Nightingales in Berlin* is his latest book, CD, and film.

Schenk, Ulrike: Born in 1983 in Germany. Studied sports science at the University of Hamburg. Several study trips to Norway inspired for friluftsliv. Started with Bea Reuter in 2008 "Friluftsliv – Leben draussen" in the South of Norway with the desire to spread the idea of "A rich life with simple means" (Professor Arne Naess). Since 2013 she works for the municipality of Grimstad.

Tompkins, Douglas: Born in 1943 in the USA. One-time businessman and founder of The North Face outdoor gear retailer and cofounded Espirit clothing. He made a fortune enabling him to save vast areas of free nature in Alaska, Argentina and Chile. He was a conservationist and conservation philanthropist, farmer, untitled architect/designer and environmental activist. The inspiration came from American natives of Yosemite, the father of the National Park idea, John Muir and in the 1970s from Arne Naess' *Deep Ecology*. He joined Yvon Chouinard and another climber in Yosemite in the early 1960s. He was known as a skier, kayaker, foil fencer, art collector, photographer and broad generalist of the Sigmund Kvaløy Setreng description. He died in 2015

Arne Johan Vetlesen: Born in 1960 in Oslo. Studied with Jürgen Habermas 1985 - 1990. Professor of Philosophy at the University of Oslo from 1998. Participates regularly in public debate. He has published many books on the relationship between nature and man

Wagle, Finn: Born 1941 in Oslo, grew up on the edge of the Nordmarka woods. Bishop of Nidaros in the Church of Norway 1991–2008. Praeses of the Bishops' Conference 2002-2006. In collaboration with the county governors of North and South Trøndelag, arranged several conferences on ethics and environmental management. Co-author of the *hustavle* "The cry from a wounded planet", 2001. Together with the Church of Norway Council on Ecumenical and International Relations, initiator of the North Sea voyage "Protecting the Riches of the Seas", 2003. Co-founder of the Trondheim branch of the Grandparents' Climate Campaign, 2006. "Life as a Reconciliation Project", article published in 2016.

TABULA CONTRIBUTORIA

Personal donators:
Aage Jensen
Arnhild Opdahl
Thomas Aslaksby
Per Bjørn Foros
Finn Wagle
Svein Loeng
Petter Erik Leirhaug

Institutional donators:
FRITT ORD Foundation, Uranienborgveien 2, 0258 Oslo, Norway
HOUDINI Sportswear AB, Finnboda Varvsväg 16, SE-131 72 Nack
ACLIMA AS, Wool Specialist, Sundvollhovet, 3535 Krøderen, Norway
NORGES HØGFJELLSSKOLE, 2848 Skreia, Norway

www.ingramcontent.com/pod-product-compliance
Lightning Source LLC
Chambersburg PA
CBHW040142270326
41928CB00023B/3322